CHRISTOPHER SANDFORD

GODFREY EVANS

A BIOGRAPHY

Statistical Index by Chris Taylor and Nicole Broderick

SIMON & SCHUSTER

LONDON·SYDNEY·NEW YORK·TOKYO·SINGAPORE·TORONTO

To my father

First published in Great Britain by
Simon & Schuster Ltd in 1990

Simon & Schuster Ltd
West Garden Place
Kendal Street
London W2 2AQ

Simon & Schuster of Australia Pty Ltd
Sydney

British Library Cataloguing-in-Publication Data available
ISBN 0–671–71007–9

Typeset in Trump Medieval 11/13 by Selectmove
Printed and bound in Great Britain by
Billing & Sons Ltd, Worcester

Contents

Acknowledgements

No book of this sort can be written without the unsung, unpaid, if not unsolicited help of those whose only connection with the author is a mutual admiration of his subject. Among those who put their recollections of Godfrey Evans at my disposal were: the late Leslie Ames, Keith Andrew, Alec Bedser, Denis Compton, Colin Cowdrey, Howard Evans, Jack Evans, Tom Graveney, Reg Hayter, Howard Levett, Peter May, Keith Miller, John Murray, John Pocock, M.J.K. Smith, Brian Statham, Raman Subba Row, Fred Trueman and Douglas Wright. To them, and to Richard Wigmore at Simon & Schuster, I am deeply indebted. Finally, my greatest thanks to those named on the cover and dedication pages. Without the early encouragement of my father, Sefton Sandford, this book would not have been started. Without the help, support and friendship of Godfrey Evans, it would not have been finished.

C.S.
London, 1990.

List of Illustrations

Introduction

THE CENTENARY TEST of 1980 enjoyed a mixed reception. Languishing on the staff of the old London *Globe*, I, for one, had been waiting eagerly. After a rain-ruined series against the West Indies, a week of nostalgia at Lord's seemed just what was ordered. Among the run-stealers flickering therein were, if not Hornby and Barlow, then Messrs. Sandham, Fender, Washbrook, Compton and Edrich, while a half-glimpsed figure seen entering 'Q' stand would materialize as Arthur Morris or 'Slasher' Mackay. It took you back.

The match itself, unfortunately, rarely lived up to its billing. After an undistinguished start, cricket, not for the first time, appeared faintly ludicrous on the Saturday, as a full house – and the world's press – sat in brilliant sunshine enduring one interminable inspection after another. Much happened that day which does not matter here: Hughes eventually scored a century and Allan Border, in his first Test in England, reached 56; the only point of the recollection is the remark of a distinguished ex-England and Yorkshire batsman sitting directly behind me, as the umpires meandered out for the third or fourth time that afternoon – ''Twere better last week at T'Oval.'

This cryptic utterance neatly summarized the previous Wednesday's fixture when, perversely, the sun had shone continually as an 'Old Australian' team subdued their somewhat older England counterparts. Little comes to mind of the England innings except some knockabout stuff by Cowdrey and D'Oliveira and, poignantly, the last sighting of Ken Barrington before he succumbed to a heart attack that winter. Some time at tea, though – if pressed, I would pinpoint it at 3.30p.m. on Wednesday 27 August 1980 – an interesting thing happened. Yet another picture had flashed on the pavilion television – Jimmy Carter, it was, exuding manic optimism about his forthcoming showdown with Governor Reagan – when out of the broadcaster's patter a voice brought me awake:

'Excuse me, master.'

I turned to make way for a rotund, white-flannelled figure making his way through the Long Room bar, seeming to list slightly, in the manner of a steamer ploughing through heavy seas, before joining his colleagues at the pavilion steps. It was Godfrey Evans. I didn't know, nor do I now, what errand had caused his divergence from the main party, but it was perhaps typical of the man that he should be in motion around the ground while others were content to take a well-earned tea. Nor was that his only distinction. At 60, Evans was comfortably the oldest of the 24 players on view (each team introducing, when appropriate, a second wicketkeeper – Evans's surrogate being the 48-year-old tyro Jim Parks) and, with deference to the bespectacled Neil Harvey, the most physically changed from his youth. Above the thickened waistline, his face, richly tinted, beamed benignly left and right, framed by an extravagant pair of bristling white whiskers. He looked like something out of an early Dickens novel. The Aussies themselves seemed to appreciate this, because there was a lot of good-natured horseplay involving the openers Simpson and Redpath. Liberties were taken with the diminished force of 'Typhoon' Tyson and a less-than-fiery Fred Trueman. On came the spin of Titmus (still, in his 48th year, appearing sporadically for Middlesex) and a nearly spherical Tony Lock. More mayhem. Then, at 79 without loss, his own score on 27, Redpath lifted a foot and, in a blur of gauntlets, retired an older, if not wiser man. . . stumped Evans, bowled Titmus. Half an hour and a half-century later, Simpson (Australian captain a scant two years earlier) came forward to the off-spinner and fell to an action, no more than a gesture, really, as delicate as a single finger laid on a piano; nothing contrived, nothing *flamboyant*, almost as if the ball itself had looped onto the wicket. . . stumped Evans, bowled Titmus. It was at this stage that the stripling Parks appeared as substitute, Australia (coincidentally, I have no doubt) going on to win by seven wickets. The point is that, beneath the Pickwickian exterior, Godfrey Evans demonstrated that day a scintilla of the footwork, anticipation and agility that, together with a personality not dissimilar to that of the comedian Max Miller, made him among the best-loved cricketers in the world from 1946 to 1959.

'Twere better at T'Oval, indeed.

Thomas Godfrey Evans is 70 in August 1990. *Wisden* itself confirms this, although no doubt Evans – as with his other notable entries between the yellow covers – will maintain an air of amused indifference. Records alone rarely concerned him. More impressed, undoubtedly, will be the formidable army of middle-aged men for whom Evans, no less than Denis Compton, represented a touch of the exotic, if not quixotic, in the austere post-War world. Youth, in many ways, provides the surest barometer of what is natural, honest and uninhibited in a sportsman, and it is surely significant that few of those who grew up in the late 1940s or 1950s were indifferent to the demotic charm of the England wicketkeeper. Even more than Compton – about whom there was always the suspicion of a more patrician leaning – Evans was truly the people's champion, of whom no less a judge than John Arlott has said he had 'greater vitality, stamina and agility than any other man in the history of cricket'. If such could be combined into a single entity, an overview of Evans's very attitude to cricket, then that entity would be *enjoyment*. Here was a man who positively relished his job. Everything Evans did, on and off the field, was characterized by a sense of exuberant, extrovert enthusiasm. Even now, veteran of 91 Tests, 50 years on, cricket still has him in its hold. Once, in the preparation of this book, I found myself declaiming on some performance of my own at the dizzy heights of the school Second XI – 'Not a bad catch, no; I remember diving a bit and taking it in front of slip. . . .' My voice trailed off as I realized, just in time, that I might have been lecturing Hemingway about the one-chapter novella I'd penned for the local freesheet. Evans's face registered nothing but good-natured interest.

Evans the cricketer had two distinct aspects, for he

in fact began his career as a batsman who sporadically kept wicket – not, as later happened, a wicketkeeper who batted sporadically. The suspicion must be that his was a character that lacked the gritted-toothed durability of the great batsman, and indeed Bradman himself wrote of the 'considerable ability behind the light-hearted smile. . . suggesting a short and happy stay at the crease'. Trevor Bailey, partner in crime in more than one Evans innings, noted his 'bright and breezy' approach to the task and his strong preference for the 'shovel shot with which he would scoop the ball out towards midwicket'; nonetheless, whatever his temperamental shortcomings, Evans's technique was sufficient to accumulate 2439 Test runs and two England centuries (one more, incidentally, than Bailey). Typically, too, Evans the batsman was untypical. While a Jekyll and Hyde approach to the art is nothing new (one thinks of Bailey himself, of Barrington and of Boycott in the 1965 Gillette Cup Final), to appear in the record books for both fast *and* slow scoring smacks of perversity. The fact is that, in going for 95 minutes without runs at Adelaide in 1947, Evans holds the record for Test Match immobility. What the record fails to state are Hammond's words to the incoming batsman – 'Stay there if you can, Godfrey' – an edict so successfully observed that, with the wicketkeeper undefeated on 10 two-and-a-half hours later, it was the Australians, fielding in 107° heat, happy to settle for a draw. Lest anyone thus associate him with the more tenacious kind of limpet, this was the same Evans who went on to score 98 before lunch in a Test Match and, for good measure, who made 47 in 28 minutes in a match at Manchester more popularly associated with the antics of Jim Laker. The fact is, here was a batsman quick, agile, deft between the wickets, yet capable of the sheet anchor role if required. A Test aggregate higher than Bailey, Benaud and Headley belies his reputation as the Cheeky Chappie of cricket. Here, quite obviously, appearances could be deceptive.

Of Evans the wicketkeeper there are two schools of thought: those who admired his brilliance and applauded it, and those who admired it and questioned it. Of the latter,

Benaud, while acknowledging Evans's wondrous agility, rates him below both Tallon and Grout, largely because he, Evans, was thought to drop more chances than they. Arlott, too, noted an early tendency to 'hold the impossible catch and miss the simple one'. If such were true, this was surely for the reason that he stood up to the stumps far more than did any other keeper. Here Evans was victim of his own genius, for natural agility allied to physical strength led him almost invariably to take up the closest available position to the action. Fearlessness will always exact its toll and Evans, with his boxer's physique, was as near fearless a cricketer as lived; a delivery that would have peppered, say, Alan Knott like buckshot, meant no more to him than the pat of a tennis ball. One suspects, too, that like many a *maestro*, Evans reserved his best performance for the big occasion, and that the bulk of such mistakes as he made occurred at moments of relatively low drama in the game. Denis Compton himself gives this as his opinion, placing Evans the 'big match' performer at the very top of the wicketkeepers' pantheon.

I have said that Evans was rarely concerned with the accumulation of records (what other sportsman underestimates his own most significant entry in *Who's Who*?), and that one of the ties which bind him firmly to the common cricket lover was his playing of cricket for cricket's sake. At the same time there is one record of which I know him to be justifiably proud – namely that, of his 1066 first-class dismissals, nearly a quarter were stumpings. Even in Tests, the ratio remains better than one in five. The reasons will be discussed in good time, but it is appropriate here to remind ourselves of modern comparisons: Rodney Marsh, who remains nearly 100 Test dismissals ahead of his nearest rival, achieved a ratio marginally better than 1 in 30; while for Knott, second in the list, the figure rises to a dizzy 1 in 14. Neither statistic reflects on those excellent cricketers who had much to contend with, including the dearth of top class spin-bowling. Nonetheless, it is instructive: Evans's instinct was to stand up to all but the fastest bowling; if this led him to occasional errors, its efficacy, not to mention its psychological effect on foe and friend alike, is there in the records.

When Godfrey Evans retired, the England selectors, unable to find another of his ability, chose a succession of batsmen-wicketkeepers who, until the arrival of Knott in 1967, only intermittently achieved excellence in either category. Not for the first time, genius was only fully appreciated in its absence. It is a loss we do well to measure, for substitutes to fill the void are few enough; with the demise of Knott, the position was again unsettled as on Evans's retirement.

What, meanwhile, of him? Evans has no substitutes for his art, although his personality remains as vital as ever. If the feet these days are a little slower, the ready smile is undiminished. The game is still active in his will and his heart; only his muscles betray him, and even that is relative. If Evans's active cricket ceased in 1959, it lives on in the hearts and minds of those who thrilled to his achievements. If now those achievements seem rooted in an almost prehistoric age, then Messrs. Simpson and Redpath are there to remind us.

Chapter One

Man of Kent

'YOU CAN'T EXPECT to make a living at cricket.'

The rebuke of the Chemistry master at Kent College, Canterbury, to the ten-year-old Godfrey Evans would be more ironic but for the fact that, in 1930, it showed every indication of being true. Only the previous year had Evans first handled a bat, and while he recalls the youthful delight of finding it 'easier than expected', little suggested that the eagerness of the boy's instincts would mature into the grown man's art. If sporting blood were inherent in the family then its primary outlets had been football, tennis and horse-riding; if an Evans *leitmotiv* existed, it had its being in sport and in dance and music. Cricket, he says, rarely exerted an influence on him until the age of ten or eleven, and not until then did he don the wicketkeeper's gauntlets. From then on, says Evans, he was to 'hover between the two worlds' of keeping and batting, in so doing establishing a reputation equal to that of any other living player.

It must have been a source of solace to Arthur Gordon Lockwood Evans, widowed from his early thirties, that he lived to see his youngest child achieve international fame. An electrical engineer who turned late in life to farming, his elder son Jack says that nothing was to give the old gentleman more pleasure than the exploits of his son Godfrey. The two boys were preceded by a sister, Violet, and it was on her that much of the responsibility of a motherless household was to fall. At best, owing to the regional nature of Arthur's work, the family was a mobile one, and remained in the rented house in Finchley, Middlesex, in which Thomas Godfrey Evans was born on 18 August 1920, a scant six months thereafter. It was at new premises at Cliftonville, near Margate, that Arthur's wife Rosie was knocked down in the street by a coal-cart, leaving her unable to walk and subsequently bedridden. Godfrey's only memory of his

Jack, Violet and Godfrey Evans, 1925.

mother was of taking a too-full cup of tea to her bedside. When she died in 1923 he was three; his sister and brother eleven and nine respectively.

If this has the ring of a childhood of Dickensian gloom, then it is a pleasure to report that such was not so. Godfrey (for whom the 'Thomas', in deference to his grandfather, was never adopted) seems actually to have relished an upbringing that would have dispatched other mortals into psychoanalysis. His father's frequent absences, as far afield as Venezuela and the Ural Mountains, he found 'exciting', while the problem of growing up at least notionally an 'orphan' seems never to have occurred to him. This may be attributed in no small part to the influence of Violet and Jack, who preceded him to Mrs Parker's boarding-school in Deal where Godfrey was lodged in 1923. It was Jack's task to 'nurse' his scarcely vertical brother, by now revelling in the nickname 'Golfball', both for his rotund shape and bouncy demeanour. Early evidence, too, was available of the stentorian voice later to raise hair on the back of batsmen's necks throughout the world. Jack gives it as one of his chief duties at Mrs Parker's to 'keep Godfrey quiet' when the latter was in full cry.

Credit for this happy early childhood must also go to the large brood of Evans uncles and aunts. Arthur, in fact, was eldest-but-one of a tribe of eleven (not yet in cricket team formation; but read on). Games were in Godfrey's blood and about him as an essential part of his youth, and it should come as no surprise to lovers of coincidence (or, who knows, fate) that from the age of six the Evans home was a twelfth-century shooting-lodge at Sheldwich, Faversham, glorying in the name of... Lords. One can imagine the agreeable shambles in the house as the sporting paraphernalia of Uncles Douglas (football and tennis), Alec (ditto), and Jimmy (horses of all persuasions) co-existed with the musical activities of their sisters May and Olive. Godfrey, having graduated to Grosvenor Court College, was influenced by all these family enthusiasms, and maintained a lifelong love of music. At the age of five he took to the stage in the guise of a Bisto Kid, and if ever there was a case of typecasting this was it. From then on Evans discovered that he possessed, for want of a better word, *rhythm*, allied to an equal inclination towards public performance. Already we can see the shape of things to come.

His father's absences continuing, much of the male influence on Evans was exerted by his three uncles, Douglas, Alec and Jimmy. The first were good enough to play football for Canterbury Waverly, while in both there was a passion for tennis. In school holidays the seven- or eight-year-old would act as ball-boy, then opponent, to his seniors. To him it was 'learning the hard way'. No quarter was given, particularly by the demonic Douglas, and to Evans's other instincts must now be added the competitive. From Uncle Jimmy, meanwhile, he was to inherit a lifelong interest in equestrianism. There is a picture of Evans atop a Guyanan Police horse at Bridgetown on the 1953–54 MCC tour that shows a rider in complete harmony with his mount; Evans sits with bolt upright aplomb while the horse is relaxed almost to the point of sleep. To his uncle, in fact, falls credit for having established the first-ever mounted Scout Troop. If not the primary passion of football and tennis, then riding was to feature more than once in Evans's life before that photograph a quarter of a century later.

The next significant date arrives in 1928 when Evans, comfortably the youngest member of the school, was sent to Kent College, Canterbury. Here, again, he was preceded by his brother, and it was the next year that, prompted by Jack, he made the significant discovery that holding a cricket bat was no great hardship. The older Evans, playing with his fourteen-year-old companions, remembers being startled by the *naturalness* of his brother's stance; so far as he, or anyone else, can remember, it was the first time that Godfrey had ever contemplated playing cricket.

From then on Jack lost no opportunity to instruct and encourage. As a prefect, it was his lot to impose sanctions if, or more accurately when, Godfrey overstepped the mark. Instead of the usual penalty, he remembers ordering his brother onto the playing fields, hitting a cricket ball as high into the air as he could, and instructing him to catch it. If an average of eight catches from ten was unattained, a more conventional form of punishment would be administered. . .with a cricket bat. Again psychoanalysts will search in vain for a subsequent aversion to the products of Messrs. Surridge or Slazenger; Evans remembers only the agreeable sensation of batting against boys a half-dozen years older than himself, and finding it 'easier than expected'.

The energy and devotion of a child in pursuit of his enthusiasm is the most ruthless spectacle in nature, and by 1930 Evans's aptitude for cricket had developed to the point of his appearance in a fixture at the Belmont estate of the Kent *eminence* Lord Harris. Nobody knows if the octogenarian's eye was caught by the ten-year-old's performance, for all that is recorded of the match is that it rained all day. Evans and his team-mates took to the house, where he has a memory of the Fourth Earl sitting alone in front of the fire. It would be tempting to make too much of this and to read into it what is unwritten; nonetheless it is pleasant to speculate on the brief encounter between these two polar extremes of greatness.

The following summer, a rare one with Arthur at home, the Evans family challenged the local XI at Sheldwich. Inclusive of uncles, cousins and brother there were ten senior members of the team, most of whom succumbed to the bombshell deliveries of the village opening bowler. Somewhat earlier than expected, the eleven-year-old found himself wending his way to the wicket with a bat several sizes too large and a pair of pads 'tight under the armpits'. Whether out of sympathy for the boy's stature or genuine fear of doing him injury, the bowler's pace slackened to allow the newcomer off the mark. This generosity was accepted with a boundary. Delivering in enthusiasm what he lacked in style, Evans soon began a display of hitting that nullified the bowler's sympathy. There was, as he puts it, 'no class' about his innings, none at all, but his eye was good enough to resist the village attack for half-an-hour, and to give him joint top score with his father. During the tea interval, Evans remembers the Sheldwich skipper, Morgan-Kirby, complimenting Arthur on his son's performance. If the phrase 'I'll be surprised if he doesn't play for Kent' now has an apocryphal ring to it, then at least *some* reference was made to Evans's future career; and he himself describes it as the first point at which he began to think 'seriously' about playing cricket.

The scene now reverts to Canterbury, where Evans progressed to the Under-14 XI, scoring a matter of six or seven centuries along the way. In the summer of 1932 the established stumper (and, writing soon after Australia's triumphs in 1989, we should, perhaps, name him: Mark Taylor) fell ill on the day of a match. Searching hurriedly for a replacement, the master in charge, Evans believes, settled on the candidate best physically equipped for the role; Taylor himself had been appointed largely because of his girth. Whatever the reason, that summer saw Evans don the gauntlets for the first time and, significantly, the first entry in the scorebook of the legend 'stumped Evans'. At Lords, he set to practising his new art until term resumed on 17 September. Whether it is coincidence that it was the very

Lords.

day that his boyhood hero set off on the most controversial tour of all time, we cannot know; but that summer Evans's future was to be determined for the next 30 years.

Leslie Ames, the late Kent and England batsman-wicket-keeper (the order, uniquely, is reversible) remains at the very acme of pre- and post-War cricket. His record is impressive enough: the only man to have played for England, become a Test selector, managed MCC teams abroad, served as secretary-manager of his County before becoming its president, and been appointed to the Cricket Council. What the facts fail to state is the enormous influence of Ames's talents on those who learnt their cricket in the late 1920s and '30s, when his combination with 'Tich' Freeman was at its peak. Obviously Evans himself belonged to this category. If it was providence that first led the twelve-year-old to don the gloves, then, by Evans's own admission, it was Ames who was to serve as a model from then on. That first experience of the keeper's art gave Evans a new outlook on the future. From 1932 he was to actively seek opportunities to play behind the stumps, even if the Kent College masters were hardly eager to give him the chance. From the age of thirteen to sixteen he was to remain a batsman who, by default, kept wicket, and it was in the former category that he impressed observers like Joe Hargreaves, the school cricket master. Hargreaves, in fact, seems to have taken his lead from Evans's brother, for he too would dispense with traditional forms of punishment in favour of an hour's work with the heavy roller. The application seems to have worked, because Evans, promoted to the First XI against the Choir School, Canterbury, in 1933, scored the small matter of 132, 128 of them in boundaries. A second century that summer brought him a Jack Hobbs trophy and he was cast, for better or worse, as a middle-order bat.

Still his hero had him in his hold. Already he had travelled to the St. Lawrence Ground, Canterbury, where both Ames and his Nottinghamshire counterpart Lilley thrilled him with their keeping to Freeman and Larwood respectively. On another occasion, Evans remembers travelling to the ground only to hear the crushing news that his hero was unfit. No sooner had the blow sunk in, than Ames himself was seen alighting from his car. An encounter took place that can with hindsight be regarded as significant: two of the great Kent wicketkeeping trio of the century met for the first time. An autograph was duly collected and the following year, 1934, Evans was at The Oval to see Wyatt's England play Australia. Ames, on that occasion, failed to make the impact of his 120 in the earlier Test at Lord's, but it can be safely assumed that he did nothing to defame himself in the fourteen-year-old's eyes.

Evans continued his agreeable existence at home and school, going on to win his colours at hockey – another sport to which he took naturally – and comfortably failing to obtain his School Certificate. The years 1935 and '36 saw the youthful consolidation of his batting and, like most who become masters, the essence of his technique was in place by his early teens. Here, it was obvious, was a natural games player who combined the eye of a hawk with an instinctive

Kent College Canterbury 2nd XI, 1933. G.E. lower right, Joe Hargreaves standing left.

sense of timing. The equation applies equally to all sports involving a moving ball and it comes as no surprise that, in later years, Evans excelled at tennis and squash. But for the influence of Ames and Hargreaves, who can say what other sport he might have adopted; but influence him they did.

In 1936 – the very week that, 200 miles to the north, the twenty-year-old Len Hutton was receiving his County Cap – Evans played the innings that was to bring himself within range of a professional career. Again the opponents were the Choir School, Canterbury; Evans's contribution was 65 out of a total of 92. More significant was the presence at the match of Alex MacKenzie, then a member of the Kent County nursery staff, who went on to play for Hampshire. Evans, in fact, had caught the young batsman's eye in an earlier encounter, and the suggestion that he, too, apply for a trial at Kent was now repeated. What had been a whimsical notion to the boy, now struck the teenager as a viable proposition. Evans, in 1936, had come to the irrevocable conclusion that scholarship was not for him, and his last report shows him failing in all subjects. A decision was taken. That summer at Lords, Arthur Evans had fallen from a ladder and damaged his ankle so severely that, in time, the lower part of his leg had to be amputated. Recuperating at home, he did nothing to dissuade Godfrey's inclination, and may even have been relieved that it would offer his son a degree of self-sufficiency. With this last obstacle removed, Evans approached Joe Hargreaves who, in a final act of benevolence, arranged for a trial at the County Ground. He arrived there late in August and, for once, both his timing and his luck let him down.

By now it was too late in the season for the County to engage new players. As to whether his performance that day had merited it, Evans is ambiguous. He remembers batting and bowling against the young Kent professionals – Wally Carter, Colin Cole, Harry Bowers – and leaving the ground feeling he had at least given an account of himself. To be given a net at all was a distinction; unfortunately for Evans, it seems to have been regarded by the County as much a favour to MacKenzie and Hargreaves as an actual assessment of his ability. Staff, the secretary explained, were not engaged in August; perhaps Evans would like to keep busy, keep fit (and, presumably, keep motivated) that winter and re-apply in May. They would be pleased to include his name among the annual trialists. And that, at least for the moment, was that.

Or was it? Faced with the sudden prospect of earning a living, Evans was again abetted by Uncle Jimmy and brother Jack, who arranged a job for him at Stewart & Ardern's, a Morris car distributor in Acton, West London. Here he secured the wage of 9s3d a week (eventually rising to 9s9d), augmenting his income by cleaning the family Studebaker at week-ends. Home during the week was Uncle Jimmy's flat at Wembley Park, and it was from there, in the winter of 1936, that he was to journey to the indoor school of Jack Durston, the former Middlesex bowler, assisted by his young teammate (and, a half-century later, County scorer) Harry Sharp. Evans remembers the 'artificial feel' of playing on matting under strong indoor lights and, whether it was this or a case of adolescent nerves, he failed to do himself justice. If Evans the batsman had a weakness – and he admits it – it was a tendency to 'have a go' at inappropriate moments, and both Durston and Sharp despaired at checking his natural exuberance. After one such session, Durston summoned the teenager to ask if he harboured alternative ambitions to batting.

'Yes, to keep wicket.'

'Then you'd better do so,' came the reply. 'Because you're no bloody good at batting, bowling or fielding.'

With enough self-awareness to take this to heart (and enough self-confidence to do so), Evans embarked on a course of rigorous application. For the remainder of that winter he put, in his own words, 'heart and soul into trying to improve a rather scant knowledge of the wicketkeeper's job'. Among his activities was to throw a cricket ball against a brick wall in the garden of his uncle's flat and attempt to take the rebound cleanly and without snatching. He bought a bicycle and pedalled daily to Stewart & Ardern's and nightly to the indoor school or, periodically, the greyhound stadium. He drank beer. He grew up.

At last spring dawned, and on the first Tuesday in May, 1937, Evans retraced his steps to the St. Lawrence Ground, Canterbury. Special permission had been obtained from Norman Collins, the manager at Stewart & Ardern's, for the excursion – although not, as we shall see, for its repercussion. Thrust into a net with the young County professionals and his fellow trialists, Evans soon displayed his penchant for full-frontal batting; and his hit-or-miss performance at least earned him the time to don a pair of borrowed gauntlets.

Here a crisis loomed. The net, he found, was pitched perceptibly at an angle and some of the bowling, more enthusiastic than exact, required a deft hand to collect. One 'big young fellow' whom Evans remembers as 'imagining himself a second Larwood', sent down a battery of leg-side deliveries which soon had the keeper in almost perpetual horizontal motion. Hardened professionals looking on noted the almost uncanny agility of the sixteen-year-old's performance *standing up* to what was, by any standards, a bowling *blitzkrieg*. At the end of the session Evans was called aside by Ted Humphreys, the County Coach, and remembers still the fulsome phrase 'another Ames' as he made his way to the Secretary's office. To be fair to Evans and his power of self-possession, he himself knew he was 'nothing of the sort'; that accolade would be won, but not before a war had been fought. That morning at Canterbury the best he could hope for was a contract on the Nursery Staff, and contracted he duly was, by the Secretary G. de L'Hough, at the startling salary of 17s6d per week. We can excuse him if, in his elation, he forgot to thank the 'big young fellow' who had unwittingly brought him to the threshold of success. Nor would the bowler himself have complained. His name was John Pocock, and more than 50 years later he served as President of the County whose net he terrorized that day.

Evans, the professional cricketer, arrived at Acton the following morning only to find that Collins, the professional manager, failed to share the general enthusiasm that his workforce was to be reduced by one. Not for the last time, Evans was forced to rely on rhetoric and, whatever he said, it seems to have worked; not only was he released from his contract, but Collins subsequently became a friend and fan. Lovers of hypothesis may speculate on the 'what if' inherent in this scenario; all we know is that Evans duly returned to Canterbury a member of the County Colts and, for £11, purchased a motorbike to celebrate. On his next birthday, his seventeenth, he was to exchange it for, appropriately enough, an Austin.

Here, at the gate, so to speak, of the St. Lawrence Ground, we leave cricket and inhale briefly the smell of sweat and embrocation associated with the last of Evans's great alternative pursuits. Virtually from the cradle, as we have seen, games of all sorts determined his life; now, at the age of sixteen, he took to that most unequivocal of sports and joined Doddington Boxing Club. At Kent College, by his own admission, he had rarely missed a chance of using his fists 'with or without gloves' and now, mindful of the seasonal nature of cricket, he applied to the Boxing Board of Control for a professional licence. Once granted, Evans (a light-welterweight) began training in earnest with Bill Gardner, then featherweight champion of Kent, and Fred

'Geoff' Evans.

Percy, who later gained Gardner's title. In the winter of 1937–38, spectators at Herne Bay or Plumstead Baths would have noted on the same bill as Ben Valentino or Ginger Sadd the presence of one 'Geoff' Evans, 'Godfrey' being considered too fastidious for his own good. Nevertheless, at the age of seventeen Evans found himself a professional boxer and in the space of three heady weeks scored knockout victories against Don Smith and Alby Bryce. Later he was to fight against the Royal Navy team at Chatham. Such successes set him wondering. Would it be better to put boxing first and cricket second; or, incredibly, to 'forget cricket altogether'? As it happened, circumstances were largely to determine events for him. A bout in the spring of 1938 broke Evans's nose and he reported for the new cricket season 'looking like an advertisement for adhesive plaster'. This was too much for de L'Hough, who promptly delivered the momentous ultimatum: cricket or boxing. Boxing lost, but with the following postscript. Evans himself states it 'a certainty' that that brief incursion into the ring improved him as a cricketer. Footwork being one of the skills fundamental to both sports, much of what he learnt at the hands of Gardner and Percy was later to be interpreted in a different arena. It allowed him, he says, to 'take those very wide balls with a quick body sway and without losing balance' and to give him greater reach than he might have had. If such was boxing's legacy then cricket owes it its appreciation.

Besides which, had it not fulfilled Kent's advice to the boy – to, at all costs, 'keep fit'? Out of the ring, Evans spent that winter and the next indentured to the Tickham Foxhounds at Newnham, and days that began at 3.30 a.m. can only have hardened the youngster's steel. He remembers entering a horsebox on such a morning and seeing the animal's hind legs stiffen and rear. Not for the last time, Evans was glad of his boxer's timing as two steel-shod hooves shot past his ear; an experience comparable, in later years, to 'ducking a Lindwall bouncer'.

What, meanwhile, of cricket? Throughout 1937 and 1938 Evans was to become a fixture in first the Club and Ground, then County Second XI, understudying at a distance his peers Howard ('Hopper') Levett and Ames himself. With two such keepers on the staff he had no illusions. Levett himself had played in a Test against India in 1933, and succeeded Ames when a back injury forced the latter to concentrate on batting. Contemporaries, in fact, were divided as to who was the better natural keeper, and for Evans they provided a unique double standard from which to appropriate and learn. If one of the two could be said to have directly influenced the *style* of Evans's play, though, then it was surely Levett. Aged 29 when Evans joined the staff, he was probably at the zenith of a career that went on, like Pocock's, to encompass the Presidency of Kent.

From Levett (for whom Evans remains 'the last of the wicketkeepers') came the memorable advice to stand up whenever possible, even to faster bowling. If his own wicketkeeping credo could be distilled into a phrase, it was: 'Be active – be involved – be *there*'. Byes he regarded as a natural consequence of his doctrine of total commitment; unfortunate but, to a large extent, unavoidable. Evans also recalls the instruction to make even the most wayward throw look accurate and, above all, to act as a transmitter of advice to the captain; in short, to be the hub of the fielding team's universe. By now it seems to have become apparent that Evans himself was no shrinking violet, and Levett's advice cast the die irrevocably in favour of a policy of maximum involvement. Years later Evans was to write a book that took as a title what was undoubtedly his own aphorism, *Action In Cricket*.

Ames he worshipped, but from afar. For one thing, in both 1937 and '38 he was engaged on Test duty against New Zealand and Australia, and seems to have had little time for appraisal of the junior County staff. It would be nice to record that the senior player's eye had already been caught by the young pretender, but the truth, as Ames himself admits, is that at this point Evans was but 'one of 30 or so hopefuls whom one occasionally saw around the ground'. Nor, unsurprisingly, does he recall signing his autograph for the thirteen-year-old on that earlier occasion. Immersed as Ames was at the forefront of First XI and Test cricket, even a junior colleague would have to do something exceptional to come to his attention. In due course Evans did.

In 1938 Evans made his first professional advance, when he was selected for the Kent Second XI, playing in the Minor Counties Championship. The promotion followed a century for the Club and Ground team against the Cyphers, at Beckenham, after scoring 57 against the same opposition the previous year. A second hundred at Tewkesbury confirmed that here was, if not a second Woolley, then a batsman of intermittent brilliance who – and the order is significant – 'could keep wicket as well'. Whatever the cause, the effect was that Evans found himself on the brink of first-class cricket and duly recorded a season's aggregate of 533 runs at an average of 26.65. During the summer, too, he worked hard to enhance his prospects behind the stumps, and seems to have realized at this stage that excellence as a batsman would, to some extent, be sacrificed in attaining it as a

Kent C.C.C. 2nd XI, 1938

wicketkeeper. In later years Evans was to write of his belief that to 'concentrate wholly on the two skills. . .would mean that, in the end, one would suffer'. Such prospects as he had to progress as a batsman at the highest level presumably died with that conviction. From then on he was to concentrate body and soul on becoming the best specialist player in the world, in so doing inducing Bradman's remark: 'One day he may decide to take batting seriously.'

In April 1939 Evans forsook riding, applied himself to the nets and continued his career on the margin of First XI selection. The day duly came, though not until mid-season and then for reasons (he later discovered) other than his own brilliance. With Ames concentrating predominantly on batting, the County knew full well that the military call-up of Levett (and by this stage, few had any illusions that called-up he would be) would create a vacancy behind the stumps. It was the Committee's intention, therefore, to acclimatize Evans to the County side and the higher grade of cricket before offering him Levett's job when the crisis arose.

It was on 22 July that he duly took the field at Blackheath in the annual 'derby' against Surrey. Ames, of course, was playing; Levett kept wicket; Evans, not for the first time, was included as a middle-order bat, whose primary instruction was to look and learn. He did. After a rain-delayed start, Surrey were dismissed for 231 and Kent collected 18 without loss before play ended for the day. At this point, and throughout the rest day, rain returned and it was an Evans doubly chastened by anxiety and impatience who entered fourth wicket down. Waiting to greet him was the distant figure of Alf Gover who dispatched a ball of electric speed, confirmed by those who saw it (and Evans, who didn't) as conceding nothing to the youngster's nerves. An over or two passed and then, once again, Evans elected to 'have a go'. Duly hooking, he awaited the umpire's signal, only to see the ball comfortably swallowed by Laurie Fishlock at fine leg. If his contribution of 8 to the total of 202 was neither disciplined nor distinguished, it was far from the worst debut ever seen; and Evans had learnt something about life at the top. Significantly, press reports mention his 'keen display' and, more improbably, his throwing 'which hit the stumps three times out of four from the deep field'. At least, as he said, it was a start.

It was more than that when, still approaching his nineteenth birthday, he was nominated to replace Levett in a match against Derby at Gravesend. Acting captain Brian Valentine lost the toss, and there was just time for Evans to consult the non-playing Levett – 'Don't worry about the byes' – before taking the field as County wicketkeeper for the first time. It was Saturday 29 July 1939. Norman Harding, a bowler of more than medium pace, sent down the second over. The second ball nipped back off the seam, clipped the inside edge of the Derbyshire skipper's bat and jagged down the leg side. Evans caught it. That is, he flung himself full length, extended a hand and, as he crashed to the turf, the ball was resting securely in his glove. Simple. The next

On the road, 1939.

morning's paper ran a photograph of it on the front page. Ames, at forward short leg, remarked that 'you may never make a better catch than that'. A half-century later, he gave it as his opinion that this was the moment 'when Godfrey arrived. . . .From then on it was up to him'.

The Committee persevered with its policy, returning Evans to the Second XI and (at Old Trafford) playing him as a batsman on Levett's return. He did a stint as twelfth man. Then, at Dover, he kept wicket in the return fixture against Lancashire. He caught Cyril Washbrook, executed two run-outs and, in the second innings, conceded no byes. Again, he achieved little with the bat, but by this point Ames, Levett and the rest had little doubt of Evans's real ability.

The strange twilight season, played increasingly in the shadow of events overseas, wavered to an end. The War affected Evans as much as it did everyone else; if it is treated here from his personal perspective, that is only because for the moment it is his perspective that matters. In 1939 Evans stood on the very boundary of professional success. For Ames and Fagg and Wright and the other Kent players he had already made his mark. He himself describes his career as 'on the brink'. The England wicketkeeper's place was at this time unsettled enough to encourage ambition and, without false modesty, he believes that another two years' continuous cricket would have seen him inherit the job. Instead he was arrested, not only in his natural development, but on the brink of fulfilling a particular ambition. The first week in September was to have seen Kent play Middlesex at Lord's, and Evans take the field at Headquarters for the first time. The weekend of 2–3 September he spent, ironically enough, at Lords, the family home. There, on the Sunday morning, he listened to Chamberlain's dismaying announcement and received news from de L'Hough at Canterbury that all contracts were to be terminated forthwith. Not only was he baulked in his desire to play at Lord's, but to the young professional it must have seemed that fate had played a trick of almost personal malice. Evans, at nineteen, was in the first flush of his prodigal gifts; the next season, and the one after, must have seen him capitalize on his promise. Instead he was confronted with the blank statement of a career checked in its tracks and, more immediately, of the pressing need to earn a living.

A cricketer in early career subjected, as he was subjected, to a six-year deferment of his active life could have been excused his moment of despair. At the height of his youthful enthusiasm he was abruptly caught short; when events permitted him to begin again he would be nearly 26; almost, in cricketing terms, middle-aged. We may speculate on this loss, and the adjustment it made to his eventual Test career, conjecturing a total of 110 or 120 possible appearances. It was not to be; but at least Evans, with his customary resilience, survived the conflagration. Others, like the Kent captain Gerry Chalk, were not so fortunate.

Chapter Two

Play Suspended

EVANS'S MAIN CONCERN, in the autumn of 1939, centred on his own predicament. He seems to have had no overview of events happening on the world stage; and, indeed, why should he? His most compelling priority that September was to find a means to continue hire purchase payments on a new car; and if this suggests an absence of *gravitas*, then surely many a nineteen-year-old's thoughts would have turned in the same direction.

In the event, help came to hand in the form of his old County sparring partner, John Pocock. The youngest partner in the family bakery of W.H. Pocock, John was keenly aware of the company's likely shortage of staff in the event of imminent conscription. Evans was duly sounded and found willing, and a place was found for him in the family home at 114 Tonbridge Road, Maidstone. So, for the duration of the Phony War, he was happily set to delivering cakes and buns to the citizens of Maidstone, pausing only to inflict grievous harm on the company van and to sampling such nightlife as existed with his patron John. It was, under the circumstances, a winter of almost idyllic content. Evans's initial despair at being checked, as he says, 'on the brink' was replaced by a sense of invigorating routine not wholly dissimilar to that of his two previous winters spent boxing and at hounds. Rising at 4 a.m. was no great hardship for one used to mucking-out at an even earlier hour, and if the advent of summer brought a pang of regret, it was soon stifled by the exigencies of War. His country needed him.

It so happened that Pocock Senior had seen service in the Royal Army Service Corps, and it was to that unit that Evans and his young colleague applied in May 1940. Here, not for the last time, military procedure obtruded. It appeared that Evans and Pocock were too young to be inducted. Crestfallen and resigned to a career in the infantry, they returned to Tonbridge Road. Suddenly Pocock Snr's detachment ended and the trio returned to the recruiting office next morning with about five pounds. The money changed hands. They were in. The full significance of the gesture was lost on Evans for some time – until, in fact, 1946, when members of his unit were demobilized in good time for the cricket season; colleagues in the infantry were to remain in the colours until the late summer or autumn of the same year. In the context of what was to be his comeback as a cricketer, the timing was surely significant.

Evans was inducted on 1 June 1940. As at other critical times of his life, he celebrated by buying a car. Unfortunately, plans to use this in reconnoitre of the highways and byways of Kent were stymied when the worsening military situation brought a posting to barracks at Staveley, near Chesterfield. He arrived just in time to join the cricket team attached to the training centre, which promptly offered Evans its captaincy. If the standard was less than first-class, at least it was a return to a more familiar pre-War existence, and in matches against other training centres in the district the unit was unbeaten.

Evans's only other memory of that summer is of embarking with Pocock on an illicit weekend excursion to Kent, when they avoided being reported AWOL by a matter of minutes. There began an almost cavalier attitude to military life, although he himself was one of the service's perennial Sergeants. Off the field, Evans completed basic training and, within reason, fulfilled the maxim 'do as the army does'; on it he developed a taste for captaincy and tested his mettle against those, like Richard Bird and Harry Halliday, who went on to represent their counties. In the winter of 1940–41 he was posted to Ossett, Yorkshire, for training (so rumour had it) to prepare for shipment overseas, possibly the Middle East. In the event, the posting never materialized, but as spring arrived he was able to sample, at first hand, the unique sporting tradition of his adopted county.

It transpired that Ossett Cricket Club had offered to find a place in one of their teams for any servicemen billetted in the district. Eager to perform at whatever level he could, Evans duly applied and was interviewed with almost cosmic disinterest by the local groundsman. Sensing that he had failed to make an impression, he remembers adding, 'I'll be glad to play for the seconds.' In truth, he nearly had to. Originally billed to bat number eleven for the reserves, justice was done only when the Ossett President received a chance telephone call from a colleague. Reference was made to 'the next England wicketkeeper, name of Evans' who, his friend believed, 'might be posted somewhere nearby'. 'I'll look out for him,' came the reply, in what was presumably a strangled croak. The team list was duly amended and, that Saturday, Evans found himself in familiar position for the First XI. It was the beginning of a happy summer, on and off, playing for Ossett. If the standard was undeniably ordinary, then it at least fulfilled the adage of 'taking their cricket seriously in Yorkshire'. More seriously, in fact, than Evans, who played on the pitted, pockmarked turf with little notion of becoming 'the next England wicketkeeper' or anything else. In fact, his thoughts at this stage are hard to fathom, and like many a conscript before him, he seems to have adopted a day-to-day resignation to events beyond his control. In Ossett, at least, he found cricketers who appreciated him for what he was; he was associated in their minds with glamour and style, and with certain other values.

In 1942 Evans and Pocock parted for the first time since induction. In the five years since their trial at Canterbury, their two careers had been strangely linked, notwithstanding (as Pocock himself puts it) the distinction that 'Godfrey was a genius'. Now Evans continued his progress northward. His next posting was to the 52nd Highland Division at Falkirk. From Pocock, though, came a postscript. In that halcyon winter of 1939–40, he and Evans had courted Maidstone girls with almost comically similar names: Joan and Jean. Pocock married the former; her friend, Jean Tritton, daughter of an electrical works manager in Maidstone, duly became, in January 1941, the first Mrs Evans. In time a son, Howard, was to be born, though not until the end of hostilities presaged a return to 'normal' existence. For the time being married life was subject, like all else, to the vagaries of War; but the event marks an important rite of passage in Evans's career. A boy of nineteen is a very different proposition to a married man

Marriage to Jean Tritton, January 1941. Brother Jack was best man.

of six years' military experience, a fact made dramatically clear when Evans returned to cricket in 1946. From then on much of what he did, on and off the field, was in conscious effort to make up for 'lost time'. In so doing he fulfilled Pocock's observation that 'here. . .surely was the greatest wicketkeeper in the world'.

The spring of 1942 saw Evans revert to two of his previous passions, football and hockey, before entering the novel world of Scottish cricket. In early divisional matches he impressed observers like Jimmy Fleming, a member of MCC, and Cecil Cook, the Gloucestershire bowler, who saw to it that Evans kept wicket in a representative match styled East v West. With Fleming, in particular, as patron, Evans was soon excused the bulk of routine duties in favour of near continuous cricket which, typically, he describes as 'good fun, at about or above Club standard'. Such it remained until, providentially, he was posted to Aldershot as a permanent staff instructor. Providentially because now, after two seasons of innocuous standard, he again stood on the brink of serious cricket.

His first match, at Buller Barracks, was for The Sergeants against The Officers. In addition to, as he puts it, 'keeping fairly well', Evans hit a lightning 46. His next two innings that week were 155 and 90. Lest anyone assume that 'serious' also meant 'easy', his next score was nought; but on the strength of those performances he was invited to play for the No. 1 Training Battalion, captained by W.H. Webster of Middlesex.

Had he remained in Scotland (or, who knows, elsewhere) there is no telling what would have happened to Evans's career. The deprivation might have tipped the equilibrium of his development, or brought him face to face with a disturbing and even demoralizing crisis. The fact is that, being returned to a higher grade of cricket, Evans now resumed an essential part of his career: competition. In addition to Webster, Evans's teammates included Hider (Kent), Brown (Middlesex) and Pierpoint of Surrey, while in neighbouring barracks a Sgt. Instructor Compton was displaying the form that had already brought him eight Test caps. With respect to Cook and the rest, it was headier company than had been available in Scotland.

Events were to take another climactic turn when an RAF side, captained by the former Sussex and England skipper Arthur Gilligan, arrived at Aldershot. Evans himself asserts that 'associating with so many well-known cricketers gave me confidence', and he hit 37 in typically brisk fashion. More significantly, he was to execute the leg-side stumping of Peter Judge, the Glamorgan all-rounder, off Pierpoint, causing Gilligan to describe it as 'the best piece of wicket-keeping since the outbreak of War'. In the context of Gilligan's continuing influence at Lord's, it was a momentous remark.

From then on Evans was to be elevated to representative cricket, first for the Army and subsequently in a number of select Elevens designed to simulate at least the appearance of first-class and international fixtures. A contrast can be made here to the First World War, when Grace himself had insisted that to play a mere game for public entertainment was, at that moment in the nation's destiny, unpatriotic. In 1939 things were different. Every effort was made to keep the sport alive in some form, not only because it did no harm to the War effort, but because, in the opinion of those like Ernest Bevin, Minister of Labour, it actually contributed towards it by showing that aspects of normal life could be maintained. To Evans it was undoubtedly a two-edged sword. While it deprived him of the chance to continue his normal development and, as we have speculated, of an additional three to four years' residency in the Test side, it also assembled wonderful combinations that would have appeared outlandish in peacetime. One such was the fixture against the RAF. As a direct result, Gilligan informed Sir Pelham Warner (whose sole previous observation on Evans had been 'That man will never keep wicket. . .he stands on his toes') that here was a star of the future. In consequence Evans at last realized his ambition of playing at Lord's and, indeed, from 1943–44 was to perform there more frequently than at any other period. Evans himself, with commendable understatement, describes these matches as 'memorable', not least because, for a time, they 'helped the crowds to forget the reality of War'. In 1940 and '41, all serving members of the forces were admitted to Lord's free; the charge to the public was sixpence. In 1942 and '43 this was made universal, and in 1944 and '45 the price was raised to a shilling. The beneficiaries of such fixtures (and, for a major two-day event, a crowd of 40,000 was not uncommon) were a variety of Services' associations and, under the circumstances, every effort was made to reconcile public and players to the reality of the situation. A scorecard for August 1942 reads:

> In the event of an air raid good cover from shrapnel and splinters should be obtained under the concrete stands. Public shelters will be found in St. John's Wood Church, Wellington Court, Wellington Road, South Lodge, Circus Road. Spectators are advised not to loiter in the street.

Evans at this point chose the moment to suffer his only wartime injury. Perhaps predictably, it had nothing to do with enemy action and everything to do with his own exuberance. Exercising in the gym at Aldershot in June

Sergeant Evans (standing, right), Permanent Staff Instructor, Aldershot 1943.

1943, he launched himself from one set of ropes only to find that the next, annoyingly, was beyond his reach; the result was a broken radius bone in his elbow and, for a month, a suspension of his own version of the war effort. Comparisons are invidious, but one is tempted to speculate on the similar mishap suffered, two years earlier, by the man who was to become Evans's England captain. Hutton's injury, of course, was to the forearm, not the elbow, and its consequences were to be more serious; the fact remains that here were two incidents involving present and future England cricketers at training in army gyms. Both could easily have checked careers with, then, a mere thirteen Test caps between them. As it was, Evans was forced to miss a match at Lord's between sides representing England and the West Indies.

He recovered by Monday 2 August 1943 when, at Warner's invitation, he represented England in a two-day fixture against The Dominions. Before a crowd of 23,000, England amassed a first-innings score of 324–9 declared, thanks largely to a century by Sq. Ldr. Leslie Ames. Evans remembers this as 'quite magnificent', and seems to have reverted to a kind of schoolboy adoration in the face of his sometime colleague. *Wisden*, while noting Compton's 'dashing' 56, allows that Ames 'hit splendidly all round the wicket'; his 133 contained two 6s and eleven 4s. Batting eleven, Evans (still, presumably, in a state of shock) scored 5. In the first-innings rout of The Dominions he caught Carmody of Australia and conceded three byes. More importantly, he had sampled life at the very top. Now that our perspective has altered, with the rapacity for Test and one-day international cricket, it is perhaps not easy to recreate the sense of occasion and atmosphere which these matches enjoyed. To Evans they were 'cricket at its very finest'; tough, competitive, but played in the full knowledge of (and, indeed, expressly for) the temporary relief they afforded from the War. When Evans, still short of his 23rd birthday, played with Compton and Robins and Ames, he was admitted into a hierarchy several light-years removed from that he had known before; it is to his credit that he held his own and, according to *Wisden*, 'displayed wicketkeeping. . .which was always high class'.

In the event, the match was won by England in dramatic, almost melodramatic, fashion. Set a target of 360 in four-and-a-half hours, The Dominions failed by just nine runs. The critical moment came when Learie Constantine ('the most brilliant, unorthodox player' of Evans's memory) was caught by Leslie Compton with his left hand at full stretch while leaning on the pavilion rails with feet on the ground. This perfectly fair catch aroused heated discussion, although Constantine himself was heard to utter only the cryptic 'That's cricket.' Its result was to deprive the visitors of their most prolific batsman and, effectively, to seal their fate. The same might be said of Evans, who, in the space of two days, was cast irrevocably as a player of, or near, international class. The match also introduced for the first time partnerships that were to extend and develop into household phrases after the War. In the England first innings,

Evans enjoyed a brief relationship with the already limpet-like 2nd Lt. T.E. Bailey, while, behind the stumps, he took his first catch to the bowling of Alec Bedser. The victim was an Australian Sergeant called Miller.

At the end of August he was at Lord's again for an almost surreal fixture billed as 'Middlesex & Essex v Kent & Surrey'. Surreal in that, with rain teeming down at the scheduled start, permission was granted for the Compton brothers to depart to play for Arsenal in the opening match of the football season against Charlton. By half-past-two, with the sun shining and Middlesex rendered Comptonless beyond recall, the covers were taken off and play found to be possible. An injury to the Essex opener, Avery, who tripped over his bag when leaving home, further contributed to the Marx Brothers-style preamble to proceedings; completed when Arthur Fagg, who should have been opening for the visitors, spent the day fruitlessly searching for his own bag as it trundled forlornly down the railway.

When play got under way, the depleted Middlesex & Essex were dispatched for 75 in just 23 overs. Gubby Allen and Walter Robins, appearing in the guise of Major and Squadron Leader respectively, offered token resistance; in other respects the match was a rout. Doug Wright returned figures of 5–3–8–3, and was judged by *Wisden* to have 'kept a perfect length with his leg breaks'. Evans, behind the stumps, caught Trevor Bailey off his team-mate's bowling.

It was the beginning of a partnership that was to extend for the rest of that decade and much of the next, as significant in its way as had been that between Ames and 'Tich' Freeman. In fact Wright's chance had come when Freeman retired from the Kent team at the end of 1936. During each of the next five seasons, excluding the War, he took over 100 wickets. Even in 1948, when a broken finger constrained him from late July, he finished with 77. To Evans he remains 'on his day, the greatest of slow bowlers'. 'On his day' because Wright, who bowled genuine leg-breaks and googlies at medium pace, remained a constant enigma: a player of prodigious gifts who seemed sometimes almost wilfully to misunderstand the situation, and who, more than most, suffered from missed chances. At Sydney in 1947 Australia were in pursuit of

214 in the last innings when at 45–1, Bradman (on two) snicked a leg-break from Wright straight into and through slip's hands at chest height. Bradman and Hassett stayed to put on 98 for the third wicket and win the match. Somehow the incident was typical of the bowler's career. It promised much, and if it delivered, at County level, over 2000 wickets and seven hat-tricks, for England it was unfulfilled. A Test aggregate less than that of Illingworth or Allen is, with respect to them, doing Wright an injustice. With his floating arms and kangaroo hop he was the most awkward and, in some ways, ungainly of bowlers, whose variation of speed required a signal between himself and Evans. Whatever its vagaries, the partnership between them, which was to reach its climax in 1947 when they combined to take 34 dismissals and which meant that, in the selectors' minds, they were often associated as a single unit (Evans himself believes that he was picked for his first tour of Australia largely because he was accustomed to Wright's bowling), was a galvanic one for both Kent and England. In which context (not to mention the subsequent career of the batsman), the notation 'Bailey c. Evans b. Wright' on 28 August 1943 was a significant harbinger of things to come.

But they *were* still to come. At Lord's, Evans contributed to the débâcle by scoring an unbeaten 56, batting, untypically, at number four. To *Wisden* it was 'further evidence . . .of his ability, following admirable work behind the stumps'. It was also the end of his cricket for the season, and the winter of 1943–44 was spent in anodyne routine at Aldershot. By now he had both met and impressed the nearby Denis Compton, who recalls Evans in 1943 as possessed of 'swift footwork, agility and neat gathering of the ball on the leg side'. Here, too, was the origin of a partnership that was to extend, as colleagues, for ten years, and as friends thereafter. For the moment it is significant only that they had met, played both with and against each other, and in Compton's case noted the presence of a 'supreme self-confidence. . .and unrufflable temperament already priceless to the rest of the team', which he rightly expected to 'hear more of' in future.

Evans's cricket in 1944 was, as in the early part of the War, subject to the rumour and eventual reality of overseas posting. On Whit Monday he was selected for an England XI whose batting order read: Barnett, Hutton, Edrich, Hammond, Ames, Robins, Allen, Bailey, Mallet, Evans, Wright. Their opponents were an Australian side of virtual unknowns, of whom only Keith Miller would be retained after the War. Hutton scored 84 in his first major innings since injury, and honour was satisfied on both sides. By now it had become clear that some form of traditional cricket would, within a year or two, be reinstated. The summer of 1944 was crowded. As if to compensate for time lost in digression, Warner and the others initiated a busy schedule. On 29 July Evans was selected for the Army against the RAF. The ground was full. D-Day had been accomplished. It was a mark of confidence that such a match was being played at all, and that day at Lord's in 1944 broke all wartime records in the matter of crowds and receipts. Evans recalls a sunlit afternoon on which, padded up, he was watching the early Army innings with friends in the grandstand. At some juncture the rumble of a doodlebug became audible, and presently increased to a crescendo. There was an eerie silence followed by a whistle. The players threw themselves down and those, like Evans, in the stands sought shelter under their seats. They waited, as he says, in 'peculiar, expectant silence'. In the event the bomb fell 200 yards short, although players and spectators felt its concussion. There was a pause and then a defiant and presumably nervous cheer rose round the ground. The players picked themselves up and Jack Robertson of Middlesex hooked the first ball he received for six, straight into the grandstand.

That ended Evans's serious wartime cricket. In the autumn and winter of 1944 he reverted, in the customary phrase, to being 'buggered about' by the army, undergoing further preparatory exercises that were to see him return to Scotland under the aegis of the 52nd Lowland Division. In the spring Warner wrote to him concerning his availability to play in the Victory Tests against Australia that summer. Before Evans could reply, news came through that, at this stage in the War's destiny, he was to be posted overseas.

His commanding officer, Major Cahill, was adamant and a few days later Evans found himself stationed with the 255 Car Company, RASC, first at Versailles and subsequently at Herx, near Frankfurt. In England the imminence of peace, at least in Europe, brought a partial resumption of first-class cricket, fulfilled by the four Victory matches against Australia. The star of these fixtures, as much for his promise as its later fulfilment, was Hutton – for the next ten years a central authoritative figure in Evans's life.

Evans himself attained a degree of authority with the birth of his son Howard Leslie (after his two County predecessors) in September 1945. Cricket, on the other hand, was at an end. True, a match was arranged in the unlikely environs of Frankfurt, but so irregular was the pitch that after the first few overs Evans gave up trying to keep wicket and became, in his own words, 'nothing more than a stopper.' For someone whose idea of wicketkeeping was, at all other times, rather more than that, the phrase conveys the very real threat he felt of being injured. The War in Europe ended on 8 May 1945 and already, under the auspices of MCC and the Inter-Services Sports Committee, something resembling a normal programme was being resumed. To Evans, with his thoughts reverting to the St. Lawrence Ground and beyond, the prospect of falling, as it were, at the final hurdle was 'simply not worth it.' Instead he spent the summer and autumn in tactical manoeuvres, and in sharpening his reflexes just as he had eight years before. Colleagues in Germany remember being asked to propel a ball at him from all angles and at speed in order for Evans to 'go through the motions'; unsurprisingly, the last person to tire of this exercise was the wicketkeeper himself. In 1937 the aim had been to refine his skills and enhance his prospects of employment. The man emerging on the other side of the War would still be ambitious; but his horizons now were altered. Within a year he would play for England.

The first thing to say about wartime cricket is that it existed. For at least the first three years of the First War, the professional game (and much else) was moribund. In this respect, Evans's experience can be compared to that of, say, Hobbs; to mention nothing of Grace and Stoddart. Nor was Evans to pay the penalty of Verity or suffer physical incarceration like Bowes. Of the five-and-a-half years of his service, five were spent in the British Isles; the remainder at relatively safe remove from the front. Having said which, it was surely the generation coming to fruition in 1939 which, in purely cricketing terms, underwent the greatest deprivation. Unlike Hutton and Edrich and Compton, tested already at international level, Evans was denied the opportunity to continue his natural development for Kent and, in all probability, England in the predicted time. He notes this himself without bitterness or self-pity, but gives it as his opinion that he lost an additional three to four years' Test experience. Moreover, until 1943, such Wartime cricket as he played was rarely above enthusiastic Club level. To a man whose first County catch had galvanized no less an observer than Ames, it must have been mortifying to be reduced, in less than a year, to the innocuous standard of battalion cricket. Only in 1943 and '44 did he regain the momentum of his early career, and then only in piecemeal form. As England's first post-War tour was to prove, the game was inherited by a mixture of those, like Hammond, whose best years were frankly behind them, and others, such as Bedser, Ikin and Evans himself, who had been denied the chance to develop professionally alongside their peers. In this respect it is salutary to note that Evans's first professional contract in 1937 and his debut for England nine years later were separated only by a handful of County appearances. To his known qualities of exuberance and agility, another attribute, less commonly associated with Evans, can now be added. As a cricketer he possessed everything, including patience.

He left the army. His cricket equipment followed him from Frankfurt to Faversham, and succeeded him by nearly eight months. At the end of 1945, the significance of Pocock's and his deceit became apparent when Evans was demobilized ahead of his comtemporaries. He returned to civilian life on 6 January 1946. Immediately he contacted de L'Hough at Canterbury and was invited to report to the St. Lawrence Ground that spring. From the army he had a new suit and some money. His battalion asked him to stay on and, under other circumstances, Evans might have considered it. But after the deprivation of war he faced the summer with renewed confidence.

Chapter Three

In Possession

EVANS RETURNED TO the circuit with much to prove. Eccentrically, he found himself in the position of having at least nominally played for his country, without first having established himself for his county. He admits to having been 'apprehensive' when he arrived at Canterbury in April for pre-season coaching; Levett had himself returned to duty and Ames's intentions remained obscure. As in 1937, Evans set himself to keeping wicket in the nets and, as before, duly impressed the County coach, Ted Humphreys. In the event, Brian Valentine, assuming the captaincy from the fallen Chalk, approached Evans with the news that Ames was to persevere exclusively with his batting, while Levett adopted the captaincy of the Seconds.

In keeping with other activities, cricket re-emerged in 1946 with no very clear identity but the ambition to establish itself as what it had once been. Yorkshire in this respect resumed where they had left off in 1939 by winning the Championship from Middlesex and Lancashire. Kent finished a respectable seventh. It was a transitional time, when curiosities like Yorkshire's 43-year-old Arthur Booth, with only a handful of previous first-class appearances, took 111 wickets for his County. Evans remembers it as a 'strange season. . .when youngsters chosen to fill the places of those who had played for the last time, had to be allowed to settle down gradually and naturally'.

One such was Evans himself. Whether it was the prospect of an overseas tour scheduled in just four months, or the fact that, in professional terms, he was no longer young, nothing about his own performances suggested that he would 'settle down', gradually or otherwise. On 19 June Evans represented the County against Warwickshire at Gravesend and scored 59 in 25 minutes, allowed by *Wisden* to have 'put Kent in a good position'. Shortly afterwards he took five dismissals in a match against Sussex at Tonbridge, watched by 14,000 spectators in the course of two days and, again according to *Wisden*, 'showing to special advantage behind the stumps'. At about this time a Test trial, to establish candidates for the three matches against India, was held at Lord's. Evans remembers listening for the names of the two wicketkeepers. His was not among them.

His disappointment was mollified by a chance meeting with A.J. Holmes, one of the England selectors, who informed Evans that he had been omitted because his abilities were better known than the two chosen keepers. Whatever the logic of this, neither the trialists, Billy Griffith of Sussex and Haydn Davies of Glamorgan, nor Evans himself, were selected for the first Test. The job went to Paul Gibb of Yorkshire. From this Evans drew what relief he could. If Davies and Griffith had failed to give satisfaction, the appointment of Gibb might be seen as a compromise, based on his presence on the last pre-War tour to South Africa. Not that Evans wanted Gibb to fail, but as he read the reports from Lord's he could be excused his moment of personal remorse. England won by ten wickets, Gibb scoring 60 and, for good measure, executing a leg side stumping off Alec Bedser. It was hardly the stuff to encourage competitors.

At this point events took a turn as decisive in its way as the match in 1943 when Evans had come to Gilligan's attention at Aldershot. Kent hosted a fixture against Gloucester at Gravesend, and among the visitors was the notable presence of Walter Hammond (who, coincidentally, made his first-class debut on the day Evans was born). The batsman, already approaching 50,000 first-class runs, was 43; war had deprived him of what might have been the six climactic years of his career. More pertinently, resuming where he had left off against the West Indies in 1939, Hammond was appointed captain of England that summer, and on the subsequent winter tour of Australia. Evans had encountered him when Hammond had appeared in wartime cricket for the RAF and 'England'; still their relationship was as apprentice to master, and Hammond did nothing to discourage it. Now, as he crouched to the bowling of Ray Dovey at Gravesend, Evans was consciously – perhaps self-consciously – trying to impress; and failing conspicuously as he saw Hammond shape to drive and, in his own words, 'anticipating the four.' The subsequent edge was comfortably dropped. From this Evans drew the conclusion that 'a wicketkeeper should imagine. . .that *every* ball is going to come through to him'. Hammond's conclusions he kept to himself. A few overs later the Gloucester player Billy Neale padded up to Wright, and the ball spun off directly into Evans's face. There was a lot of blood. The Kent players, reinforced by Hammond and Neale, urged him to retire. He refused. Wasting no time to put his new theory into practice, Evans sank groggily to his haunches for the next over from Dovey. Hammond came forward, overbalanced, and the ball turned off the edge for a catch behind. 'Plucky,' murmured the outgoing batsman. Evans beamed.

Coincidentally or not, Evans was selected for the second Test trial, held at Canterbury in early July. Encouragingly, he was included for 'England' under Hammond; his opposite number for the 'Rest' was Griffith. At least, thought Evans, he wouldn't fail through the strangeness of the surroundings; only, as it transpired, through inertia, as, one by one, the 'England' batsmen went through the motions to gentle derision from the crowd. The day passed slowly, and at 5.50 Evans found himself striding to the crease to join Norman Yardley. When he returned, after 25 minutes and an equal number of runs, he modestly hoped he might have 'livened things up'. Certainly the crowd, among whom were Evans's family and friends, appreciated the belated pyrotechnics. Hammond, from the pavilion, signified approval.

As a postscript, the match improved on its start, with the Rest failing by just twenty to achieve a target on the last day. Among the dismissals was Laurie Gray of Middlesex, for whom the entry 'st. Evans b. Bedser' must have impressed Hammond and others. Satisfied with his performance, Evans returned (insofar as he had ever left it) to Kent, for whom he was awarded his County Cap on 3 July 1946. It was during a match against Sussex at Tunbridge Wells, and, while other aspects of his career were progressing satisfactorily, the timing of the award stunned, and still stuns, him. He played miserably against Sussex. An aggregate of three and an indifferent performance behind the stumps was hardly the expected prelude to praise, but here was Valentine with the new blue cap and words of fulsome encouragement. Typically, Evans remembers being 'inspired by the occasion', and promptly took four victims to compensate for his earlier lapses. Throughout his career he was to respond to challenge in equal measure; so much so that, in time, his phrase 'We shall be there at the finish' was adopted as a kind of *leitmotiv* by successive England sides. For the time being it was enough that he had been recognized by his County and, in short order, repaid them. The champagne flowed that night at Tunbridge Wells.

The notion now spread that Evans might be on the brink of full England selection. Gibb did not have a happy time behind the stumps in the second Test at Old Trafford. Evans's colleagues and supporters began to back their assumption by laying bets with him, in shillings, half-crowns, drinks, ten shillings, pounds; anything. Evans himself went about his business, representing the Players against the Gentlemen at Lord's on 17–18 July. *Wisden*'s laconic assessment that he 'kept wicket well' underestimates his contribution: five dismissals and no byes conceded in the Gents' two completed innings. It was at 6.30 p.m. on 18 July 1946, as he left the field at the conclusion of play, that Evans noticed someone waving from the old players' balcony. It was his County colleague, Leslie Todd. It happened that Kent had no fixture that day, and Todd was enjoying a busman's holiday at Lord's. Gradually his gesticulation took the form of a thumbs-up sign. Evans knew that the selectors had been meeting that afternoon to choose the first twelve players to travel to Australia that winter. Hardly believing his eyes, he sought Todd's confirmation in the dressing-room. It was true. He, Evans, had been selected, and could he, Todd, please have the pound previously wagered on the event?

The rest of that evening and the day that followed passed in a blur. When Evans appeared at Blackheath next morning to represent Kent against Surrey, among the first to congratulate him was Ames. 'A different world,' he warned of Australia. For the time being Evans's only horizon was the field at Blackheath where, seven years earlier, he had made his first-class debut and where the crowd now gave him a 'warm reception'. One assumes it was more so than that afforded him by Jean, when he joined her that night without having established his whereabouts for the previous 36 hours. Somehow one recalls a comment by Trevor Bailey: 'You could be angry at Godfrey – but never for very long.'

Three weeks later news came through that Evans had been selected to play for England in the final Test at The Oval. The call-up itself was anodyne. Over the years, England players have learnt of their inclusion – or, more memorably, exclusion – from Test and touring teams in an assortment of car-parks, dressing rooms and pubs. Evans himself more than once heard the news through a shouted remark from the boundary. On this occasion, the soothing medium of the BBC informed him that Gibb (like himself, selected for Australia) would not appear at The Oval; in due course a confirming letter arrived, requesting him to report to the Great Western Hotel and offering him £25 (this at a time when his annual salary from Kent was no more than £350). Nervous as never before, he duly awaited the start on Saturday 17 August.

Here fate was to play a callous (and, in England, not unfamiliar) trick. It rained almost continually throughout his first Test. At the scheduled start, and at lunch, the gates were shut to the public and Evans was left to speculate on how to cope with the habitually erratic opening overs of Edrich, and the fast bowling of Gover, on a slippery and rain-soaked surface. At five o'clock he found out. The England team followed Hammond onto the sodden pitch, succeeded by the two great Indian openers, V.M. Merchant and Mushtaq Ali. Immediately a ball from Edrich vectored up off the seam and had Washbrook failing by inches to catch Merchant at cover. The first day ended with the openers still in uneasy possession.

Sunday 18 August was a rest day. It was also Evans's 26th birthday. He spent it in London, reflecting on the fact that Test cricket, like any other, was too absorbing to accommodate nerves. Those had left him at the instant of Edrich's first slinging delivery. When play resumed on Monday, Evans found himself actively involved in, and even directing, play; in short, fulfilling Levett's maxim that the fielding side should at all times be overseen by its wicketkeeper. The presence of Hammond (never one to sully his whites) at slip may have been a restraining influence, but there was nothing inhibited about Evans's appeal for run-out against Mushtaq Ali; nor, for that matter, against Merchant, when Compton (reverting to his Arsenal persona) side-footed the ball onto the stumps.

And that, as far as the Test was concerned, was that. Eventually India reached 331, of which Evans conceded a single bye. It was a ball from Jim Langridge which bounced awkwardly over his gloves; before Hammond could retrieve it, the batsmen had crossed. England did not complete their first innings; Evans did not bat, and rain ruined the match finally on the third day. As on his County debut, Evans had spent much of his time in the pavilion awaiting resumptions, and had felt anxious only when denied the chance to perform. It is one of his endearing qualities that, in every aspect save talent, he was as near 'normal' a cricketer as ever lived; his career never bears the stamp of omnipotence or infallibility, and his emotions at The Oval in 1946, no less than at Blackheath in 1939, are those of the common man. He was in turn proud, nervous, irritated (the bye) and relieved. Relieved because he had emerged with his stock intact, and even, on the basis of his performance, enhanced. He was, at last, in possession.

How good, technically, was Evans at this stage in his career? According to Arlott, 'basically sound, in the orthodox, two-handed method', but capable of amazing improvisation that had him gathering throws from the field one-handed and making catches 'incredibly wide' of the line of the stumps. The inference is that, while Evans was always liable to try the daring or dramatic, he never did so at the expense of basic principles; in other words, he was correct before he was clever. On arrival at the wicket, he would invariably mark a line with his left foot on the off stump; when standing up (which he did to all but the fastest bowling), he placed his left foot on the mark and his right a comfortable distance from it. This, he discovered, would afford him not only the clearest sight of the ball, but the ability to ride with it to his left (over the stumps) without moving his feet. As every schoolboy knows, the wicketkeeper should stand either directly up to the wicket or well back; strangely, when Evans himself obeyed this precept not all his contemporaries approved. But stand up, if humanly possible, he did, and at such an angle as to allow him the widest view of the ball. Lest anyone assume from this that he was interested only in the dramatic catch or quickfire stumping, it should be noted that Evans's tolerance of byes was grudging to the point of parsimony. When now he recalls his career he is likely to record 'only two extras' in preference to 'three or four catches'. At Sydney and Melbourne, the Australians were to experience this parsimony to their cost. To achieve it required not only lightning reflexes, agility and Evans's patented stance behind the stumps; the secret lay in Warner's observation: 'That man stands on his toes.' For Evans, as he crouched to the oncoming bowler, did indeed balance on his toes. At the moment of release his weight was thus thrust forward, enabling him to make in effect a flying start to the wayward delivery. The technique was equally effective to the edged catch in either direction. Nothing about Evans was ever static or tiresome and his wicketkeeping, too, was rarely predictable. But it was founded on sound principles, learnt at the hands of Levett, Ames and others, and allowed improvisation only insofar as this augmented certain basic truths. At this stage he had not toured overseas and observed Tallon or, of an earlier generation, Oldfield. Nonetheless, he was at the very zenith of his enthusiasm and, by his own admission, would sometimes attempt the one-handed catch or dazzling dive purely for effect. The season he played for England, lest we forget, was his first in continuous first-class cricket.

On 31 August 1946 the RMS *Stirling Castle*, an unconverted troopship, left Southampton with the twenty members of the MCC party to Australia. Few were ever to lack a dance partner; on board were 900 war brides returning to men whom they scarcely knew and whom they had met in brief wartime encounters. Less agreeably, the ship was designated 'dry'; to Evans's chagrin, the strongest refreshment available was orange juice. Few on board were under illusions about the undertaking before them; the England party was a curious amalgam of those, like Hammond, Langridge and Voce, clearly past their peak, and others, like Ikin, Bedser and Evans himself, undertaking their first overseas tour. The Australians, for whom the War had brought no significant disruption of domestic cricket, were captained by Bradman and boasted two young bowlers of whom Evans had 'heard much' and was to hear more: Miller and Lindwall. Their effect on the series, and on series to come, would be, in Evans's words, 'like a flame burst open'.

The *Stirling Castle* docked at Freemantle on 25 September. On 3 October Evans had his first experience of keeping on an Australian wicket when he was selected for MCC against a team representing Northam & Country Districts outside Perth. Off the first ball sent down by Voce, he learnt a lesson which he retained throughout the remainder of the tour. He was standing well back, in his customary position, when the ball burnt through the air into his chest; later, keeping to the spin bowlers, the bounce was 'like that of a tennis ball on a hard, as opposed to grass court'. Evans adjusted his stance accordingly. As Ames had forewarned, it was a 'different world'. Different in every sense, as the subsequent three-day train journey across the Nullarbor Plain confirmed. To alleviate the boredom of the Australian bush, Evans accompanied Dick Pollard on the saloon piano. He arrived in Adelaide bronzed, fit and, ominously for Paul Gibb, 'gaining in confidence'.

Against South Australia, Evans was to encounter Bradman for the first time. Looking frail after a long illness, the Australian contented himself with 76; and that only because Evans dropped him twice off Pollard at 15 and 58. It was the beginning of a relationship that, over nine Test Matches, saw Evans fail to once obtain the great man's dismissal. Had he done so early in the match with South Australia, it is conceivable that Bradman might have withdrawn from Test cricket there and then. As it was he was able to retrench and demonstrate at least a modicum of his pre-War brilliance. To Evans, he was 'absolutely concentrated and determined. . .with a backlift away and out towards point which would come down in a circle, finishing straight to the line of the ball. Neither elegant nor spectacular. But a genius.'

The word was far from Evans's own epithet as, fielding in the deep as twelfth man against Victoria, he dropped Lindsay Hassett in front of 60,000 derisive Antipodeans. From there things deteriorated to the point where he missed Bradman, again, behind the stumps against an Australian XI at Melbourne. When the first Test team was announced at Brisbane, it was almost a relief to be omitted.

This was the match whose outset was designated by E.W. Swanton 'the day of might-have-beens'. Australia, from 46-2, recovered to 322–3, due largely to centuries by Bradman and Hassett. With the captain on 28, a catch was held by Ikin that appeared to the fielding side, and much of the 20,000 crowd, as near conclusive a dismissal as possible. Bradman and, decisively, the umpire demurred. Less contentious was the moment when Hassett, on 50, snicked a ball into and out of Gibb's hands off Wright. According to Swanton, it was a 'plain miss', and did much to allow the eventual score of 645. England never recovered and lost the match by an innings and 332; Miller took 9 for 77.

That night Hammond set off by car (a Jaguar) for Sydney. His passengers were Hutton and Washbrook, who spoke among themselves while the captain brooded throughout the 900-mile journey. Among his contemplations, it can be assumed, was the question of team selection for the second Test. In the event there was a single change. Evans took the field on 14 December on the second day of his second Test, with the daunting task of following Tallon's four earlier dismissals. After a delay of three hours for rain, Australia set about compiling the small matter of 659–8, with Bradman and Barnes contributing an identical 234. On the fourth day (and, to the England team, it must indeed have seemed a match of Biblical proportions), Evans took his first Test dismissal: Miller caught off Peter Smith for 40. When he left the field at 12.45 on the fifth day, Evans had fielded in 100° heat for a total of eleven hours 40 minutes throughout what remains the highest home Australian total against England. Of that there was not a single bye. According to 'Tiger' O'Reilly, not one to over-praise, 'Evans's performance was equal to the great keeping of Don Tallon'. In the words of *Wisden*, 'Both Tallon and Evans performed magnificently.' The explanation for what was, by any standard, a feat of epic endurance is twofold: during the intervals at Sydney, Evans had sought out the great pre-War Australian keeper, Bertie Oldfield, who listened sympathetically to the younger player's complaint of difficulty in judging the apparent speed of the ball. It was then that he gave Evans his advice to physically link the two little fingers, the right over the left, so that the two hands, thus joined, would move together. According to Evans, 'if it was good enough for Oldfield, it was good enough for me', and he duly retained the technique for thirteen years and 89 subsequent Tests. In addition to proving infallible against the 'skier', it also meant that the coupled hands represented a sizeable impediment to byes. It was the last technical adjustment of Evans's apprenticeship and represented at least half the reason behind his performance at Sydney. And the other? 'Enthusiasm'.

Evans spent Christmas Day at the novel pursuit of surfing before setting off with the rest of the party (save Hammond, in Jaguar) for Canberra. There he met the Governor-General, the Duke of Gloucester, before taking part in a knockabout affected (as was much else this tour) by rain. Two Tests down, England arrived in Melbourne for the first international fixture of 1947. On the eve of the match, Langridge was injured at net practice and the following morning Edrich, fielding at short leg, was nearly obliterated by Barnes's hook. At this point, and when Voce, in full flight, pulled a muscle, England could be forgiven for regarding fate as distinctly partisan. In front of 60,000 spectators the abridged England attack performed heroically to dismiss Australia for 365. Again there were no byes. By this point word had spread that the red-faced tyro who had dropped Hassett had metamorphosed into a wicketkeeper of equal or even greater ability than Tallon, and reports continually refer to their 'neck and neck' performances. Evans regarded it and regards it today as the 'greatest tribute' to be placed on a level with his Australian counterpart. Despite this (and with endearing fallibility), he dropped Morris in the first innings and Bradman in the second. Both were chances perceptibly easier than others he did hold. In the England first innings, Washbrook, Ikin and Yardley contributed to a total of 351, Swanton from the press box noting 'a tendency which has shown itself on the tour towards public criticism of the decisions of umpires', specifically of lbw verdicts against Compton and Edrich. Evans scored 17 with a borrowed bat. The next day a turning ball from Wright twisted down the leg side, and the first byes in a total of 1,054 Australian runs were recorded. To complete a performance of epic endurance, Evans was at the crease with Norman Yardley when, on a worn wicket in sizzling rain, England defied Lindwall and Miller to earn a draw.

The fourth Test at Adelaide demonstrated at least one of Evans's prime attributes: resilience. It was preceded by a memorable sojourn with the comedian Tommy Trinder, with whom one suspects he had more in common than cricket. The influence seems to have paid off because, bowled for nought by Lindwall in the England first innings, Evans improvised a little cameo of his own; hurrying from the middle he selected the wrong gate to the pavilion and found himself stranded in a crowd of apoplectic Australians. Surviving the ordeal rendered the next day's play relatively straightforward, and he duly caught Arthur Morris down the leg side off Bedser. To quote the Adelaide press: 'Some of his takes on the leg when Bedser was bowling with the new ball were remarkable.' Australia finished 27 ahead, and at 5.15 on the fifth day, when Evans returned to the crease, only Compton remained of the recognized batsmen. At 255–8 and more than a full day's play to come, rarely can a captain's order to a number ten batsman to 'stay there' have been more heartfelt. The temperature in the middle was 107°.

Compton's promise to 'farm' the bowling soon developed into a pantomime of refusing singles on any but the last or penultimate ball of the over. Sensitive to this, Bradman would adjust his field so that the players moved to and fro like the breathing of a sleeping dog. Forty-five minutes later Evans left the field, scoreless but intact. The crowd gave him an ovation. Next morning the ordeal resumed; so sweat-soaked were their gloves, neither Compton nor Evans could take a firm grip of their bats. Bradman complained to Compton about the England tactics and the fact that he, Compton, was allegedly roughening the pitch in advancing on Colin McCool. 'I always move my feet to the spinners,' came the reply. Bradman retreated.

Evans eventually went 95 minutes without a run; his score of 10 not out took more than two-and-a-half hours. He himself attributes his tenacity to 'bloody-mindedness'; to *Wisden* it was evidence of a 'splendid defence'. The former Australian captain, Warwick Armstrong, congratulated him and the *Sydney Sun* ran a cartoon commemorating the event. Almost lost in the eulogy was the fact of Compton's second successive century and the subsequent draw. When Evans and the rest of the party were celebrating their achievement that evening he was handed a telegram by Arthur Gilligan. It read: 'Never did one man bat so long for so little.' The signature read, simply, 'Churchill'.

After these heroics the final Test at Sydney proved an appropriate climax. Its chief distinction was a first-innings century by Hutton (compared by Swanton to 'the great Hobbs') which, in the event, proved his last contribution of the tour. After the rest day, Hutton registered a temperature of 103° and was dispatched to hospital with tonsillitis. Despite the exertions of Smith and Wright on a turning pitch, Australia won by five wickets a match that, until the last two hours, they could conceivably have lost. Evans caught Barnes off Bedser in both innings and, in the second, broke what threatened to be an opening stand by running out Arthur Morris. It was a an appropriate finale to the tour.

How had Evans himself emerged from it? In simple terms, his nine Test dismissals equalled Tallon's; more significantly, critics like O'Reilly now bracketed the two players together, while Woodfull believed that, if anything, Evans emerged ahead of his counterpart – an astonishing achievement for one who had played his first Test less than six months before. *Wisden*'s summary is the most comprehensive: 'Only the second choice wicketkeeper at the beginning of the tour, Evans never looked back when picked for the

Test at Sydney. . .with his place certain, he became more confident in everything he did.' At 26, Evans had been the youngest member of a party of which only Bedser, Ikin, Compton (all 28) and himself were under 30. The average age was 33; Hammond, the captain, 43. The latter provoked criticism from some, like Swanton, for letting the game run on the field and from others, like Compton, for his remoteness off it. But Evans found him 'among the finest skippers' under whom he played and bore Hammond no ill-will for his detachment: 'If I'd had a Jaguar, I would have used it too.' It is hard, in fact, over a first-class career spanning twenty years, to find a single cricketer whom Evans admits *not* to liking, even among those, like Hutton, who undoubtedly saw life through different eyes. He even formed a relationship, of sorts, with Bradman, to whom Evans chatted affably in the middle. The remarks were rarely returned. He was fortunate, too, to have as a room-mate his colleague Wright, who had played in South Africa with England before the War. If the tour itself had been undistinguished (of the seventeen first-class matches, thirteen were drawn) and bedevilled by rain, Evans, without doubt, emerged from it with credit. In all four Tests in which he played he left a decisive mark either in front of or behind the stumps; and, in common with Hutton, Compton and Wright, left Australia with a reputation enhanced.

In early March the party, save Gibb, Hardstaff, Langridge and Hutton, flew to New Zealand. After the cauldron of Sydney, the fresh grass and morning dew reminded Evans of Kent. He duly celebrated by scoring 101, his maiden first-class century, against Otago on 15 March 1947. His partnership with Ikin of 171 extended for precisely 90 minutes. In the subsequent Test at Christchurch he scored a rapid 21 not out, then watched the remainder of the game from the pavilion as rain ruined the following three days and the extra day that followed. Earlier, Hammond, in what was to be his last appearance in senior cricket, had scored 79 of the England total of 265–7 declared. Both sets of players applauded him from the wicket.

After that there was little to do but celebrate prior to taking to the air for the seven-day journey home. A route that saw the advance party of Evans, Washbrook, Compton and Voce touch down at Darwin, Surabaya, Singapore, Karachi, Calcutta, Bahrain, Cairo and Sicily terminated at Poole barely a month prior to the start of the 1947 season. There to greet them was Jean Evans, brought to the airport by John Pocock. There was a reunion with the infant Howard at Maidstone. Everywhere he went, Evans was accosted by those who had risen in the early hours of raw winter mornings to listen to Gilligan's distant commentaries from Australia. Praise and plaudits attended him; more tangible recognition followed in the form of a television set and engraved cigarette case purchased by public subscription in Maidstone. The benevolence was appreciated: Evans returned from a seven-month tour, during which he had played five Test matches and established two world records, with a net remuneration of £200. It made him laugh.

The summer of 1947 will forever be associated with Compton and Edrich, who scored mightily for both county and country, and for the radiant weather that attended them. For Kent, too, it was a propitious season. The County rose to fourth in the Championship, and, according to *Wisden*, 'save for one lamentable period in August' might even have exceeded that. For his County Evans took 46 catches and fourteen stumpings (nearly a one-in-four ratio) and scored 691 Championship runs. His combination with Wright secured 34 dismissals.

The association was in evidence from the first match, against Derbyshire at Canterbury. Evans conceded no byes in either innings and claimed eight victims – seven of them off Wright. Interest in the background significance of domestic cricket was already high when England took to the field at Trent Bridge on 7 June for the first Test against South Africa. Norman Yardley, as expected, succeeded to the captaincy vacated by Hammond. Throughout his tenure, the sole criticism that seems to have been levelled at the Yorkshireman was that he was 'too nice'; that and the suspicion that, in purely technical terms, he was not always worth his place in the side. The team from Australia was remodelled to include Dollery, the Warwickshire batsman, the slow bowlers Cook and Hollies, and Evans's Kent teammate Jack Martin, whose stuttering delivery stride restricted his pace to medium. Inexplicably, the selectors omitted Wright. According to Arlott, 'there was no justification for such a decision'; but decided it was. Leg spin was provided by Eric Hollies, who returned the remarkable first innings figures of 5–123 off 55 overs.

Hollies was something of a humorist, and needed to be as a 319-run partnership developed between Melville and Nourse that saw South Africa to 533. After an early shower, the pitch had become an invitation to runs of which Melville, in particular, took full advantage; the timing of his cover drives rivalled that of Hammond. When Compton was out playing an 'airy flick' early on the third morning, the England innings never recovered. The last eight wickets fell for 54 and by lunch they were following on, 325 behind. It was at this point that Compton, abetted by Yardley, proceeded to reconstruct the match to an extent that, theoretically, meant that England could have won. He scored 163, batting, according to Arlott, 'with the air of improvisation of a boy at play on the beach'. When Evans appeared at 407–5, the ground was still galvanized by his performance. Yardley met the new batsman with the question, 'Can you stay here half-an-hour?' 'Half-an-hour?' said Evans. 'Just watch me.' He then proceeded to score 74 runs in even time. His innings altered the entire atmosphere of the match. The fire went out of the South African attack and their eventual target of 227 in 138 minutes proved too much. They finished at a creditable 166–1. It would have been two, but for Evans dropping Melville off Compton on 96. The South African became the first to score a hundred in each innings of a Test. At the end of the over Evans pointed out the salient fact to the aggrieved bowler. 'Fair enough,' said Compton.

The most memorable fact of the second Test at Lord's was the crowd of 30,000 on the first day who saw Compton and Edrich score 216 in 200 minutes, subsequently enlarged to 370, then the highest ever scored for the third wicket in a Test. That and the royal visit of the King, Queen and two princesses. Evans remembers the party 'showing quite an interest' in his hands, which, unlike a later period of his career, bore relatively few signs of damage. After the England offensive, South Africa performed manfully to reach 327 and 252, Melville scoring his third successive century. Evans conceded three byes. England were left 26 to win and Hutton and Washbrook made them easily enough; one up and three to play. For Evans it had been 'the best-spirited' Test (the eighth) of his career. It neatly foreshadowed the match at Old Trafford where, of the 26 innings played prior to the Test, only four had reached 300. Under the circumstances, South Africa's total of 339 in wet, wind-racked conditions, did them credit. In reply, Compton and Edrich restricted themselves to a partnership of 228 at a run a minute; and that, in effect, was that. On the last day Hollies, Wright and Compton did the damage on a wicket that tested Evans no less than the departing batsmen. Arlott remembers him 'now squatting, nose behind stumps, as the bowler's arm came over . . . leaping, reaching, stretching and urging – absolutely in his element'. As at Lord's, England reached their last-innings target, though with less than an hour in hand. It was the first Test at Manchester brought to a conclusion since 1937.

After this performance, Evans had an agreeable interlude appearing for the Players against the Gentlemen from 16–18 July. The side was captained by Ames. Evans achieved a quick 22 and three dismissals (including Bailey) before rain, perversely in this fine summer, intervened. Then and for Kent he was clearly a man in form; less than a year after his England debut, rivals like Brennan, McIntyre and Griffith were forced to the realization that Evans had made the wicketkeeping job his own. It was agreeable, too, to be winners of the series, and England's success gave them confidence; too much, perhaps, as the side dispatched to the West Indies that winter had a suspicion of complacency – not, however, evident as Evans and, incredibly, Hutton played their first Test on Yorkshire soil that July.

Again there was a crowd of 30,000 to see Hutton play the pivotal innings in the England total of 317; his score, exactly 100, lasted five hours and was, according to Arlott, 'faultless'. Again, England were left with a modest last-innings total and, again, they achieved it. Despite capturing

'Leaping, reaching, stretching and urging'–in action against South Africa, 1947. (Sport & General).

only two victims, Evans felt he had given the crowd 'value for money', chiefly in taking the lively deliveries of Harold Butler, moving both ways off the wicket at speed. In the South African first innings there were no byes.

It is perhaps instructive to place Compton's and Edrich's achievements that summer in context. In scoring 3816 and 3539 runs respectively, both surpassed Tom Hayward's outstanding record of 3518 runs in a season. Compton also broke Hobbs's record of sixteen first-class centuries; his double century for Middlesex against The Rest was his eighteenth, eleven of which came in a phenomenal five-week surge at the end of the season. As a modern comparison, Graeme Hick's 1988 aggregate of 2443, formidable enough in itself, contained half the number of Compton's centuries, at an average of 76 versus 90. Lest anyone assume that Middlesex's ascendancy was a two-man performance, it should be remembered that the County openers, Robertson and Brown, scored nearly 5000 runs between them and Jack Young, the rotund slow left-arm bowler, took 159 first-class wickets.

So much the better, then, for Kent's two performances against the Champions in July and August. The first, in a gloriously hot Canterbury Week (attended by 50,000 spectators in five days), saw Kent reach a first innings total of 423–8 declared. The Middlesex reply, according to Arlott, 'crystallized into a contest between two of the most gifted cricketers in England' – Compton, who made 106 (c. Evans b. Wright) and Wright himself, who took 6–87 and forced Middlesex to follow on. After centuries by Robertson and Edrich, Kent, set a target of 232 in two hours, eventually achieved a draw; no small achievement, given that Middlesex were held to only one other such result all season. Evans turned in his 'usual spirited performance' behind the stumps. In the return fixture at Lord's, Kent triumphed five minutes from the end of extra time after one of the most exciting matches of the season. Again Wright did the damage, with a first innings analysis of 7–92, twice accounting for Compton (admittedly, in the second innings, after he had scored 168). For Kent, Evans played an innings of 56 in better than even time, and Middlesex were set a target of 397 to win in 260 minutes. They failed by 75 runs. In both Middlesex innings, 550 runs on a turning wicket, there were no byes. Evans made the short journey to The Oval justifiably feeling that, for county and country, he was performing as well as he ever would.

The fifth Test confirmed this. The match was played in heat such as at times seemed to tire even the South Africans. As in 1976, the outfield was bleached to a shade of burnt yellow and white; the ball travelled to the boundary with convulsive speed. Evans's contribution to the England total of 427 was 45, and might have been more but for a farce of Karno-like proportions involving Cliff Gladwin. On Monday, his 27th birthday, Evans hit a ball to deep extra cover and called his partner for one. Gladwin's decisive reply, 'Nay, lad', left Evans stranded in mid-wicket. According to Arlott, it was 'unpardonable'; to Evans, 'soon forgotten', particularly when Gladwin redeemed himself with an innings of 51 not out. The South African reply of 302 was notable for a century by Mitchell – that and Dick Howorth's first ball in Test cricket, which tempted Dyer to drive; Dyer accepted and the lofted shot was caught by Gladwin at cover. In the second innings Compton made 113, of which the last 60, 'full of glorious improvisation', came in 40 minutes; at the other end, Howorth admitted that he had enjoyed the performance so much that he felt it anti-climactic to play a shot himself. But play he did, improvising a partnership of 58 with Evans, who 'cut, hooked and flashed merrily' to allow an England declaration 450 ahead. At 232–2, few would have put the total past South Africa's reach; then came the melodrama which ensured the draw. Yardley brought back Howorth to check the scoring rate, and he duly bowled Nourse a ball to which no stroke was offered and which appeared to brush the back of the batsman's leg. Howorth appealed for lbw. There was a click, and Evans appealed for a catch at the wicket. Both were met in the negative by the umpire at the bowler's end. It was at this point that Robertson, fielding at square leg, noted the salient fact of the leg bail lying on the ground. A third appeal, for 'bowled', was duly lodged and found proven. Nourse had scored 97 and from then on the visitors, despite Mitchell's sheet anchor, were all at sea. At the end they were 28 short and England had won the series by three Tests to nil. From it Evans emerged with fourteen dismissals and a batting average of 41.80, marginally below Hutton's and above that of his captain Yardley.

Evans concluded his *annus mirabilis* by representing the South versus the North at Scarborough. Hutton, in trying to hook Alec Bedser, mistimed the ball. It caught the top edge and flew in the general direction of fine leg. Evans, after a 40-yard sprint, caught it. Hutton's comment was unprintable.

Home now was a semi-detached house, 'The Wickets', at Bearsted, near Maidstone. Ames and John Pocock both lived nearby. Evans's opportunity to enjoy a rare Christmas in their and his family's company was denied when, at the last moment, MCC brought forward the departure of the touring party to the West Indies to 23 December. For Jean, it was the second in a series of deprivations, though she would later have the consolation of visits to the Carribean and Australia; for Evans, a continuation of the merry-go-round that eventually saw him make eight overseas tours. If he was already aware of the strain of international cricket, this was mitigated by the experience he now had of it. Although he had played his first Test only sixteen months before, Evans, it should be noted, was in the senior half of the party to the Carribean. His cricketing development in 1947 had been dramatic and he anticipated, at 27, a virtually limitless future. For the moment, that meant the West Indies.

The tour itself was the product of gentle deceit by the home Board of Control. Karl Nunes, its President, had asked Warner to use his influence to have a side sent out as soon as possible after the War; adding, for good measure, that the home team would be 'not very strong'. The result was an England party from which Hutton, Compton, Edrich, Bedser and Wright were omitted; the captain was the 45-year-old Gubby Allen. For the second year in succession, MCC set off under the leadership of a great cricketer no longer great, and in no more comfort than before. The SS *Tettela*, a banana boat with accommodation for fewer than twenty passengers, pitched and rolled its way across the Atlantic. Christmas dinner was notable only for the large number of vacant chairs around the table. The party was three days late in berthing at Barbados, and never can cricketers have been so glad to see that idyllic island. More than one felt moved to kiss the ground.

Here arose one of the perennial complaints of all overseas teams. Due to the *Tettela*'s late arrival and the congested nature of the itinerary, only a single day remained before the first fixture of the tour. In consequence the match was hopelessly lopsided; all Evans could hope for was a degree of acclimatization to the sights and sounds of his new surroundings – particularly the latter, which he compared to 'playing cricket inside an enormous beehive'. As vivid as the huge cap of January sun overlying the ground, the incessant blare of drums and hooters attended the crowd

MCC in the West Indies, 1947–48.

who, dressed in tones of fiery red, darted and flapped like a shoal of carnivorous fish. Bets were wagered on every day, every session, every ball; on even the speed of the two drink-boys to and from the wicket.

Within the party, the bet was that the series would not be the picnic that Nunes had predicted. Already, at Barbados, Evans had noted the presence of two West Indians, of whom one scored 118 and the other kept wicket 'with almost equal brilliance' to his batting. Their names were Weekes and Walcott.

As in Australia, the radically altered conditions forced Evans to reconsider his technique. As a batsman, with the ball coming off the pitch quicker and lower, he realized he had to commit to a stroke as late as possible; as a wicketkeeper, he was forced to adjust to the slower ball bouncing higher than in England. In common with all but Robertson and Hardstaff, Evans never successfully mastered the West Indies attack; his Test aggregate of 128 runs at 18.28 was respectable, no more. Behind the stumps, he delivered in concentration and agility what he lacked in experience – so much so that, at the end of the tour, Walcott was to admit how much he had learnt from his opposite number. With its usual perspective, *Wisden* concluded that Evans 'delighted the native crowds with his spectacular wicketkeeping, but as a batsman. . .accomplished little'. Except, of course, his own further education.

To emphasize the point, West Indies had comfortably the best of the first (drawn) Test at Bridgetown. England were hindered by the absence of Allen and Harold Butler, both of whom had pulled muscles; the attack was opened by Cranston and Tremlett, neither of whom could be classified as electric. Later in the match Dennis Brookes broke a finger and was unable to play again on the tour. For England, Hardstaff batted heroically for 98, bettered only by Christiani, who scored 99 on his debut for the West Indies. Evans made, in his own phrase, a 'merry' 26, and was chastised by the watching Warner for 'not taking it seriously'. His reply was to flay the Trinidad attack in the next match. This was Evans's first experience (at least since Durston's school) of playing on matting. As a wicketkeeper, he found it ideal for keeping to pace – if not to men like Laker, for whom the ball bounced even higher than before. As a batsman, he frankly revelled in it. The ball came through at an even height, save for the occasions when it struck one of the restraining steel pegs; Evans himself achieved this when bowling in the nets and nearly decapitated Laker. In the second match at Trinidad he went one better and, with Griffith behind the stumps, sent down three overs of lively medium pace for eight runs. His room-mate Howorth's comment, 'I've seen better bowlers in a second-hand tailor's,' was a little unkind.

In the second Test the folly of England's selection, and the ruinous succession of injuries, was fully exposed. Hardstaff, Place and Brookes were all unavailable. In consequence Griffith was called on to open the innings with Robertson.

He responded with 140, his maiden first-class century. Laker, in his second Test, scored 55, and the England total of 362 was, under the circumstances, relatively respectable; relatively. For West Indies George Carew scored 107; the first wicket went down at 173; and Frank Worrell, on his Test debut, proceeded to 97 before Cranston found the edge and Evans completed the catch. The result was that West Indies were left needing 140 to win at two runs a minute. They were achieving them when Butler came in to bowl to Weekes. Allen had set a defensive field. Weekes got a hard edge and the ball vectored between the non-existent second and third slips. Evans took off, dived, and caught it. The crowd, remarkably, fell quiet. Weekes himself appeared to take some time to comprehend what had happened. It was, by any standard, an epic feat of agility and anticipation. The West Indies duly settled for a draw.

To celebrate, Evans and others attended the Trinidad carnival. Confronted by the native pageantry, he had to fight his theatrical longing – the longing to join in. This had to be resisted. Allen was a fine captain, who retained at least a vestige of the fast bowler's art, but dissolute he was not. Evans must have paused for five or ten seconds before accepting Victor Stollmeyer's offer of the loan of a native woman's costume. Thus disguised, he oscillated into the crowd of local partygoers, singers, dancers and MCC tourists. One of the last, Dick Howorth, appeared to show definite interest in the sturdy, well-built woman wearing the colourful mask, terminated only when a request for 'the time' revealed the hirsute Evans forearm. Howorth's response made Hutton's at Scarborough seem mild by comparison.

Hutton himself appeared when an emergency call brought the news that Compton, Allen's first preference as reserve, was unavailable. Hutton was duly sounded and found willing, and arrived in Georgetown by way of Lisbon, Dakar and Brazil. Two days later he played an undefeated innings of 138. The effect on the touring party was electric. Evans felt the atmosphere perceptibly changed and praises to this day Hutton's innings (and his second, of 62) in conditions removed, to say the least, from those of midwinter Yorkshire. Evans's own contribution was restricted by a bout of prickly heat induced by extreme humidity. At the ground, nine feet below sea level, steam could be seen rising from the pitch. In some discomfort, Evans was dispatched to patrol the boundary while Griffith kept wicket. Few of the party were distraught when rain ended the final fixture before the third Test.

Here Hutton again distinguished himself in response to the West Indies' 297, of which Worrell made 131. After a promising start, England collapsed and followed on. At this point, on a worn wicket, a rearguard action to which Evans contributed 37 meant that the West Indies would at least bat again; and against Laker, to boot. At one stage, chasing 78, they were 26–3, and the looks from the home dressing-room were anything but sanguine. Had Gomez not been dropped five times, England might even have forced an improbable win. But dropped he was, and the home side prevailed by seven wickets. Evans's reaction was relief that the party promptly decamped for Jamaica.

Hutton, having played on the island a dozen years earlier, made a century at Melbourne Park, discovered since his last visit to have acquired a 'ridge' just short of a length. In the Test at Sabina Park, he and Robertson put on 129 for the first wicket; the remaining nine fell for 98. The West Indies won by ten wickets. Evans achieved little except to be present when Weekes scored the first of what were to be five consecutive Test centuries. With the serious cricket completed, MCC received and complied with a request to play an additional two-day match along the coast at Montego Bay. They duly recorded their sole victory of the tour, a fact communicated by Swanton in previewing the coming series against Australia. Evans and others resented it. The vagaries of team selection had been beyond their control, as were the catalogue of injuries and illnesses that attended them. Evans, the perenially cheerful tourist, personally enjoyed the experience. His most abiding wish was that, in future, the selectors would decide to send a full complement of players of Test standard. On a technical note, he was given the opportunity of studying the potent batting of Weekes, Worrell and Walcott, even if the last suffered from his concentration on wicketkeeping. Evans himself emerged with credit behind the stumps, and, as when catching Weekes at Trinidad, demonstrated the full brilliance of his play reinforcing his maturity. From now on, he was to be not only an automatic, but senior member of overseas tours. Fourteen successive Tests had consolidated his position, and his reputation among the public; even in New York, *en route* to London, he was heralded as 'some kind of English big-shot'. The phrase, in its less pejorative sense, seemed highly appropriate.

At the conclusion of the final Test of 1948, England were observed by Arthur Gilligan to have lost 'not only the Ashes, but the sackcloth as well'. From the moment of their arrival, the Australians proved themselves worthy of comparison with their illustrious predecessors: Darling's side of 1902, Armstrong's of 1921 and, more recently, Bradman's of 1938. Bradman himself was past his peak, but held in such regard that bowlers were intimidated by his mere presence. A batting order of Morris, Barnes, Bradman, Hassett, Miller, Harvey and Loxton was one which, against the England attack, could scarcely go wrong, and the proof of its strength was that Brown, with a Test average approaching 50, could be omitted. The bowling was spearheaded by Lindwall, with Miller and Bill Johnston in support. Tallon, behind the wicket, was 'magnificent'. The Australian, on his first overseas tour, took catches – such as that diving left-handed to account for Hutton at The Oval – which proved that, at 32, he remained the only other currently playing wicketkeeper of Evans's stature. Only in leg-spin were the tourists deficient; Ring was an adventurous but unpredictable proponent who never fully mastered English conditions. It might be argued that, with the new ball available to Lindwall and Miller after just 55 overs, he never needed to.

From the start the Australians proved a formidable combination. Against Essex at Southend they scored 721 runs in a day, with Bradman and Brown sharing an extraordinary partnership of 219 in 90 minutes. Against Gloucester at

Bristol, Bradmanless, they declared at 774–7, with Goddard returning figures of 0–186. For Tom Graveney, this was the moment when he 'knew England were in trouble'. According to Evans, no attack led by Lindwall, the classic fast bowling schizophrenic ('Hated you on the field, loved you off it') was going to be easy; not with Miller, Loxton and Johnston to sustain it. The early season was disappointing for Kent; eventually they were to drop to fifteenth in the Championship and Valentine relinquish the captaincy to David Clark. To Evans, the start of the Test series came as a relief.

The first Test at Nottingham saw the enforcement of a rule, now laughably archaic, that jeopardized England's hopes. Throughout the first day, the light varied from ashen to stygian grey, with the then limitation of one appeal per innings meaning that play continued in deepening shades of Nottingham gloom. Yardley, restored as captain, had elected to bat in conditions of bright sunlight. No sooner had the match started than did the rain. When play resumed the wicket became greasy and Lindwall, Miller and Johnston dismissed England for 165; it would have been less but for 63 by Laker, batting number eight on his home debut. Evans's contribution was twelve, notable only for the unique experience of being dropped twice by Bradman, fielding at cover, off successive balls. Shortly afterwards, Arthur Morris – enjoying, by his own admission, 'a quiet doze' at silly-mid on – was roused by a lofted drive which, as much from surprise as instinct, he caught. Evans departed. Yardley's response was to restrict the Australians' scoring, implementing his credo that the opposition had not so much basic weaknesses as basic strengths; and by avoiding them, one could impart a superiority. The plan appeared to work when Barnes chopped a ball from Laker which Evans anticipated, sighted. . .and missed. Fortunately for him, if not for Barnes, the ball rebounded off his thigh and, pivoting, Evans held the catch both sideways and backward of his normal position. Barnes himself believed no one else could have achieved it. Frank Chester, the umpire, declared it the finest wicketkeeping catch in living memory. England collectively drew strength from it and, with Laker dismissing Miller first ball, only Bradman and Hassett of the recognized batsmen remained. They made 138 and 137 respectively. England began their second innings 344 behind, led, as Arlott put it, by 'two great batsmen batting at their greatest'. The first, Hutton, made 74 after surviving an onslaught from Miller; the second, Compton, 184 in an unwonted display of textbook determination. It ended when Miller, who, if tending to 'signal' his bouncer, could still unleash it from a disarmingly short run, delivered a ball which forced Compton onto his stumps. Evans then scored 50, thanks to which the Australians were at least compelled to bat again. It had been an ill-tempered Test, aggravated by the Nottingham crowd, who (perhaps remembering the reception afforded Larwood in comparable circumstances) roundly booed Miller in bowling successive bouncers at Hutton. He at least had the satisfaction, in the brief Australian second innings, of catching Bradman for nought.

The achievement was repeated at Lord's where, for the third successive time, the Australian captain was caught at backward short leg off Bedser. With Hutton also catching Barnes without score, Australia owed everything to Morris's century in reaching 350. With respect to the late umpire Bill Reeves, who advised disgruntled bowlers to 'look in the morning paper' for confirmation of his decisions, it is tempting to speculate on Australia's score had, on 52, a decision been awarded against Morris. Both Wright and Evans are convinced to this day that he snicked the former into the latter's gloves, and Morris himself confirmed it in the safety of the pavilion. His hundred, too, should be seen in context of Jack Fingleton's observation that 'in this Test. . .the playing area seemed very small. Under the circumstances, a century score hardly compared with one when the ground was not circled off.' Certainly the crowd, excited by the first Australian presence in a decade, restricted the boundary; in which case, England's reply of 215 was all the more abject. The critical moment occurred when Barnes, whose tour up to then had been disheartening, appeared in the second innings on a 'pair'. After twenty minutes of utter misery, he advanced down the pitch to

Caught by Miller off Johnston. 2nd Test at Lord's, 1948 (Sport & General.)

Laker. The ball turned, past Barnes, past Evans, and passed into the crowd for four byes. 'Thanks,' said Barnes. 'I'll make use of that.' He did, scoring 141. The upshot was an England target of 596, which they spectacularly failed to achieve, despite a last-wicket rearguard between Evans and Wright. Fifteen minutes later the clouds opened and rain would undoubtedly have ended the match, had Lindwall (8–131) not done so already. It was the 150th Test between the two countries.

The next, at Manchester, was preceded by a sensation. Hutton was dropped. England's shock at this announcement was matched only by Australia's. Evans, for one, could scarcely credit it. The sole justification for the decision seems to have been the conviction that Hutton had played below himself and that, at Nottingham, his confidence had been undermined by Miller. In the event his replacement, Jack Emmett, soon departed. Worse was to come. Compton, in attempting to hook a short-pitched ball from Lindwall, edged it onto his forehead. In his own words, it was 'comparable to the blow of a sledgehammer'. When Compton weaved into the dressing-room, the doctor was waiting for him. A dozen stitches and a 'quick net' later, he resumed his innings with England 119–5 and proceeded to score 145 not out. It was an epic performance, inspiring Evans to produce a cameo of his own: 34 out of a partnership of 75 with Compton, in whose company he invariably revelled. In the closing overs of the innings Barnes, at silly-mid on, was struck in the ribs by a full-blooded drive by Pollard. He tried to resume, but subsequently collapsed at the wicket and spent ten days in hospital under observation. The incident unnerved Australia, who were dismissed by Bedser and Pollard for 221, a first innings deficit of 142. At one stage Edrich approached Evans and advised him to 'stand well back' as he intended to 'slip in a few'. The resulting barrage was met with rapturous applause, after which Lindwall, the batsman, was heard to mutter words about the cyclical nature of cricket. In the first over of England's reply Emmett was caught behind, whereupon Washbrook and Edrich dropped anchor. Had rain not intervened, washing out the fourth day, England must have prevailed; as it was, Yardley was compelled to declare at 174–3 in an attempt to force victory. He failed. It was the eighth successive Ashes Test at Old Trafford to be drawn or abandoned, and meant that England could not now win the series.

For the Headingley Test Hutton was restored and on his home ground made 81 out of 458. For once the sun shone constantly and, as at Lord's, the crowds were so tightly packed that some squatted on the grass inside the boundary. The Australian reply was led by a nineteen-year-old making his debut in England. Neil Harvey, a Victorian who had impressed Evans in a State match eighteen months before, now produced an innings of astounding maturity. His 112, and Loxton's run-a-minute 93, meant that the first innings deficit was restricted to 38. It was a situation custom-made for Evans, who responded to Yardley's request to 'have a go' by scoring an undefeated 47 between 5.50 and the close of the fourth day's play. At one stage Yardley called out the England team to watch; Evans waved. Australia were left 404 on the fifth day, a winning total never before achieved.

Had Hollies, or Wright, or Young been playing – and had their fielding not collapsed – England must have won. Instead Laker and Compton were unable to exploit a turning pitch. As the certainty of their position subsided, so did England's morale. Crapp dropped Bradman twice in the slips. That was bad enough, but when Morris advanced to a full toss from Compton, Evans made the cardinal error of anticipating the boundary instead of the ball. The resulting stumping chance was missed; Morris went on to make 182. To compound this, Evans promptly dropped Bradman when a thick edge off Laker bounced over his shoulder for four. At this stage it became apparent that it was not to be England's day, and Evans concedes that the team, not least himself, 'took things too lightly'. From a position of being certain to win, by tea on the last day they appeared likely to lose. Australia achieved their target with fifteen minutes to spare. Bradman scored his nineteenth and final century against England and deliberately allowed Harvey to make the winning run, a gesture unexpectedly significant in light of his subsequent innings at The Oval. While the champagne flowed in the visitors' dressing-room, Evans made for his car and left the ground within ten minutes of the finish. He spent the evening of 27 July driving the 250 miles to Maidstone after the worst performance of his international career.

The Oval, 1948, will forever be associated with one innings. It says much for Bradman that a score of nought has eclipsed in the imagination the artistry of Morris; the tenacity of Hutton, Compton and Edrich; the fire of Miller and brimstone of Lindwall; and the sustained brilliance of Tallon. The fact is, when Bradman appeared at the wicket in the late afternoon of 14 August, the cricket world experienced something approaching a collective breakdown.

Normal protocol was suspended in the extraordinary circumstances that left the world's greatest batsman, after a Test career encompassing twenty years, appearing at the crease for the last time needing four runs to achieve an average of exactly 100. It is part of folklore that he failed to attain it. Lest anyone assume that a score of nought was indicative of Bradman's declining power, it should be recalled that his previous innings, at Headingley, had been the small matter of 173 not out. Charity was the last thing on Evans's mind as he and the rest of the team cheered Bradman to the wicket. Having been dismissed earlier in the day for 52, their smallest total this century against Australia, England were in no mood to prolong the sentiment. Evans confirms that there was never a thought of 'giving' Bradman a four; to have done so would have diminished the occasion. When Hollies bowled what, to the wicketkeeper, was an 'obvious' googly, there appeared only two explanations for Bradman's ensuing dismissal: that his normally hawklike concentration on the ball was impaired by emotion; or, in Evans's words, that he 'simply missed' it. It has been said that tears were rolling down Bradman's cheeks as he took guard. Evans, a yard away, saw only 'the usual determination to make a hundred, and then two, and so on. It was the same Bradman as before.' With this in mind, Evans's remark, as the bails fell and a sigh of emetic release rose round the ground, stands alone:

'Hard luck, mate.'

Bradman blinked and departed.

England emerged from the series overwhelmed by a side that, according to Swanton, was 'not properly tested' by the opposition. If certain aspects, such as the limitation of appeals, the near-constant availability of the new ball and the extension of the Tests themselves to five days, could be said to have gone against England, there was no denying the Australians' technical supremacy. No team before had won four Tests in an English summer. From the carnage Evans, notwithstanding Headingley, emerged with his reputation intact. His twelve Test dismissals equalled Tallon's and a batting average of 26.85 was exceeded only by Hutton,

Compton, Washbrook and Edrich. When the subsequent touring party to South Africa was announced, Evans was again included – as was his deputy, Griffith.

First, a disappointing season reached its climax. Returning to Kent, Evans bore the leg-pulling of his colleagues concerning England's performance with his usual equanimity. Fresh from the Test, the Australians arrived at Canterbury on 21 August. The home team's dismissal for 51 (one fewer than England's) left Evans 'unsure whether to laugh or cry'. In the Australian innings Bradman, on 50, appeared to snick a delivery from Eddie Crush; Evans, untypically, suppressed his appeal, only for the batsman to subsequently confirm the catch. Evans brooded until the Kent second innings when, (wagered £5 against scoring 50) he indulged in a stand with Tony Pawson of 71 in 32 minutes. On 49, he came down the wicket to Johnson, pushed the ball past mid-on and ran. He was still running when Pawson, who remained completely immobile, greeted him at the other end: Evans run out 49. It was that kind of season, and marked the beginning of a decade in which Kent never rose above the lower half of the table. Ames, though capable of sporadic genius, was past his prime; Wright broke his finger early on; Norman Harding, tragically, had died of polio; and Evans himself was absent from half the programme on Test duty. Only Fagg, with 2,423 runs at an average of 53.84, supplied consistency in a changeable team. After the torrid summer before, the weather again reverted to type and no fewer than eleven of Kent's fixtures were drawn or abandoned. A commentary on the season is provided by the fact that Glamorgan, for the first time in their history, won the Championship, almost exclusively on the basis of their superior bowling and fielding. Evans's consolation was to indulge in a series of functions for the retiring Brian Valentine; and if Championships could be won by enthusiasm alone, then Kent would surely have emerged with honour.

George Mann of Middlesex, artful diplomat, astute tactician, amateur cricketer, was appointed to captain the MCC side to South Africa. Off the field he led with considerable charm; on it his main asset was boundless enthusiasm which communicated itself to his young team. Evans recalls him 'chasing and diving to save a single run. . .always returning the ball straight over the stumps'; his kind of cricketer. As a result, Swanton predicted 'a tour. . .no less enjoyable either for those taking part or the friends they made', and when MCC returned in April 1949 they brought with them a party, nearly as large as their own, of English professional coaches who had worked tirelessly throughout the Union. The Nationalist Party had only recently come to power, and, to observers like Swanton, there was no evidence of the 'harassment of non-whites. . .apparent when MCC next toured South Africa eight years later'. Arlott, later so critical of the State regime, detected 'not the slightest suggestion' of unrest. Characteristically, Evans declined – and still declines – to cast the first stone against his hosts, who offered him only 'warmth, hospitality. . .and the heart-stopping sight of Table Mountain emerging through the mist'. He was there, after all, to play cricket. If in today's context that sounds helplessly naïve, then it stands alone as a statement of pure intent. Others, perhaps, have not been so forthright.

Evans found conditions more to his liking than on any other tour, save perhaps New Zealand. His comment to Wright on first entering the ground at Cape Town was that 'this could be Kent'. The ball certainly kept lower than in Australia or West Indies, and came through to the wicketkeeper proportionately slower. Batting conditions, too, appeared to suit him: against Western Province, Evans scored 52 not out in company with Mann, who produced an 'inspiring' 112. It was the start of a five-match winning sequence by MCC, for whom Hutton, Compton, Washbrook and Alan Watkins all made centuries. Evans himself at one stage boasted a batting average of 196, and only the sight of a nineteen-year-old fast bowler from Natal impaired the generally buoyant mood of the party. Cuan McCarthy, rated by Hutton 'as fast or more so' than Lindwall, came perilously close, in Evans's opinion, to contravening the law; and, three years later, playing in the same Cambridge University side as May and Sheppard, was duly 'called' for throwing. By then McCarthy's international career was over, but in the first Test at Durban his 6–43 raised eyebrows among the tourists. In the end reservations about McCarthy's action were suppressed in the climactic English victory. Set a target of 128 in two-and-a-quarter hours, they achieved it when Cliff Gladwin ('Cometh th' hour, cometh th' man') aimed an almighty heave at the last ball of the match, missed, and was called for a leg-bye by his partner, Bedser. To Swanton this was 'just about as good a Test' as one was likely to see; such had been the tension of the finish that, when all was over, the players had been too overwrought to collect the stumps. Evans, from the balcony, collected the bets.

The second Test at Johannesburg was played on the new ground at Ellis Park, 6000 feet above sea level. In front of the largest crowd ever to watch a match in South Africa, Hutton and Washbrook established a still-existent England record of 359 for the first wicket. Later – much later – Evans was run out for 18, trying to liven things up. In a match in which the bat dominated the ball, Evans terminated the South African innings by stumping Tuckett and Mann off Alan Watkins and Roly Jenkins respectively. The inevitable draw was leavened by the irony of Eric Rowan's match-saving innings of 156, played in the knowledge that he had already been dropped from the next Test starting two days later. England spent the first of them in mass transit to Cape Town.

The subsequent Test presaged a crisis in Evans's career. The match itself dwindled to a draw, South Africa declining to accept Mann's challenge in the final innings. On the last day Evans accounted for three of the four wickets to fall. He and the party decamped for a week's holiday at Victoria Falls, convinced that certain of the home team, Mitchell and Melville among them, were apparently more interested in their averages than in obtaining a result. The team arrived, in the rainy season, at Salisbury, and what had been billed as an agreeable interlude in Rhodesia (with two former Worcester players, Martin and Singleton, appearing for the opposition) ended in some acrimony. Evans was not the only one to feel that the two umpires were unduly biased, but he was alone in protracting a long, quavering appeal after a verdict of 'not out' had been already recorded. Manners making Mann, a rebuke was promptly issued. It was the first time in his career that Evans, who sometimes came perilously close to it, had officially exceeded the boundary of acceptable conduct. It was followed by another. At the subsequent 'Saturday Night Club' the usual light-hearted fines were imposed on those whose performance, either on or off the field, had been considered deficient. Evans took exception and the result was a glass of beer upturned on the imposing head of Brigadier Green, the former Gloucestershire and Essex player serving as team manager. Returning to the Langham Hotel, Johannesburg, on the night of 12 February, Evans was met with a handwritten note at the desk. It was from Mann. In delicate, well-rounded terms, he informed Evans that he had been dropped. Griffith, who all agreed had done an outstanding job, replaced him for the remaining Tests. The selection was vindicated and England went on to win the final match when, set a target of 172 in 95 minutes, they achieved it by three wickets with one minute to spare. The series was won two-nil.

Up to this point in his career, Evans had survived and even prospered from a reputation as someone willing to speak his mind. Now this had brought him to a crisis, ending a record sequence, for a wicketkeeper, of 22 consecutive Tests. It was, by his admission, his own fault. At the same time, it is hard to escape the conclusion that his omission was as much in consequence of the 'totting-up' rule as for any specific offence, and embodied the feeling by Green and others that disciplinary action was due. For disciplinary it was. While Wright, too, was omitted from the fourth Test, to connect his exclusion with Evans's (as some did) was pure fiction. Little wonder that Evans felt disappointment when he learnt not only that he had been dropped, but in favour of a player who, while performing well, had an undoubted social affinity with Mann and Green. He was out and Griffith was in.

Evans recognized that, for him, the tour was over. He set about converting it into something akin to a paid holiday, the climax of which was a golf foursome in which he partnered Bobby Locke (and won). For Evans this first visit to South Africa remains one of his most enjoyable tours, surpassing others where, in purely cricketing terms, he was more successful. From his three Tests under Mann he scored a total of 49 runs at 12.25 and accounted for ten dismissals, equally divided between catches and stumpings. The tour itself saw MCC emerge undefeated and contained the drama of the first and final Tests, and of Compton's 300 in three hours at Benoni. Compton himself felt that 'one could see signs of development in South Africa', but that a number of the host's more established players were past their peak; when South Africa appeared for the return tour of England, Melville, Mitchell and Viljoen were all omitted. For England the chief successes were Hutton and Washbrook with the bat, and the Worcester leg-spinner Roly Jenkins with the ball. The last took sixteen Test wickets on his first and only tour, and had both Evans and Griffith in a state of near apoplexy as batsmen 'came, saw and scrambled back just ahead of the stumping'.

The England party left Cape Town on 17 March 1949. On the return voyage they were entertained by the sight of Evans in skirt, hat and slippers, exotic fruit tied to his (excessively hairy) knees, in unique representation of Carmen Miranda. If the period 1946–49 marks the first phase of Evans's international career, in which he made the wicketkeeper's job his own, then it is salutary to note that little about him changed during the three years. Evans in 1946 was party to others' merriment; in 1949 he *was* the party. Reticence was not his way, though it is self-evident that Evans took cricket as seriously, when the situation required, as did any Yorkshireman. Such was the man who embarked on RMS *Stirling Castle* in 1946 and who returned, on the same vessel, some three years later. He now stood on the brink of his greatest achievements.

Chapter Four

Glory Days

THE *STIRLING CASTLE* docked at Southampton on 1 April 1949. Less than a month later Evans was in action for Kent, whose season continued their post-War decline. Under the captaincy of David Clark they finished thirteenth, an improvement of only two places on the débâcle of 1948. Evans scored 870 runs at an average of 21.21, and it says much for his reputation as a batsman that this was considered by *Wisden* to have 'fallen below expectation'. If so, then others were equally deficient.

In June New Zealand began only their third (and first undivided) tour of England. It was preceded by a Test trial at Birmingham in which Don Brennan, the young Yorkshire amateur, was Evans's counterpart. Both performed creditably, Evans effecting two catches and a leg-side stumping. With the first Test to be staged at Headingley, he was understandably apprehensive that Brennan, on his home ground, might be preferred. In the event Evans, whose batting was acknowledged as superior, regained his place and held it throughout the four-match series.

Of the tourists there were two contrasting opinions. Generally acknowledged as pleasant and affable and by *Wisden* as 'arousing nothing but admiration', they nonetheless contributed to a series as monotonous as any played. Compton, for one, found it the most boring season of his career. Evans, too, believed that New Zealand went into every match playing for a draw and duly achieved it on each occasion. With the Tests restricted to three days' play, it might be argued that much of their work was done for them. Among the successes were Tom Burtt, a jaunty left-arm spinner; the captain Walter Hadlee; and the eminent left-handers Sutcliffe and Donnelly. The last had distinguished himself in England in 1947 when, appearing for the Gentlemen, he scored 162 at a run a minute, assessed by Swanton as 'one of the classic innings of modern cricket'. If so, it was reiterated only in the second Test, when Donnelly scored 206, completing a sequence of three successive three-figure innings at Lord's.

For England there was the consolation of two notable debutants. Brian Close, in his first Test at Manchester, obtained a wicket when he bowled Wallace a full toss in his second over. The New Zealander promptly dispatched it over square leg, where it was caught by Washbrook in front of the pavilion. More significantly, the series saw the introduction of Trevor Bailey, recently down from Cambridge and already playing, in Compton's words, 'like someone who had been in Test cricket for years'. Behind the stumps Evans had a reliable rather than remarkable series, taking twelve dismissals and scoring 61 runs at 15.25.

Three further matches are worthy of comment. In July, for the Players, Evans distinguished himself by scoring an all-run six, without overthrows. Bailey, from the Nursery End, bowled a full-length ball that was dispatched to the (untenanted) long-on boundary. By the time Mann, from mid-on, had retrieved it, Evans and his partner Close were contemplating a seventh. Swanton, in the commentary box, was overwrought; as was Evans when, on a turning wicket, he and Jenkins achieved a fourth-innings victory.

For Kent against New Zealand in August, Evans claimed five first-innings wickets and four of the five to fall in the second; one can speculate on the final total had the tourists not declared, but an aggregate of nine remains his highest in a single match. Afterwards his opposite number, Frank Mooney, acknowledged Evans's example; shades of Walcott in the West Indies.

For Kent against the Combined Services at Gillingham, Evans took note of a 'tall, shy, long-legged youth' of whom the coach George Geary confided, 'this gentleman will play for England'. After the laughter had died down, the nineteen-year-old in question proceeded to carve the first ball he received for six. He went on to make 52, and Evans was forced to the realization that here, indeed, was a star of the future. His name, they told him, was May.

*

Evans had now played near continuous cricket for three years. The winter of 1949–50 represented a welcome respite from touring, and with it the prospect of much-needed supplementary income. His gross salary from Kent and England in 1949 amounted to £500, no undue amount on which to maintain a wife and a son about to enter school at Ellesdon Court, Maidstone. Resuscitating a friendship from Kent College days, Evans entered into partnership with Doug Yates, a director of the jewellery firm Reeve Carter. Eventually restyled Yates & Evans, in 1949 the firm was a Birmingham-based concern for whom Evans consulted and returned happily to Germany to study design and manufacture. Reverting to another schoolday association, he resumed playing hockey, appearing both for Maidstone and Tunbridge Wells Wednesday. Against Kent College he scored nine goals for the Old Boys. His position, appropriately enough, was centre forward.

In the summer of 1950, England called on no fewer than 25 players, two more than against the same opposition in 1988. No one can disrupt the pattern of a team like the West Indies. With Compton out of action for much of the season with his knee injury, and Hutton, Edrich, Bedser and Evans himself sidelined at various times, the selectors experimented with a strange amalgam of established professionals and recent Cambridge graduates. Of the latter, Dewes, Insole, Doggart and Sheppard failed to impress, while for the fourth Test Freddie Brown, himself a pre-War Blue, assumed the captaincy from Yardley. At the end of a series won three-one by the visitors, Evans concluded that 'even more than 1947–48, the tour forced England to take the West Indies seriously'. That they did so was due largely to the inclusion of two twenty-year-old spin bowlers, shrewdly picked by their captain, which was more than they were by the England batsmen.

'Sonny' Ramadhin and Alf Valentine arrived in England unknown. They left it four months later with 59 Test wickets between them. The former, first in a succession of East Indians to be chosen for his country, turned the ball both ways with a quick, finger-spin action; Valentine, a left-armer, lacked his partner's guile, but imparted such turn on the ball that, according to Evans, you could *hear* it fizz. Later in their careers both were 'found out' by opposing batsmen, and a tendency to over-bowl Ramadhin, in particular, invoked the law of diminishing returns. But, in 1950, the pair represented, in Graveney's words, 'as close to unplayable an attack' as then existed. Under the adequate captaincy of John Goddard and growing influence of Weekes, Worrell and Walcott, the West Indies henceforth indeed deserved to be 'taken seriously'.

Little of this was evident on 31 May when, in the Test trial at Bradford, Laker returned figures of eight wickets for two runs. Evans performed outstandingly. His dismissal of Don Kenyon, off Laker, in front of the wicket was considered by many (including Evans) to be among his finest catches. His opposite number, Dick Spooner, also distinguished himself, and now formed a triumvirate with Brennan and McIntyre (Griffith concentrating on journalism) of pursuing players. In time each would be afforded his chance, but for the first Test at Old Trafford Evans retained his place. From the outset the wicket caused both lift and turn; Hutton was hit on the forefinger and forced to retire before Valentine demolished the middle order. When Evans came to the wicket the scoreboard read 88–5; and there were still ten minutes to go before lunch.

The first ball he received reared over Evans's right shoulder. From then on he and Bailey were continually hit as they went on to establish a then record sixth-wicket stand against the West Indies. According to *Wisden*, they 'wrested the initiative from the bowlers in a splendid partnership of 161'; according to Evans, they 'bloody well fought [their] way out of it'. The stand remained intact throughout the session until tea, when, to Evans's astonishment, he discovered his own score to be 97. His terrific concentration had, he says, precluded even perusal of the scoreboard. After the interval Evans swung mightily at successive deliveries from Valentine, causing apoplexy among the England team watching from the balcony. In inimitable fashion, he then reached his century – his first in Tests and, indeed, in England. His 104 and Bailey's 82 not out completely altered the complexion of the match. The West Indies visibly wilted in the face of an innings which, in *Wisden*'s words, 'neglected no opportunity to hit the ball hard'. In all Evans scored seventeen boundaries; his innings, played on a spiteful pitch on which Valentine took the first eight wickets to fall, lasted two hours twenty minutes. Without it England would have been pressed to save the match.

Goddard's appreciation of the pitch was reversed when he himself came to bat on it. By the second day, both Berry and Hollies were achieving turn such that, on more than one occasion, the ball went direct to first slip without Evans touching it. The West Indies clearly did not relish the situation and employed varying techniques to counter it. Worrell, for one, elected to come down the wicket to Berry; missing the ball, it duly lifted over the top of middle stump. Evans flung up a hand to prevent it hitting him in the face; the ball rebounded off the centre of his glove onto the wicket and Worrell departed stumped. With a first innings lead of 97, England added 288, thanks to Edrich and Bailey, and West Indies collapsed on the fourth day to 183 all out. Notably, Evans allowed only four byes in two completed innings, thirteen fewer than did Christiani (deputizing for Walcott who, remarkably, opened the West Indies bowling) in one. Immediately after the England victory, Goddard issued a public complaint about the condition of the pitch. Strangely, he had failed to do so on the first day when, until Evans's arrival, his own bowlers had so relished it.

That was the turning-point of the series. At Lord's the tourists achieved their first victory in England, accompanied by an impromptu carnival in front of the pavilion. In the decisive West Indies second innings of 425–6, Walcott scored an immaculate 168. But for an almost comic mishap it would have been significantly less as, on 50, Walcott advanced on and missed a Jenkins googly. Evans duly collected the ball, along with a liberal portion of his own shirt. By the time the ensuing melee was resolved the batsman had recovered his crease. It took some time for the laughter to die down. The upshot was the Godfrey Evans Cricket Shirt, a close-fitting garment designed to prevent the sort of Chaplinesque antics witnessed at Lord's.

Gomez (W.I.) stumped Evans, bowled Berry at Old Trafford. Earlier Evans had scored 104. (The Cricketer).

In retrospect, this was the match in which a major shift in the balance of power was discerned in Test cricket. During five days at Lord's, witnessed by a crowd of 112,000 (including the King himself), West Indies decisively outplayed England in every department. The steel drums and claxons that for the first time accompanied a home Test seemed only to underline the altered state of international cricket, in which England and Australia would no longer contest, as if by divine right, the unofficial championship of the world. In light of subsequent events, Thursday 29 June 1950 may be seen as the day on which West Indies, and much else besides, came of age.

To Evans also it was the dawn of a new era, that of the commercial exploitation of his own name. As far back as 1946, Slazenger had contracted him to market his own patent wicketkeeping gloves; these were designed to Evans's specification and featured a red rubber surface similar to that of a table-tennis bat. In time the colour became an Evans trademark, but in truth it was originally preferred simply because it was immediately available. Beneath them Evans wore chamois 'inners', bolstered by a pad of cotton wool sewn into the palm. Slazenger also provided him with the majority of his personal equipment, although Evans, like Denis Compton, was not averse to experimenting with any available item that caught his eye, and, indeed, to providing his own on the same basis; in 1946 Sam Loxton scored 132 wielding an Evans bat. On the Australian tour of 1948 Brylcreem contracted Evans, Miller and Lindwall to join Denis Compton in promoting their product, an association that ultimately ended in some discord but at the time provided the basis of much good-natured banter. Finally, in 1950, came the eponymous Cricket Shirt and, the following year, an autobiography, *Behind The Stumps*. If the combined income from these pursuits was rather less than to encourage thoughts of retirement, it nonetheless provided a valuable source of additional income. And as fast as Evans made it, he spent it.

The third Test, at Trent Bridge, started on an ominous note when Hutton, suffering from lumbago, dropped out on the morning of the match. The ensuing side, adjusted to incorporate Dewes and Insole, promptly collapsed to 25–4, largely thanks to Worrell's new-found ability to swing the ball. When, at 70–5, Evans found himself, for the second time in three Tests, required to bat before lunch, he shared in a stand of 77 before being bowled by Ramadhin. Worrell the batsman then played an innings of 261, sharing in a partnership with Weekes (129) of 283 in 200 minutes. The tourists' lead was 335. In England's reply, Washbrook scored 102, Simpson 94 and Evans 63. It was a model rearguard action, ended only when Stollmeyer, at fine leg, made a catch that only he could have reached. Valentine bowled a Test record 92 overs; Ramadhin a mere 81; and England succumbed by ten wickets. As the inquest began, Evans left for London for the annual Gents v Players fixture the following morning.

This was the match which determined beyond doubt the captaincy for the ensuing winter tour of Australia. Freddie Brown, the only Peruvian-born player to be afforded the honour, was duly confirmed at the conclusion of play. The announcement succeeded an innings of 122 which, in Swanton's words, 'reminded one of how cricket used to be played'. Fingleton exceeded even that by declaring it 'one of the greatest innings in the whole history of such matches'. For the Players Evans scored nineteen and nine, and was undoubtedly one of the first under consideration when, in the Gentlemen's second innings, Brown retired to the Committee Room to ponder candidates for the tour. For Evans, it was to be the fourth in as many years.

It was preceded by a calamity. Batting for Kent against Middlesex at Canterbury on 10 August, Evans was struck on the glove by a rising ball from Warr. He played on. After some memorable one-handed strokes, he was dismissed and retired to hospital. The diagnosis, a broken thumb, led him to miss the final Test. More immediately, he missed the *dénouement* of the match at Canterbury where, in the final innings, Ames scored his hundredth first-class hundred. It would be his last for Kent. After leading a Commonwealth side in India that winter he broke down with back trouble in the first match of 1951 and announced his retirement. For Kent it was the end of an era. As much in anticipation of future success as in recognition of an outstanding career, the County hosted a party that, even by Kent's standards, excelled itself. Evans, in hospital, twiddled his thumb.

For the fourth Test he was elected a member of the Old Players' Club and sat at The Oval in the company of Hobbs, Woolley and Sandham. It was, as he says, compensation. His deputy McIntyre took three catches and, ironically, kept outstandingly to the recalled Wright. The West Indies won by an innings. From his abbreviated series Evans emerged with nine dismissals (of which, strikingly, two-thirds were stumpings) and a batting average inferior only to Hutton, Washbrook and Bailey. He was one of the successes of an indifferent England performance. For the tourists Worrell scored 539 Test runs at an average of 89, in a style 'heartbreakingly beautiful from the England point of view'.

Walcott was tough in the sense that certain Australians have merited the description; Weekes held a bat 'as a lumberjack holds an axe'. Between them they scored over 1,000 Test runs; Ramadhin and Valentine took 33 and 26 wickets respectively. After their departure, England were never to look at the West Indies in quite the same way again.

For Kent it was a year of relative success. Ninth position in the Championship was to remain their highest until, under Cowdrey, they went one better in 1958. Cowdrey himself appeared in the traditional fixture against the tourists at Canterbury. During it the non-playing Evans asked Walcott to nominate his most enjoyable match of the tour. 'This one,' he replied. Valentine, at his elbow, nodded assent. In the Kent second innings he took five wickets for six runs.

Evans spent the month following his 30th birthday at home in Bearsted, at Canterbury, and in fashioning plans with Doug Yates. It was an unaccustomed month with Jean and Howard, now five. In retrospect, the summer of 1950 was a kind of Dunkirk; a comprehensive English defeat which, in some quarters, was perversely regarded as a triumph over the primitive forces which had found their expression in the riot at Lord's. Evans himself had no such illusions. The months from June to August had belonged to the West Indies; he and others who had participated in them knew that, for them, life would never again be the same. It was a lesson still being absorbed when he was passed fit to play in September. September meant Australia.

The SS *Stratheden* set sail from Tilbury. On board was a party of sixteen cricketers, two managers (among them Evans's friend Brigadier Green) and thirty journalists; two Lancashire bowlers, Tattersall and Statham, would be recruited later due to injuries. Brown, as captain, was blunt, direct and, in Evans's words, 'John Bull-ish'; the players respected him and the Australians admired his straightforwardness. Compton, his deputy, was less confident. When he captained the side he was sometimes successful, sometimes not, the latter involving a tendency to lose control of the game. In four Tests in Australia, his batting average would be 7.57.

Evans, on his fourth tour, was afforded a place on the Selection Committee. His fellow members were Green, Brown, Hutton, Compton and Washbrook. It was a significant tribute to his development as a player, and, for that matter, to the conciliatory nature of the man who had dropped him on his previous tour. The Saturday Night Club duly resumed on the outward voyage, although in more subdued form. It was a happy party which disembarked at Colombo, where McIntyre not only kept wicket but scored a brisk century; enough to keep even a selector on his toes.

Arriving at Perth, Evans was greeted by the same driver who had met him four years before; they followed the same route through King's Park and arrived at the same hotel. Other comparisons were more diverse: under Hammond, the side had been widely criticized for its age; under Brown, it would be for its youth. The relative inexperience of players such as Close, Dewes, Sheppard and Warr was fully exposed in the run-up to the first Test. The side's only success came against South Australia at Adelaide when, on the final day, 31 October, MCC were left a target of 185 in a hundred minutes. With twenty still required, captain joined wicketkeeper at the crease. 'We'll get them in singles,' said Brown. 'Agreed,' said Evans, whereupon he struck five fours in an over. MCC won by seven wickets.

On 30 November the Selection Committee met to determine the side for the first Test at Brisbane. The inclusion of Evans's deputy, McIntyre, as a batsman was the only revelation of an order that read: Hutton, Washbrook, Simpson, Compton, Dewes, McIntyre, Bailey, Brown, Evans, Bedser, Wright. Or such was the intention. The truth is that the match was a freak which, in the *Telegraph*'s words, 'baffled all prophecy'. Australia batted first on a perfect wicket, on which a total of 228 spoke volumes for the bowling of Bailey and Bedser. Then came the rainstorm that entirely washed out the second day's play. When cricket resumed on Monday 4 December, the England order was swiftly re-arranged to counter the ensuing 'sticky dog'. Evans, sent in third, emerged with a second top score of sixteen. The resulting declaration at 68–7 stands alone as an indictment of conditions; it was immediately re-iterated when Hassett ended the Australian reply at 32–7. At this stage fourteen wickets had fallen for exactly 100 runs. The eventual England target was 193. With the wicket fluctuating from vindictive to merely spiteful, Evans began confidently enough against Johnston and Iverson. For a quarter of an hour all went well, at which point he pushed forward to a ball from Johnston and was caught at short leg. Compton followed in the same over. England were 22–3, 23–5, 46–7; only Hutton, 'blazing away volley after volley of the most brilliant strokes imaginable' suspended the inevitable. England lost by 70 runs and, although there was disappointment at losing a match which, against the odds, might easily have been won, Evans and others took solace from the fact that, technically, they had exceeded expectations. Unfortunately, so had the weather.

MCC entrained to Toowoomba where, against a Queensland Country XI, Evans acknowledged Compton's advice to 'have a go' by scoring 94 in even time. Despite the debacle at Brisbane, spirits were high as the second Test began at Melbourne. This was the match that contained the finest sustained performance of Evans's career. In front of a crowd in excess of 60,000, Evans, Bedser and Bailey performed heroically to contain Australia to 194. In 90° heat Bedser bowled nineteen eight-ball overs and took 4–37; Evans, reverting to his normal practice, stood up to the stumps. On the greenest pitch he, or any of the team, had seen in Australia, Evans conceded a total of four byes, when a Bedser leg-cutter turned perpendicularly off a length. It was an epic performance, reminiscent of his displays at Sydney and Melbourne four years earlier. Immediately Evans followed it by scoring 49 of the England reply of 197. *Wisden* praised his innings for 'courage and determination'; Evans, more prosaically, considered himself 'a fool' for getting out to Iverson in attempting a four that would have achieved an England lead and his own fifty. (He *did* achieve his 1000th Test match run.) The upshot was a target of 178, which England failed to reach by 28. Such had been the quality of their performance that Swanton, in the press box, asserted that 'the home crowd almost to a man wanted the visitors to win'. As Hassett led in his side

Great Evans – Sydney, 1950–51. (Hulton Deutsch).

the spectators seemed merely to melt away. One left behind a banner affirming simply, 'Great Evans', a sentiment shared by players on both sides.

Evans himself felt the teams to have been unequally matched due largely to decisions taken at Lord's the previous August. With respect to Sheppard, Dewes and Close, the non-selection of Edrich and May unnecessarily weakened a batting order already undermined by Compton's virtual non-performance in Tests. As for bowling, the selectors' options were limited: the debut of Trueman was not yet, and, in Bailey and Bedser, England had an attack that compensated with skill what it lacked in pace. More remarkable was the omission of Laker, who finished the 1950 season with 166 wickets at an average of fifteen. Evans attributes this – and, indeed, Laker's subsequent exclusion from the tour of 1954–55 – to events off, as much as on, the field. Both Brown and later Hutton were known to have reservations about the bowler's character; in his infamous memoir, *Over To Me*, Laker asserts that Brown, 'to the discomfiture of the other selectors', personally insisted on the inclusion of Close over himself, while both Hutton and May later expressed doubts about the off-spinner's commitment in adverse conditions, culminating in May's comment following a Surrey v Kent fixture in 1958 – 'I don't think you were trying to bowl them out.' Whatever its cause, the effect was to severely limit the tourists' effectiveness against Morris, Miller, Hassett and Loxton, all of whom scored freely against a spin attack limited to Wright and Compton. This was the series, too, in which Harvey confirmed his status as the most distinguished batsman of the post-Bradman era. The reticent nineteen-year-old encountered at Headingley had seasoned into a player who would in time score six centuries and 2,416 runs against England alone, and who represented from 1948 as near a sheet anchor as Australia or any side possessed. For England, only Hutton fulfilled the same role. It was a disparity keenly felt at Melbourne, where, other than Evans, Brown, Bailey and Bedser, the *Telegraph* felt England carried 'too many passengers.' If so, it ironically foreshadowed the subsequent complaint by Bedser that 'selectors don't make players – they pick them'. The Committee's hands had been tied.

If the first two Tests had been, respectively, a farce and a tragedy, then the third, at Sydney, was a comedy of errors. It started on a note of expectation. Brown won the toss, England batted and matters were proceeding satisfactorily until, in short order, Bailey broke a thumb and Wright, in attempting a short single, tore a muscle in his leg. That left an England 'attack' of Brown, Bedser and Warr. With Iverson, an oddity who flicked the ball either way with his middle finger squashed back under the seam, taking 6–27 (and Compton still becalmed), England lost by an innings. Evans was not alone in wondering what Wright, let alone Laker, might have achieved in similar conditions.

Until then England had at least maintained an appearance of parity. From Sydney things deteriorated. Immediately following the Test, MCC played an up-country game against a South Australian X1 at Renmark, where the opening

Taking down the leg side, Melbourne 1950–51. The bowler is Bailey. (Hulton-Deutsch).

batsman, in his enthusiasm to dispatch Compton to the boundary, instead dispatched Evans to hospital by hitting him in the follow-through. That concluded proceedings until the Test at Adelaide, where the surrounding bush blazed in temperatures exceeding 100°. It was a baptism by fire, in every sense, for Tattersall, recently arrived from wintry Lancashire. Brown lost the toss yet again and Australia batted first on a placid pitch. Equally placid was Morris, who played and missed his way to a half-century, displaying the rare ability to dismiss each previous *faux pas* from his mind. Evans awaited the inevitable. At 50 Morris opened up, and from then on played beautifully for 206. Burke, in his first Test, also reached a century, of such monotony that one wag was moved to observe, 'I wish you were a statue and I were a pigeon.' For England Hutton made 156.

The same score by Simpson brought victory in the fifth Test at Melbourne – the first such against Australia in thirteen years. The local press actively welcomed the result, as did Evans tending the dressing-room champagne. In retrospect, this was the turning-point in English post-War cricket; henceforward they were to remain unbeaten in home series for a decade. It was also the dawn of an era of heightened press scrutiny of Test cricketers abroad, leading Evans to observe that 'this was the tour when off-the-field incidents were first written about'. One such was the occasion on which Compton injured himself in Melbourne. Compton's own account is unambiguous. At a private party at the home of Bill and Margaret Gluth, the England vice-captain took the opportunity to demonstrate a cricket shot (one hesitates to suggest the cut). Unfortunately, his host chose that precise moment to push Compton good-naturedly in the back, causing him to fall against a static water nozzle concealed in the lawn. Compton got up, laughed, and resumed the demonstration. It was only later that he noticed the blood pouring into his eye, and later still that the press began to speculate on its cause. To Evans (who confirms Compton's account in every detail), it was evidence of the desire to undermine the tourists' morale by explaining their relative failure on the field in terms of their conduct off it. On this occasion, not for the last time, irresponsible conjecture caused a player to suffer unnecessary anxiety that, by his own admission, further impaired an already distressing tour. If Compton could be so perturbed, what hope was there for a twenty-year-old making his first overseas appearance? Just such a player made a resolution then and there to keep his head down on all future public occasions.

The tour was a triumph for Hutton, who achieved a Test average of 88.83; for Bedser, who took 30 wickets; on occasion, for Bailey; and, emphatically, for Evans, who emerged with an average superior to Washbrook, Sheppard and Compton and who took eleven catches. His performance in the second Test was, in the opinion of those who saw it, among the finest witnessed at that level. To Bailey, Evans 'never put a foot wrong'; in Bedser's assessment, he was 'bloody marvellous'. Once again, he returned to England with a reputation enlarged and extended.

On the debit side, certain of the younger players failed (as they had against the West Indies) to inspire; and Close, for whom hopes had been so high, ended the tour disillusioned by Brown's apparent indifference to the role of team motivation. Conversely, the captain was universally admired by the more established members of the side, to whom, in Evans's words, he was 'magnificent throughout'. Like Mann, Brown led by example and in the last Test at Melbourne, despite a shoulder injury sustained in a car accident, he 'bowled all day' and fielded brilliantly. His 210 Test runs and eighteen wickets exceeded all but the most extravagant forecasts made on his appointment.

From Melbourne, the party flew to New Zealand for the usual summary, if not summery, excursion. The Test in Christchurch was played in bleak, dripping conditions reminiscent of Kent in November. Bailey's 134 (his only Test century) barely animated an otherwise lifeless match. In late March the party came to Wellington, where England won by six wickets. Brown, Hutton and Simpson all contributed, and even Compton, subdued for much of the previous half-year, demonstrated touches of the old genius. Evans took three dismissals and found the opposition, despite

Sutcliffe's century at Christchurch, much diminished since their last appearance in England. He himself was at the end of a long, frequently arduous tour and registers surprise at the story, endorsed by more than one of those present, of his hurtling sideways to take a sharp catch off a distinctly lively Bedser leg-cutter. After the usual enquiry of 'Howzat?' the umpire paused for some time before delivering his reply: 'Bloody brilliant'. And, for good measure, 'Out'.

The party returned home by air, flying across the Pacific. They had a day in Honolulu (where Evans distinguished himself at hula-hula) and were invited to play a match in Hollywood. Those in favour, including Evans and Compton, were outvoted by a majority eager to return home by the shortest route possible. Compensation followed in the form of a stopover in New York where, in addition to an evening at the Waldorf Astoria, Evans reverted to his boxing persona and 'had a few' with Jack Dempsey in the latter's bar. From there the party flew to London, where Compton felt moved to admit that the Ashes might have been won had he himself performed better. The press converged on Evans and it was some time before he was able to join his wife and son. Later still he received his cheque for the tour of Australia and New Zealand; six months overseas, encompassing seven Tests and protracted scrutiny of his every move both on and off the field. The total was £31.

The 1951 season started on an auspicious note when Evans was nominated by *Wisden* as one of its Five Cricketers of the Year. The award, which recognized his outstanding achievements in 1950, was shared by Ramadhin, Valentine, Weekes and Worrell. Evans's citation noted that 'in an age in which possibly too much first–class cricket has caused some of the game to look routine, Evans remains the embodiment of energy and enthusiasm. To play with him is as much a tonic to the jaded cricketer as to watch him is a source of delight to the spectator.' The author then asserted that, on the basis of his performances in 1950, Evans was 'without an equal in the world as a wicketkeeper'. Above all he had the virtues of 'inspiring the bowler and worrying the batsman', echoing Brian Statham's observation that

Evans's mere presence 'was worth a wicket before a ball was bowled'.

It is salutary to note that the following edition of *Wisden* considered Kent's performance in 1951 to have been 'their most depressing since the turn of the century'. The County collapsed to sixteenth in the Championship, mitigated only by the 'advance of an eighteen-year-old former Tonbridge captain' named Cowdrey. Compounding the decline was the retirement of Ames, who thus frustrated the Committee's intention of appointing him captain in succession to Clark. Clark himself had had a distinguished career in the Second XI and, in Evans's words, 'was, as a trier, unsurpassed'. This begs the question as to whether, in purely technical terms, he was worth his place in the team. The captain's shortcomings in time communicated themselves to the players and contributed to an unusually subdued dressing-room atmosphere. The Australian tour marked Evans's apogee as a Test cricketer. Yet only a month later he found himself exhausted and, incredibly, lacking enthusiasm for the game. Wright, too, decisively lost form; for the first time in years he failed to take 100 wickets in a season and in consequence Kent lacked the ability to bowl the opposition out. In retrospect, Evans feels, both players suffered a reaction to the tour of Australia. The raw spring and early summer seemed to forecast a season in which Evans would be dropped from the Test side and omitted from the winter tour of India. Yet, even at this moment in his career, his influence on those who watched and played cricket was inescapable. That spring a teenager on the ground staff at Lord's celebrated his sixteenth birthday by donning a pair of gauntlets for the first time 'due entirely to Godfrey's influence'. To John Murray, even a subdued Evans was inspirational.

For Kent the season started ominously. Against Worcester at Gravesend, Evans scored a 'pair' and, in the field, found himself 'failing to get down the leg side quickly enough'. Throughout May he proved adept at standing back, but lacked his normal agility in keeping to Wright. In certain games he was reluctant to turn out, so short was he of confidence; in others rain cut play to the bone. By the time

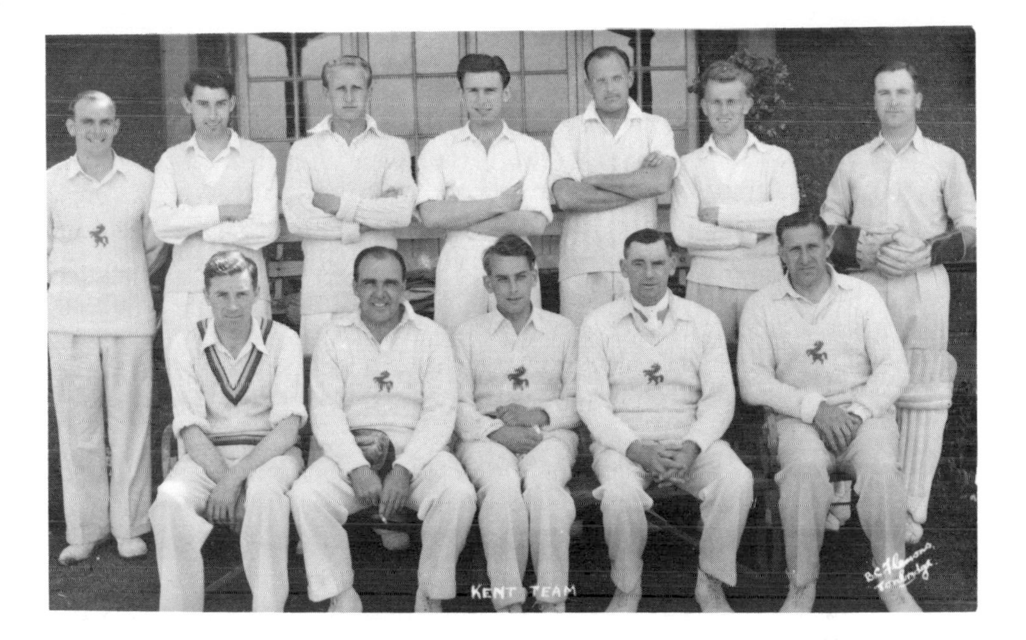

Kent C.C.C. under David Clark.

of the first Test in June, far from being 'the embodiment of energy and enthusiasm', Evans considered himself fortunate to be selected.

This was the match when South Africa achieved a first innings total of 483, of which the captain Nourse scored nearly half. More strikingly, he did so with the handicap of a broken thumb. Evans, behind the stumps, winced vicariously at each rasping blow from Bedser. For England Simpson and Compton (reverting, in *Wisden*'s words, to his 'gay cavalier' role) scored centuries. And then it rained.

In the radically altered conditions Bedser took 6–37 and South Africa (with Nourse declining to bat) were dismissed for 121. At this stage England were confronted with their nemesis McCarthy, who confirmed Hutton's assessment of being 'faster than Lindwall' by promptly hitting him over the heart. Hutton departed for eleven and England failed in their pursuit of a relatively modest target of 186. Evans's contribution had been to stump Jackie McGlew, playing his first Test, off the bowling of Bedser. Even the South Africans applauded.

The second Test belonged to Roy Tattersall. After England had scored 311, the off-spinner took 7–52 in 28 overs. He owed much to excellent close catching by Brown, Ikin and Evans. Evans himself felt his keeping, particularly to Wardle, to have been somewhere approaching his normal standard. South Africa followed on, exceeded England by just 16 runs, and the match was won by ten wickets.

Between the second and third Tests Hutton scored his 98th and 99th first-class centuries, and the teams arrived at Old Trafford amidst press agitation for the hundredth. In typically bleak conditions Nourse eccentrically elected to bat, and Bedser took full advantage to dismiss the visitors for 158. Chubb, a bowler in the Bedser mould, then achieved similar results to remove England for 211. The eventual target was 139. At lunch on the final day, England were 135–1 with Hutton 91 not out. It was raining. There was considerable dressing-room speculation on the chances of Hutton's achieving his own and England's objective, with Evans offering evens on the weather precluding both. He had a personal interest in that, too, since, possessing a ticket for the Randolph Turpin-Sugar Ray Robinson title fight that evening, he was anxious to leave the ground at the first opportunity. Eventually the clouds parted, Hutton took three off McCarthy and then faced Mann requiring six for his century and a single for victory. Intending to achieve both he lifted the ball high over cover, where it fell a yard short of the boundary. Hutton returned cursing his bat. Evans departed for London. It was Tuesday 10 July and, though he was not to know it, his last international appearance for nearly a year.

In the three matches to date Evans had taken five dismissals, appreciably fewer than his career average of 2.4 per Test. His batting, too, had declined to an average of 1.75. More significantly, in the South African second innings at Manchester thirteen byes had been conceded of a total of 191. To a man who considered a ratio of approximately 1 bye per 100 to have been acceptable, his performance at Old Trafford was galling. He attributes it to lack of concentration, a diet of ten home and away series in five years having sated even his rapacious appetite. Evans returned to Canterbury to resuscitate the season for Kent as best he could. Somehow it always seemed to be up to him.

For a time he considered withdrawing in favour of his deputy, Derek Ufton. Clark was sympathetic to this. Ufton was a capable young player. Moreover, for Evans to be available for Kent from mid-July was itself a novelty, and a system to accommodate both players was duly improvised. Brennan, meanwhile, was selected for England, appearing at both Headingley and The Oval. At the former May made 138 on his Test debut, after which he appeared for the Gentlemen at Lord's. Evans watched as May resumed where he had left off at Leeds; he, Graveney and Cowdrey, though at different stages of their development, all came to prominence this year. The last had appeared for Kent in the closing weeks of the previous season. His reputation as an 'on-side player' had preceded him to Canterbury, where Evans at first declared himself disappointed by the reticent seventeen-year-old who greeted him. All that changed in 1951, when Cowdrey scored over 800 runs, impatient, as he puts it, to 'establish [himself] at first-class level'. To Evans, the two players provided a contrast in styles. When May hit the ball, 'it stayed hit'. Cowdrey at least invited an excursion to the boundary.

Evans returned to something approaching his normal form at the end of August. Against Gloucestershire at Dover he scored 52 in a Kent second innings of 135, described by *Wisden* as 'rousing' and by Evans as 'more like it'. On the evening of 24 August he drove to Leicester, where a three-day fixture started the next morning. By close of play Evans had scored 101 of a total of 158, including two sixes and fourteen fours. It was his first first-class century for Kent. Cowdrey (who himself scored 87 in the second innings) describes it as 'vintage Evans', and *Wisden* as 'fearless' – the two not being entirely incompatible. Evans recalls only his dismissal, caught on the long-on boundary by the back-peddling R.C. Smith. But for a headwind, 'it would have cleared the sightscreen'.

Immediately following the match at Leicester, Evans returned to Canterbury to face South Africa for the first time since being dropped. In the interim, the tourists had respectively drawn and lost the remaining Tests. Brennan had done nothing to disgrace himself, although as an amateur with increasing business commitments outside the game, he represented only a short-term option. A number of the South Africans registered surprise at Evans's exclusion, which they assumed (wrongly) to have been for off-the-field infractions. At Canterbury Evans played superbly. Cowdrey, too, distinguished himself with an innings of 71. 'Right from the start,' he says, 'I set my heart on playing for England.'

At season's end Evans was invited to tour India with an MCC 'A' team. Torn between his inclination to play and the certainty that his loss of form was due to a long and almost continuous diet of first-class cricket, he sought out his former teammate, Griffith, by now a respected journalist on the Sunday Times. Griffith's advice was decisive. Evans wrote to the Committee asking that he not be considered for selection.

The wicketkeepers chosen were Brennan and Spooner. According to Graveney (who himself returned with an average exceeding 60), both played well, with Spooner preferred in the Tests due to his superior batting. Brennan's two matches against South Africa were to remain his only international appearances. Spooner proved more resilient, deputizing for Evans in the West Indies and subsequently at home against South Africa. Meanwhile, at The Oval, the player described by Bedser as 'the best day-in, day-out wicketkeeper on the circuit', Arthur McIntyre, continued to press his own claims, pursued in turn by a diminutive seventeen-year-old making his first appearances for the Surrey Second XI. Evans recalls the name Roy Swetman being mentioned that summer as a prospect for England, little realizing that it would be fulfilled at his own expense.

Evans spent the winter of 1951–52 at home in Maidstone. He fought off the impulse to rest and played competitive hockey. He resumed his relationship with Yates. Having lost his form, been dropped, and prospered again for Kent, as spring dawned he felt himself 'more eager for cricket' than ever. He was ready.

India will always hold a prominent place in Evans's memories. It was against them that he made his Test debut in 1946. Now, six years later, he was to enjoy his finest season against the same opposition. Unconsciously tautening his abilities while Spooner, Brennan and the rest toiled on the sub-continent, Evans approached the season with the conviction of one with a point to prove; it so happens that many of the brightest phases of his career followed a period of relative decline.

Before play began, Tom Crawford, a Kent member and sometime Second XI captain, approached Evans with a 20–1 wager against his scoring 1,500 runs in the season. It was accepted. Crawford's stipulation was that the runs should be made 'for the side'; Evans's that they be scored from a position no lower than three in the order. The new captain was found willing and Evans promptly opened his account by scoring 137 against Gloucester at Bristol. Graveney remembers the ball 'travelling like a rocket to all points'. A month later against Somerset Evans scored 144 in 110 minutes, described with some understatement by *Wisden* as containing 'forcing strokes all round the wicket'. At season's end the almanack praised his overall performance as 'among the most heartening features' of a County 'once again amongst the weakest sides'.

The Kent captaincy had passed to Bill Murray Wood, another player of Second XI pedigree who was to be dismissed before the end of his second season in favour of Wright. The County thus followed the precedent established by England in choosing Hutton as its first professional captain. The Selection Committee of Yardley, Brown, Wyatt and Ames were unanimous in concluding that this was the moment to consolidate on the successful series against South Africa, and the press in general concurred. *Wisden* declared that, in future, all captains of England should be 'worth a place in the side', and Evans typified the general view that 'once Brown had withdrawn, Len was the obvious choice'. Only Swanton, who was to remain an attentive critic of the new captain, expressed concern about 'the native caution said to be characteristic of the Yorkshireman', a suspicion for which there was ample justification in the years ahead.

Hutton took the field as England captain on 5 June 1952. Also present was a young Aircraftsman granted permission to play by his Station Commander at RAF Hemswell, Lincolnshire. Fred Trueman, bowling up the Headingley hill (the opposite to his usual preference) had the unremarkable figures of 3–89 in India's first innings, which, thanks to the captain, Hazare, and a century by Manjrekar, reached 293. England's reply began after rain fell overnight. As Evans went out to bat on Saturday morning, Hutton stopped him with the question, 'Do you think you can score twenty?' 'Watch me,' said Evans, whereupon he struck 66. Hutton produced champagne. Graveney, for one, believed that the innings (which saw England to a lead of 41) 'completely demoralized' the Indians. Their second innings included the most photographed scoreboard in the history of cricket: 0 for 4 at the close of play. Trueman took 4–27 and, in *Wisden*'s words, 'upset the opposition by his fiery pace and hostility'. The epithet stuck and the bowler who left the field that evening was established forever in the public imagination. India (among others) had no answer to him.

Between the first and second Tests the tourists recruited Vinoo Mankad from Harlingden in the Lancashire League. It was an inspired decision. At Lord's he scored 72 in the first innings and 184 in the second, bowling the small matter of 73 overs in between. If, for sheer all-round excellence, it was thus 'Mankad's Match', then Evans's contribution was far from negligible. It was the most memorable Test of his career.

On Friday 20 June England began their reply to the Indian first innings. Hutton made 150. That evening Evans and other members of the team assembled in a night club off Regent Street. Some time later they were joined by two of the England selectors. The upshot was that Evans went out to bat on Midsummer Day 1952 (a wicket having fallen on the last ball of the previous evening) nursing a hangover 'of gale-force dimension'. Two hours later, he was 98 not out. Graveney, his partner, was content to 'stand back and let

[Evans] take it out on the bowling'. More pertinently, he was content to let Evans take the strike, affording him the lion's share of a then record sixth-wicket partnership. At 1.28 Evans was ready to face what he assumed to be the last over before lunch. Hazare, to bowl it, set his field in slow motion. The Indians had been run off their feet for two hours and looked it. Finally Hazare reached his mark. He turned. At that moment the umpire, Frank Chester, raised his artificial arm, gesticulated at no one in particular and announced theatrically, 'Time, gentlemen – please.' Evans had been denied by two runs the chance to become the first Englishman to score 100 before lunch in a Test match.

'It showed Frank off to advantage,' says Graveney. 'Unnecessarily.' During the interval Chester himself expressed regret at the decision, which he attributed to the Indians' field-placing. Immediately on resumption Evans completed his century, according to *Wisden* 'declining to pay the least respect to the bowlers'. The journalist John Woodcock went one better and commended Evans's 'extraordinary flair for imprinting his sparkling presence on a Test match'. His 104 lasted marginally over two hours, contained sixteen fours and allowed England an unassailable first-innings lead. Hutton led the applause from the balcony. For the second match in succession the champagne was waiting on Evans's return.

On Monday 23 June, the Queen paid her first visit as sovereign to Lord's. She congratulated Evans on his century and on his 100th Test dismissal – Shinde, stumped off Watkins in the first innings. The final act was then played out by Mankad, whose speed between the wickets and acute judgement of a run contributed much to his 184. At 2.30 he was bowled by Laker, driving over a half-volley. India finished 76 ahead and, after a false start by Simpson, England prevailed on the final morning. According to Swanton, the match had been one of 'brilliance followed by futility, timidity by aggression. . .a Test which divided itself into separate chapters each distinct from the last'; and punctuated throughout by the brilliance of Mankad and Evans.

INDIA

First Innings		Second Innings	
V. Mankad c Watkins b Trueman	72	-b Laker	184
P. Roy c and b Bedser	35	-b Bedser	0
P. R. Umrigar b Trueman	5	-b Trueman	14
*V. S. Hazare not out	69	-c Laker b Bedser	49
V. L. Manjrekar lbw b Bedser	5	-b Laker	1
D. G Phadkar b Watkins	8	-b Laker	16
H. R. Adhikari lbw b Watkins	0	-b Trueman	16
G. S. Ramchand b Trueman	18	-b Trueman	42
†M. K. Mantri b Trueman	1	-c Compton b Laker	5
S. G. Shinde st Evans b Watkins	5	-c Hutton b Trueman	14
Ghulam Ahmed b Jenkins	0	- not out	1
B 7, n-b 10	17	B 29, l-b 3, n-b 4	36
1/106 2/116 3/118 4/126 5/135 6/139 7/167 8/180 9/221	235	1/7 2/59 3/270 4/272 5/289 6/312 7/314 8/323 9/377	378

Bowling: *First Innings* – Bedser 33–8–62–2; Trueman 25–3–72–4; Jenkins 7.3–1–26–1; Laker 12–5–21–0; Watkins 17–7–37–3. *Second Innings* – Bedser 36–13–60–2; Trueman 27–4–110–4; Jenkins 10–1–40–0; Laker 39–15–102–4: Watkins 8–0–20–0; Compton 2–0–10–0.

ENGLAND

First Innings		Second Innings	
*L. Hutton c Mantri b Hazare	150	- not out	39
R. T. Simpson b Mankad	53	- run out	2
P. B. H. May c Mantri b Mankad	74	-c Roy b Ghulam Ahmed	26
D. C. S. Compton lbw b Hazare	6	- not out	4
T. W. Graveney c Mantri b Ghulam Ahmed	73		
A. J. Watkins b Mankad	0		
†T. G. Evans c and b Ghulam Ahmed	104		
R. O. Jenkins st Mantri b Mankad	21		
J. C. Laker not out	23		
A. V. Bedser c Ramchand b Mankad	3		
F. S. Trueman b Ghulam Ahmed	17		
B 8, l-b 5	13	B 4, l-b 4	8
1/106 2/264 3/272 4/292 5/292 6/451 7/468 8/506 9/514	537	1/8 2/71	(2 wkts.) 79

Bowling: *First Innings* – Phadkar 27–8–44–0; Ramchand 29–8–67–0; Hazare 24–4–53–2; Mankad 73–24–196–5; Ghulam Ahmed 43.4–12–106–3; Shinde 6–0–43–0; Umrigar 4–0–15–0. *Second Innings* – Ramchand 1–0–5–0; Hazare 1–1–0–0; Mankad 24–12–35–0; Ghulam Ahmed 23.2–9–31–1.

Umpires: F. Chester and F. S. Lee

Between the second and third Tests Evans scored his 144 against Somerset. On 17 July he reported for duty at Old Trafford where, despite constant interruptions, play was completed in three days. Evans scored 71 of the England first innings of 347, 'bringing gaiety to the cricket' (*Wisden*) and at one stage scoring fourteen from four consecutive deliveries. At the other end Sheppard played a cameo of 34. The 23-year-old, after a discouraging tour of Australia, was in the throes of a season that would see him lead the first-class averages with 2,262 runs at 64.62. The following year, as captain of Sussex, he led the County from thirteenth in the table to runners-up. To Evans, Sheppard shared many of the qualities enjoyed by May, while lacking the latter's 'decisive genius'. Sheppard's shots tended to find the field; May's transfixed it. At Manchester Sheppard distinguished himself not only with the bat but in the extraordinary sequel that saw India dismissed twice in a day. The perpetrator was Trueman. He took 8–31, supported by English fielding in which Evans, Sheppard and the debutant Lock were outstanding. At one stage Trueman's field consisted of three slips, three gullies, silly point and two short legs and, in his own phrase, had the Indians 'mesmerized'. In the second innings Bedser took 5–27 and the match ended that evening.

At this point Hutton's record as captain was unblemished. He himself had scored centuries at Lord's and Manchester. Yet doubts remained. Compton, who had had the feeling 'that Len's way of playing would not be mine' agreed with Swanton that there remained limitations in the captain's appreciation of the broader scene. His management of Trueman, for one, inclined to despair at the latter's 'difficult' nature; although, to be fair to Hutton, Trueman was indeed 'difficult'. According to Evans, at this stage 'you either liked Fred or you didn't'. (He liked him.) Another player, Graveney, was thought 'too carefree' for the captain's taste, although again it says volumes for Hutton's management that he adapted to the psychology of an individual like Evans – witness the champagne. Coincidentally or not, Evans considered Hutton 'magnificent'; from the point of view of policy and strategy, the best under whom he played. Undeniably Hutton strived to win – or, failing that, not to lose. The adjustment of the over rate, and his own batting, as a tactical ploy was a Hutton refinement. In the fourth Test at The Oval (where admittedly rain had fallen overnight) he and Sheppard scored only 45 before lunch against an indifferent attack. They eventually made 86 and 119 respectively; India collapsed once more and the match ended in monsoon conditions that must at least have made the visitors feel at home. In the four-match series, Evans had taken eight dismissals and, significantly, finished second in the averages with 242 runs at 60.50. Lest this be construed as accidental, no less a judge than Graveney asserts that Evans's innings at Headingley and Old Trafford were among the finest of the series, 'not least in the way he scored them'. As for the century-that-should-have-been at Lord's: 'phenomenal'.

What, meanwhile, of Kent? The County rose to fifteenth in the Championship, with only Evans (when available), Cowdrey and Fagg offering resistance. In early August the County played Essex at Southend with Evans's aggregate on 1,469. He duly scored 32 and was caught at extra cover attempting a six. Two results followed: Essex were beaten with four minutes to spare and Tom Crawford came forward to celebrate Evans's achievement. By his own admission, the runs from then on dried up, lending credence to the Hutton/Crawford theory of inducement; if, as Evans asserts, playing cricket was still reward enough itself, then the presence of additional incentive seems not to have hurt.

His only remaining representative match was, as usual, for the Players at Lord's. They won by two runs. The chief distinction was a century by the Leicester captain Charles Palmer. According to Swanton, Palmer 'played all the strokes', displaying 'exceptionally fast running' between the wickets. At one stage he and Insole rushed six while Laker retrieved the ball from inside the boundary. Palmer's reward came twelve months later when he was appointed player-manager of the touring party to the West Indies. This involved the contradictory position of being under Hutton's jurisdiction on the field, yet otherwise responsible to MCC for the administration and discipline of the team, including presumably the captain. Evans, among others, had reservations about the arrangement – though not about Palmer's innings at Lord's. As with Brown in the corresponding fixture two years before, it was a classic case of the psychological moment being seized. At Scarborough the same sides met again, with Cowdrey running out Hutton on 99. Even this left its impression – Cowdrey cites the match as the one where 'Hutton first began to watch [me] closely'; Evans as the moment that 'the on-side player' came of age. The same week Cowdrey scored 101 for Kent against India.

England, alone of the Test-playing countries, had no fixtures in the winter of 1952–53. For Evans it afforded another chance to consolidate his business dealings with Yates; that and the familiar routine of squash and hockey. Home now was a detached house named 'Wild Acre' (actually 1½ acres) at Aylesford, an establishment indicative of his enhanced earning power outside cricket. In addition to a net, rose garden and soon-to-be-installed swimming pool, there was ample space for Evans's newly acquired car. It was a Bentley.

A mere study of the records gives no indication of the excitement generated from match to match in the Test series of 1953, or of the passion expended in the matches themselves. To Arlott it was 'the most dramatic Ashes series' in memory. To Evans the prelude to the first Test was one of 'unprecedented optimism', based on the evidence of the tour of 1950–51, and, in particular, of the final Test at Melbourne. As a backdrop, the series was played in the wake of the June Coronation and the ascent of Everest, both of which contributed to a mood of extravagant national confidence. However incongruous it may seem to connect these events with cricket, connected they were – and in August the celebration echoing over England indeed 'crowned the year', in Jack Fingleton's apposite phrase.

Evans's first sight of the enemy was not encouraging.

For MCC in mid-May he contributed ten of a first innings of 80, in which the leg-spinner Ring took 5–36. The tourists, meanwhile, proceeded to win six of their first eight matches by an innings. Thus it was an England side 'fully aware' of its responsibilities that took the field at Trent Bridge on 11 June. The team had been adjusted to incorporate the Worcester batsman Kenyon, who would open (unsuccessfully) with Hutton. The attack was led by Bailey and Bedser, of whom the latter laboured heroically on a dead pitch to take the three Australian wickets that fell for 157. After rain fell overnight, the second day, characteristically, brought a reversal. While Hassett, a captain and batsman in the Hutton mould, endured to score 115, the rest of the side collapsed; among them the 21-year-old Richie Benaud who, attempting to glide a ball from Bailey, was disconcerted to see Evans diving full-length to his left to catch it. Australia never recovered, and from 237–4 were all out for 249. Unfortunately England responded in kind, with Lindwall, Miller and Jack Hill, a leg-spinner of Wright-like velocity, dismissing them for 144. In yet another reversal, Bedser (7–44) bowled out Australia for 123, in so doing passing Sydney Barnes's record English total of 189 Test wickets. Barnes was on hand to congratulate him. The match was perfectly balanced for a finish when rain obliterated play on the final two days, with England on 120–1. The winning target of 229 had been, in Evans's words, 'distinctly feasible'. Both sides emerged from the encounter with wary respect for the other, like boxers who had achieved a double knockout. For England Bedser had been outstanding.

The sides regrouped at Lord's with England holding a moral advantage. The match was played in balmy weather, before capacity crowds. Fingleton noted:

> *25 June 1953*: To Lord's by underground and a strange sight all along the tube stations of blackboards with chalked notices – 'Cricket: Test match at Lord's. Ground full.'
> *26 June 1953*: The same blackboard tale on the underground route to Lord's – 'Ground full. Gates closed.'

> The streets outside the ground this morning are an awful litter of old newspapers, the remnants of the all-night camp by many people. Scalpers are on the job. . . . They ask £5 for a £1 reserved seat.

For those inside, the death throes of the Test were acute. England started their second innings in the late afternoon of the fourth day, needing 343 to win. The wicket was deteriorating. They then declined to 73–4 when, towards the close of play, Watson joined Compton, replaced at lunch the next day by Bailey. For the rest of the session, and the one that followed, Evans remained padded-up in the dressing-room. At times he stretched out and slept. At tea the two batsmen 'slumped, hardly speaking, and sat quite still'. According to Arlott, 'news of their resistance spread round London' and the crowd increased. Hassett unloosed Lindwall and Miller with the new ball; thrice Bailey was hit on the hand. 'This suited me,' he says. 'I enjoyed batting when the pressure was on.' Then, in quick succession, both players were out: Watson, 109 in 346 minutes; Bailey, 71 in a mere 257. Evans appeared. Gil Langley, deputizing for Tallon, appealed first ball: Benaud sent down a full toss; Evans lunged out, his weight on the front foot, and missed it. Langley removed the bails and the close-fielders (all nine of them) 'leapt like kangaroos'. Gauging the mood to perfection, Evans observed, 'That was close.' The reply was unprintable. At the other end, Freddie Brown, recalled for one match, struck a succession of fours – they took up more time, he said. On his departure Wardle joined Evans at the crease. They played out the last over of an epic stalemate.

Bailey, says Evans, was 'out of the Hutton school'. He batted uncompromisingly. As a bowler he had been disabused of any notions of speed by the sight of Lindwall and Miller in 1948. Instead he settled for a life of military medium precision. He also varied his approach to the wicket: Evans remembers his footmarks as being 'two or three feet apart', meaning that the batsman was constantly attacked from a different angle. Bailey was a strategist. He would provoke Miller into a rash stroke by deliberately shutting up the game. 'He was always thinking,' says Evans. 'And most of the time he was thinking, someone was hitting

Catching Harvey down the leg side off Bedser, Old Trafford 1953. The batsman's expression says it all. (The Cricketer).

him.' Most of the time.

At Old Trafford Edrich and Simpson returned to reinforce the batting. Rain restricted play to only thirteen hours, during which Harvey made 122. It would have been less had Evans caught a straightforward chance off Bailey.

> It happened like this. I watched the ball off the bat and it seemed to me as though it would be a waist-high catch. But the ball must have been travelling faster than I expected. Instead of following a normal trajectory, it kept coming up and up, and as it approached, my hands moved further and further back into my chest. At last they were tucked right into my body, and it was too late to step back. So the ball hit the base of my thumbs and bounced out.

So much for the theory that Evans was already throwing up the ball as he caught it. That particular chance proved expensive in that Harvey went on to make a century; had he and Davidson (dropped behind in the second innings before scoring) departed early on, the match might have been won. Arlott, in the commentary box, took the opportunity to remind his listeners of 'Evans's miss', redeemed when, off Bedser, he brought off an outstanding leg-side catch to dismiss the same batsman. In the England reply Evans shared a seventh-wicket stand of 60 which averted the follow-on. There followed an astonishing Australian collapse to 35–8 at the close of play. It says much for Hutton that he introduced Wardle and Laker so early in the day; rather less that he had previously omitted to declare. It was the ninth successive match between England and Australia at Old Trafford to be drawn or abandoned. From it Evans emerged with six dismissals, 44 runs and the absolute conviction that the Australians were sooner or later, going to be beaten.

At Headingley, Hutton again lost the toss; he threw away the coin. Both he and Compton made nought as England subsided to 142–7, with Bailey the sole remaining recognized batsman. Next morning Evans ran him out. It was a classic case of 'Yes – No – Sorry', the last sentiment being Evans's as Bailey passed him on the way to the pavilion. The England total of 167 was less abject than it seems. Benaud remembers the pitch being 'so green it could hardly be distinguished from the square'; Hassett's insertion of the opposition was the first by an Australian Test captain in 44 years. Eventually the tourists were presented with a target of 177 in two hours. It is part of folklore that, largely thanks to Bailey, they failed to achieve it. Of the five batsmen who had successfully reached a total of 404 on the same ground in 1948, four still remained; the fifth, Bradman, was in the press box. The critical difference was the presence of Hutton as captain. Having opened with Lock, he saw the Australians proceed to 66 after 45 minutes. Only two wickets had fallen and, after consulting Evans and Compton, the captain reverted to defence. Bailey appeared and proceeded to bowl six overs of leg theory for nine runs. The target receded and England achieved, rather than earned, a draw. The goodwill engendered by both sides was suspended, and Swanton noted that, following the match, 'some of the Australians had to clutch pretty hard at the last remnants of their good humour'. Among them was Benaud, who asserted that 'time-wasting saved England'. Even Compton, of a more mercurial school than Hutton, felt that 'the Australian anger was justified'. Not surprisingly, his advice to the captain had been to attack. The critical influence was Evans, who had seen Morris and Harvey deliberately set out to destroy Lock's confidence. He indicated as much to Hutton, adding, 'If we keep this up, we'll lose.' The Australians were livid with Hutton, Bailey and Evans; 'rightly so', he admits. As a postscript, one wonders whether they themselves would have declined such tactics under similar circumstances. The match, like its predecessors, had fluctuated wildly over the five days, with the crowd of 150,000 rarely disappointed; even in the last climactic 45 minutes, twelve overs had been bowled – by modern standards, almost cause for celebration.

The five-act drama reached its climax at The Oval. Trueman was introduced to the side for the first time, and in Bedser, Lock and Laker possessed three colleagues appearing on their home ground. The Australians omitted Benaud. A further refinement was added by the tourists' objection to Frank Chester, previously known to answer appeals with the phrase, 'Not bloody out.' Despite their own altercation the previous year, Evans thought Chester the best available, and detected in the Australian protest a suggestion of panic. It was reinforced when the first ball of the match, bowled by Bedser, left a mark '. . . as if someone had crushed the pitch'. Hassett, the batsman, turned to Evans and remarked sardonically, 'I can see who this has been made for.' At the end of the first day Australia had scored 275, in conditions suggesting that the turning-point, literally, was around the corner. When Evans appeared the next afternoon the England reply stood at 170–5; Lindwall had just taken the new ball. Not being in exceptional form, Evans promptly elected for the most reliable form of defence: he hit Lindwall for ten in an over and proceeded to 28; 'not allowing,' says *Wisden*, 'anything to worry him.' At this stage Evans discerned the need to open up and duly smote

The England XII at The Oval, 1953. Standing (left to right): Bailey, May, Graveney, Laker, Lock, Wardle, Trueman. Sitting (left to right): Edrich, Bedser, Hutton, Compton, Evans.

his first ball from Archer to square leg. What he failed to discern was Alan Davidson, who, forgetting Hassett's instruction to 'drop back when Evans is batting', was quietly discussing matters with the square-leg umpire. Alerted by Bailey, Evans turned, slipped and slid down the wicket on his back. Recovering, he made for the crease. For a moment it seemed his corkscrewing approach had succeeded. Then the finger rose. It was a moment worthy of Chaplin, a nearby Kennington native. More pertinently, it meant England were on equal terms and eventually achieved a first-innings lead. Still, they would have to bat last.

The critical moment of post-War Ashes cricket was enacted on Tuesday 18 August 1953. It was Evans's birthday. That afternoon Australia were dismissed for 162, due entirely to Lock and Laker. The ball at this point was 'turning at right-angles' and Bedser, for one, believed that an equally heroic role was played by Evans in restricting byes to eleven.

England needed 132 to win and ended the day at 38–1. That night Evans indulged in a preliminary celebration with his brother and father, the latter given to excitedly indicating newspaper reports and exclaiming to complete strangers, 'That's my boy.' In the event Edrich and May batted with considerable poise when play resumed in front of a full house the following morning; television, uniquely, broadcast the match throughout the day. Evans (forsaking his normal habit of sleeping with his pads on) watched from the balcony; at the fall of the second wicket he was instructed by Hutton to be ready. It would have crowned his own year had Evans then been required to bat; but Edrich and Compton remained until lunch, when, with the score at 101–2, the outcome was inevitable. Evans recalls 'a considerable amount of champagne' accumulating in the England dressing-room and, whether as an extension of the previous night's revelry or the commencement of another, he found himself devoid of pain when, at 2.53, Compton achieved the winning run. In the five Tests Evans had scored 117 runs at an average of 23.40 and taken sixteen dismissals; according to Swanton, he had been, 'apart from a few off-moments at Old Trafford, quite admirable'. On the balcony both Tallon and Langley sought him out with congratulations. Below 15,000 spectators clamoured in front of the pavilion. The Ashes had been won for the first time in nineteen years, and for the first time at home in 27. 'It was,' says Evans, 'the most memorable day – and night – of my life.'

Hassett accepted defeat with the same equanimity that characterized his own batting. 'Not bad,' he told Walter Robins, 'considering Lockie threw us out.' Lock had been no-balled three times in the Surrey v India fixture the previous year and, according to Swanton, 'everyone knew. . .that he threw his faster one.' If so, there was evidently a conspiracy of silence. Not until the 1958–59 tour of Australia, when Bradman produced photographic evidence, did Lock (to his credit) significantly modify his action. At this stage he was, and remained, a 'cricketer's cricketer'. Unlike Laker, irritants such as a raw or bleeding spinning finger rarely inhibited him. As a batsman, says Evans, 'he had certain limitations'; diffidence not among them. The theatrical touch was most evident in Lock's fielding, particularly his work at short leg. He and Evans were akin in that both had the ability to take catches which no one else would have considered chances. Although recognized as a specialist, Lock in time became an outstanding fielder in the deep. His throwing was particularly accurate – as one cynic suggested, it might have been. He remains, in Evans's view, 'one of the two outstanding reasons' England won the Ashes that year.

The other? Bedser. Bailey concurs that 'he worried everyone with his nagging accuracy, movement in the air and off the pitch, and his ability to produce the really devastating delivery even on a docile track.' He and Evans both nominate Bedser's dismissal of Hassett at Trent Bridge as the consummate delivery: starting outside off, moving in, pitching leg and hitting middle. In the match Bedser had figures of 14–99; in the series, 39 wickets at an average of seventeen. It was an epic performance, bolstered by his ability on more than one occasion to score vital runs. Few lower-order players have been able to hit the ball off the back foot more impressively. 'Marvellous,' says Evans. 'It gave you confidence just to see him there.' The feeling was mutual.

For Kent the season continued their post-War recession. In August the captain, Murray Wood, was dismissed in favour of Wright. Evans immediately declared the action misguided. Certainly the Committee's handling of the affair left much to be desired; the senior players (including Evans) first hearing of it was when informed by the captain himself. Wright, like Hutton, proved himself on the cautious side, and (again like Hutton) was oppressed by the additional responsibilities of the job. The County finished sixteenth in the Championship. In a generally depressing review of the season, *Wisden* declared that 'another disappointment was the falling-off of Evans's batting. . .although his wicket-keeping was as brilliant as ever.' His fund-raising, too, seems to have flourished in this, his benefit year. Eschewing tradition, Evans organized no Sunday matches ('Six days' cricket a week was enough') and allowed a collection only in his nominated match, against Hampshire at Canterbury.

Thus it was that on August Bank Holiday Monday Evans joined Cowdrey at the wicket before a crowd of 10,000. By an extraordinary coincidence he reached 50 just as the collection box was circulating, and, a few minutes later, received word from Brian Valentine that a second half-century would ensure an additional offering. He was out for 71. At the end of August the Australians appeared at Canterbury and a party was held in Evans's honour. The details are sketchy, but are thought to include Hassett drawing the winning ticket in the raffle and subsequently discussing the meaning of life with Evans until four in the morning. When all the figures were added up, the benefit was found to be worth £5,259, a Kent record. If not in the same league as Compton and Washbrook, it was, as Evans says, 'a very tidy sum', and represented close to the net amount he had then earned as a professional cricketer.

Immediately following the Headingley Test, the first ten names for the winter tour of the West Indies had been announced, Evans's among them. His deputy was Spooner. A conspicuous absentee was Bedser, who had asked to be omitted in order to prepare himself for the 1954–55 tour of Australia. Statham and Trueman were brought together for the first time, with spin provided by Lock, Laker and Wardle. The only notable controversy was the inclusion of Palmer as player-manager. This was in defiance of Hutton's stated preference for 'the Colonel' (Griffith), who had left his position on the staff of the *Sunday Times* and been appointed assistant-secretary of MCC. As Swanton put it, 'if ever there was "a natural" for the managership it was Griffith.' The Committee demurred and appointed Palmer. He, Hutton, Bailey and Compton formed the tour committee. It was, says Evans, an ominous note on which to start the tour described by *The Times* as 'the second most controversial in cricket history.'

Chapter Five

Action in Cricket

THE PARTY WHICH LEFT England on 14 December 1953 was the first to do so under a professional captain this century. It was also the first to travel by air. From a mild English winter the group found themselves stranded by engine trouble in Newfoundland, clad only in their tropical suits. It was 'just preferable' to the crossing on the SS *Tettela*, says Evans. 'Just.'

The first port of call on arrival was Bermuda, where MCC played three fixtures at Hamilton. Hutton distinguished himself by being bowled off the first ball of the tour. The results were, respectively, an MCC win and two draws. From the first shot of *his* tour, Evans scored six, batting on a mat with a concrete base. Lock, not surprisingly, was able to extract considerable bounce and made life 'interesting' for his wicketkeeper. Improbably, it rained all week.

The serious cricket started on 2 January 1954 with a Colony match against Jamaica. Here the party met the great Headley, the 'Black Bradman', brought out of retirement in England at the age of 44 by public subscription. More ominously, Evans and others noted a distinct tension absent on Allen's tour six years earlier. Certain elements of the press endeavoured to instil a political aspect to the match, and suggested that the teams were engaged in something more than a game of cricket. On the eve of their departure MCC had been briefed by the Colonial Office, which left no one in any doubt of the changed political reality in the islands. 'At times we were used,' says Evans. 'People seemed to think we were representatives of "the system". We weren't.' Considerably more in sorrow than anger, he notes that the 'siege mentality', later to characterize almost every modern overseas tour, first became evident in 1954. Swanton himself wrote that there was an element of 'political prestige' attached to affairs both on and off the field, and that lessons were to be learnt 'as regards the management and organization of future tours'. With commendable understatement, Hutton later reported that 'our friends in the West Indies actively connected with cricket could be numbered with one hand. This contributed to a rather strained atmosphere on occasions.'

One such was the Colony match against Jamaica, where, as Evans says, the thunder-flashes exploding at the fall of each MCC wicket 'made it difficult to maintain the calm dignity expected of the occasion'. MCC won by an innings and 21. In the return match Headley's 53 was greeted by a reaction comparable only to Evans's when catching Holt off a 'huge deflection' from Wardle. The batsman was given not out. It was an early indication of the umpiring which, in Hutton's report, 'except on one or two occasions, was appalling throughout'. MCC approached the first Test at Kingston convinced, in Evans's words, that they 'would have to be one-and-a-half times as good as the West Indies to beat them on their own ground'. They weren't.

Despite a first innings deficit of 247, England entered the last day needing only 230 with eight wickets in hand. They lost by 140 runs. A contributory factor was Evans, who had been invited the previous evening to a private party at Blue Mountain Inn. Given the precarious state of the match, Hutton had imposed a 10 o'clock curfew and promptly informed his wicketkeeper that non-compliance would be dealt with accordingly. Evans (in his 50th Test) felt this 'unnecessary' and retired to bed in a state of brooding resentment. This was exacerbated when, next morning, he learnt that Hutton had attended the same party in his absence. That afternoon, with victory 170 runs off, Evans joined Bailey at the wicket. 'Play yourself in,' said Hutton. 'Don't do anything rash.' 'Right,' said Evans, whereupon he advanced ten yards down the pitch and was bowled. 'It was madness,' he admits, and words were exchanged with the captain in the dressing-room. The upshot was that both men apologized and Hutton, Evans believes, subsequently acknowledged that 'each player should be handled as an individual'. The axiom applied not only to Evans, but to Laker – in whom Hutton was to note 'a strong tendency to be afraid of certain batsmen', and whom he found personally difficult. Wardle and Trueman – his fellow Yorkshiremen – he placed in the same category, Hutton's attitude to the latter's indiscretions remaining one of passive resignation. Swanton recalls an incident on Trueman's birthday in Barbados when 'a certain robustness of phrase' had offended residents of the team hotel, and Evans himself believes that 'Fred would in no way have been harmed had Len applied more discipline'. The balance was obviously a fine one.

In the Test itself Hutton had displayed uncharacteristic generosity by allowing Headley off the mark. Possibly he feared the consequences of not doing so. Evans remembers the sound of machine-gun and automatic rifle fire punctuating the stands and one of the umpires, Perry Burke, was physically assaulted for his decision against a local batsman. On the field Ramadhin and Valentine enjoyed their customary share of wickets; Weekes made an imperious 90 and West Indies introduced a new wicketkeeper, Clifford McWatt. During the series he frequently approached Evans for advice, which was freely given. Hutton, no doubt, would have disapproved.

From Kingston the party flew to Antigua, where, eschewing the two-day match, Evans went sightseeing with Trueman – 'always an experience'. Evans's room-mate on the tour was May, who confirms that 'Godfrey's company was a lively introduction' to his first overseas excursion. Rarely an evening (save that at Kingston) passed without Evans engaging in some form of revelry, and the journalist Reg Hayter recalls him 'sprinting from the field at the end of a long, hot day, as though already late for a prior engagement', which quite probably he was. May found his enthusiasm both on and off the field 'invigorating'. Graveney adds that 'Evans's head never dropped. He was the same sparkling personality at six in the evening as he had been at eleven that morning. . .and as he would be at twelve that night.'

Evans's humour was temporarily diminished by the cyst that had developed on his shoulder. After the Kingston Test he reported to hospital, where, under local anaesthetic, he watched a team of surgeons 'cutting and sawing away for an hour'. The result was that, after recuperating in Antigua, he stood down from the Colony match against Barbados, which MCC won off the last ball. On 6 February he declared himself fit for the second Test at Bridgetown, which West Indies again won handsomely. This was the match adjudged by Swanton, among others, as jeopardized by Hutton's tactics in restricting strokeplayers like Compton and Graveney. Evans confirms that the captain's pre-match instructions had consisted largely of the phrase 'Don't get out', and Graveney, for one, fell to a full toss that he would normally have struck for four. 'Len's policy was not to lose,' he recalls. 'He never realized there was more than one way of doing it.' For the West Indies Walcott scored 220, during which Evans witnessed 'easily the best over' of his professional career. It was bowled by Bailey. Each ball was near-perfect; each was hit by Walcott 'like a bullet'; each brilliantly fielded and returned without score. Evans himself had returned to form and conceded no byes in the West Indian innings of 383. Set an eventual target of 494, England failed by 181. Hutton, May, Compton and Graveney all scored respectably, and, in Graveney's case, at noticeably increased tempo. At the conclusion of the first innings (England at one stage scoring 128 in a completed day's play), Evans and Compton had approached Hutton with the suggestion that batsmen be allowed to play 'naturally'. Somewhat reluctantly Hutton agreed, the upshot being that Compton scored 93, batting, says Evans, 'as though it were 1947 again'. Another consequence was the relative demise of Valentine, who failed to take a wicket in England's second innings. Although continuing to play Test cricket for another eight years, the series marked the end of his partnership with Ramadhin as a virtually unplayable spin attack. It was the one psychological advantage England held as they embarked on the remaining Tests, two-nil down in the series.

By the time the party arrived in British Guiana there was, says Evans, a perceptible mood in favour of adopting a more positive approach on the field. Off it, conditions remained as oppressive as ever, and of Georgetown Evans wrote:

> You could cut the humidity with a knife. You were soaking wet and yet it wasn't really hot. You knew the sun was up somewhere but it never seemed to shine

> through. A very heavy and unpleasant atmosphere came up from the dykes which run along either side of every roadway. They smelt musty and were full of dirty water. The houses were often on stilts, with a contrivance like an upturned cup fixed on each stilt to prevent the white ants getting into the house and eating the place down. The ants were everywhere.

In the Colony match, Watson scored 257 and Graveney 231 of an MCC total of 607. Guiana were bowled out twice and lost by an innings. This was the moment, says Evans, when a number of players – Graveney and himself among them – determined that from henceforward the best form of defence would be attack. Hutton had objected to the standard of umpiring in the Colony match and his request that officials be imported from Barbados was supported by the West Indian captain Stollmeyer. In the event the Board appointed the local groundsman, Badge Menzies, who throughout the Test could be seen supervising the preparation of the pitch in addition to his duties as umpire. It was a fateful decision. In the West Indies first innings, Worrell – much diminished, in Evans's opinion, since 1950 – was caught behind in the first over. Stollmeyer and Walcott followed, leaving the home team on 16–3. The crowd, already in a state of latent hostility, took exception to the dismissal of McWatt, run out when attempting the single which would have achieved a hundred partnership for the eighth wicket. Evans, who broke the stumps, estimated that the batsman was at least three yards out, and Menzies's decision was at best academic. The players were already congratulating themselves when their attention was drawn to the sight of McWatt sprinting for the safety of the pavilion. He was followed by a volley of bottles raining onto the outfield. 'They came in a burst lasting perhaps half a minute,' said the *Telegraph*. 'No one knew quite what caused them, perhaps a little rum, a certain amount of betting and possibly there were political origins too. British Guiana was going through a difficult time.' The England team reacted in their different ways: Wardle abated the crowd by raising a bottle to his lips and pretending to drink; Compton bated it by returning at least one receptacle to its owner.

Probably the calmest man on the ground was Hutton, who kept Menzies and his colleague on the field and declined to lead the team off. His statement signifying he wanted 'a couple of wickets tonight' was, says Evans, 'a classic Huttonism'; unwitting, unruffled and unmoved. Without doubt, his grace under pressure communicated itself to the crowd who, in Swanton's words, 'at once became perfectly normal again'. Having resumed play, England secured one of the two wickets specified that night. Between then and the resumption, the Governor of British Guiana offered Hutton military protection if required. It was declined. On Tuesday 2 March England duly won by nine wickets, their first Test victory in the West Indies since 1935.

The press were unanimous in asserting that Hutton's courageous and masterly handling of the situation had won the day, and to some extent it was this, rather than the Oval Test of 1953, that finally established him as England captain. A congratulatory cable from Aird, the secretary of MCC, confirmed this. It was a team considerably buoyed by, in Wardle's words, 'Len's victory' that flew to St. George's, Grenada, for their second experience of playing on matting. The episode at Guiana seemed to have animated Hutton, and Graveney recalls him speaking 'quite excitedly' about the team's prospects in Australia that winter.

The team's prospects in the fourth Test at Trinidad were impaired when an infection to Evans's foot caused him to report unfit. Spooner had just time to thank him for 'ruining an otherwise agreeable holiday' before taking the field on 17 March. This was the match, played on jute matting, that Trueman asserts 'cut down my life by a year or two', and by the time West Indies declared at 681–8 the same bowler was comparing the experience unfavourably to serving a term of hard labour. After nine overs Statham pulled a muscle and was unable to bowl again on the tour. Confined to his hotel, Evans received nightly reports of the Test which neither Hutton nor Stollmeyer expected to reach a conclusion. Nor did it. During the match MCC were guests at a reception hosted by the West Indies Board of Control at which the president expressed regrets at some of the crowd behaviour throughout the series. He refrained from specifically mentioning the umpiring, which again at Trinidad verged on the capricious. Early on England were convinced that Weekes was caught by Spooner; the umpire demurred and the batsman scored 206. On the final day Evans appeared at the ground 'still agreeably full of aureomycin and penicillin', a state presumably envied by the England bowlers.

At the end of March the party returned to Jamaica, where, for the first time on tour, Evans was joined by his wife, Jean. Dorothy Hutton arrived at the same time; earlier Compton's wife, Valerie, had appeared in Barbados. Evans recalls that, while MCC gave permission for the visits, they certainly took no responsibility for travel arrangements or expenses. Having spent five out of eight winters abroad since the War, he felt that 'after a certain number of tours, a player should be offered the privilege of a free passage for his wife to join him. Not for the whole tour, of course.' More than 30 years later, the suggestion remains.

On losing the toss at Sabina Park, Hutton gloomily anticipated a West Indies total somewhere in excess of 500. An hour later the score was 13–4, due largely to Bailey, who eventually took 7–34 in sixteen overs. Among the victims was Weekes, caught by Evans off one that 'came back like a rocket'. Bailey's secret, as such, was to bowl on a length, and, in his own words, 'let the wicket do the work'. Ten minutes after the last West Indian was out for 139, he and Hutton opened the England innings. A day later Hutton was 93 not out. 'He didn't hurry,' says Evans, who gave a fair impersonation of his own rearguard at Adelaide by scoring 28 in two-and-a-half hours. Hutton eventually made 205 and entered the pavilion at the end of the third day yearning 'for a cup of tea and the luxury of putting my feet up'. No sooner had he done so than he was accused of insulting the Chief Minister, a man whom Evans had previously noted as being 'accompanied throughout by a bodyguard of gigantic proportion, whose jacket bulged very significantly by one armpit'. The incident, given full prominence in the Jamaica *Daily Gleaner*, to some extent detracted from the match in which West Indies began their second innings 275 runs behind. If the credit for the England victory belonged to Hutton, who over the five Tests scored 677 runs at an average of 96, then supporting roles were played by Evans, May and Compton and, at various times, by the bowlers who laboured on a succession of pitches as hard as concrete, which they occasionally were. In the West Indian second innings, Evans employed some elementary psychology by instructing the close-fielders to 'wildly applaud' the fourth ball of a Trueman over, irrespective of its merits. Trueman's reaction on seeing a long-hop ecstatically received by his wicketkeeper and slips was to visibly accelerate a gear, nicely complementing Laker at the other end. The off-spinner bowled from lunch to tea on the fourth day without change, eventually taking 4–71 in 50 overs. Two things became obvious to Evans that afternoon: firstly, that Laker, whatever his difficulties with Hutton and others, was capable of unrivalled subtlety and variety, a fact reluctantly confirmed by Lock; secondly, that a seventeen-year-old making his debut for the West Indies, bowling slow left-arm and batting 'as though his life depended on it', was a player of whom the world would hear further. His name, apparently, was Sobers.

So ended the tour then second only to that of 1932–33 as the most controversial of all time. From the outset, Hutton's instinct had been to defend; in this respect, the private meeting of the senior players on the eve of the third Test, at which Evans urged a more positive approach, can be seen as decisive. To recover from the Barbados debacle in which, in Swanton's words, England reached 'rock-bottom' to a position of squaring the series represented a remarkable revival. Whatever his shortcomings as captain, Hutton the batsman led by example, and by the end of the tour Graveney, for one, considered him outstanding. Evans's own performances had been mixed, and he emerged from the series with six dismissals and a batting average of twelve. In Kingston, he freely admits, he disappointed. Players at the outset of a tour are subject to the additional pressure of acclimatizing both to their surroundings and themselves, and on this occasion Hutton's intransigence touched a nerve. He, Hutton, was later to report cryptically of Evans: 'I feel that you know all there is to know about him.' If so, that would surely have included the fact that, based on his performance in the Caribbean, Evans remained outstandingly the best Test wicketkeeper in the world, capable, in Bailey's words, 'of making catches and stumpings which no other man would have considered'. He returned to England in April with his reputation intact.

Rarely can a season have begun more auspiciously. In Kent's first fixture of 1954, against Derbyshire at Gravesend, Evans scored 109 in the first innings. Immediately afterwards, the County beat Worcestershire at the same ground; Evans scored the winning runs by the simple expedient of striking successive sixes over the sightscreen. That season Kent were to rise five places in the Championship.

On the circuit Evans had begun to notice a gratifying number of impersonators; the 'old solid-footed wicket-keeper' was gone, replaced by the 'greater mobility' patented by himself. One such convert was Tony Catt, who now competed with Ufton as Evans's County deputy. The dilemma of retaining an outstanding prospect whose own First XI appearances were necessarily limited in time contributed to Evans's decision to retire; meanwhile he afforded the younger players the maximum encouragement he could, recalling the days when Levett and Ames had done so for him.

1954 was one of the wettest summers on record. England and Pakistan arrived at Lord's on 10 June woefully short of match practice, a condition exacerbated when the first three days of the Test were rained off. As compensation the teams were invited to a reception at Buckingham Palace on 12 June. The rain ceased over the weekend and play eventually started on the fourth afternoon. On a sodden wicket, Pakistan were dismissed for 87, with Statham finally establishing himself at the forefront of the England attack. The Lancastrian was, says Evans, 'the complete fast bowler'; more given to seam than swing, Statham's stock delivery moved into the right-handed batsman, the ball invariably leaving the pitch faster than expected. Statham was double-jointed and used to amuse his teammates by removing his sweater with both hands arched behind his back. He was, notwithstanding, the straightest of bowlers: Statham's maxim, 'If they miss, I hit', was demonstrated more than once that afternoon as he captured the last four wickets to fall for ten runs. In the England reply, Evans scored 25 out of 117; for Pakistan a nineteen-year-old named Hanif occupied the crease for six hours to ensure a draw.

Before the second Test Hutton withdrew from the captaincy. The West Indies tour had left him mentally and physically exhausted and already he had experienced the rheumatism that would enforce his retirement. Speculation grew as to whether Hutton would lead the team again, and, indeed, whether he was the right man to do so in Australia. The alternative candidate was Sheppard. By now reading theology at Cambridge, he had proved an outstanding captain of Sussex in 1953 and appealed to those who believed in the tradition of amateur captains from the ancient universities. The issue now seems absurd, but in 1954 there was sufficient apprehension at Hutton's appointment for the player to write formally to the Board of Control indicating his willingness to tour in whatever capacity. Sheppard, meanwhile, was appointed captain for the second Test at Trent Bridge.

There Appleyard took a wicket with his second ball in Test cricket; Bedser and Wardle lent support and Pakistan were dismissed for 157. Evans dramatically caught Maqsood off Appleyard and spent the following two days watching England accumulate 558–6 in reply. Compton, having been dropped on 20, made 278, his highest Test score. The second half of his innings was played, says Evans, in limited-overs fashion: 'Denis would charge down the pitch, check, adjust and still score four. The Pakistanis had never seen anything like it.' In contrast, Hanif again proved obdurate in scoring 51, while, at the other end, Maqsood made 69 in an hour. The tourists, while individually talented, appeared to have little or no notion of teamwork. At Trent Bridge they lost by an innings.

The third Test at Old Trafford saw the introduction of a 22-year-old included as a specialist batsman. Jim Parks would, in time, become Evans's 'second-finest wicketkeeper-batsman ever' (behind Ames). At this stage of his career, Parks's greatest assets were his footwork against spin and the cuts and glides responsible for more than half his runs off fast bowling. At Old Trafford he batted proficiently until bowled behind his legs by Fazal; Wardle scored a rapid 54; and Evans himself contributed 31. Confronted with a total of 359–8, Pakistan made 90, the Glamorgan off-spinner McConnon taking 3–19. The tourists were 25–4 in their second innings when rain intervened.

On 27 July, the last day of the Test, the touring party to Australia was announced. Hutton was captain. Sheppard, having declined to tour in a lesser capacity, was excluded. The manager was Geoffrey Howard, an occasional Middlesex and club cricketer and subsequently secretary of Lancashire and Surrey. The scorer, George Duckworth, had kept wicket for England 24 times between 1924 and 1936. At Hutton's insistence a professional masseur, Harold Dalton, was also included. More notable were the omissions: Trueman, Lock and Laker. Evans's deputy was the 24-year-old Northampton player Keith Andrew, who was joined by his teammate, Frank Tyson.

On 28 July Kent played Northamptonshire. Tyson duly bowled Cowdrey (another surprise selection) at a pace Evans found astonishing on a docile wicket. On his day, Tyson was to prove, without doubt, the fastest bowler to whom Evans kept wicket. That 'day' was to extend from the summer of 1954 to 1956; thereafter, in the bowler's own phrase, 'it became increasingly difficult to turn the switch which unleashed (the) pace'. Few who saw Tyson in the late summer of 1954 doubted that the switch was capable of electric power.

Hutton returned as captain for the final Test at The Oval. Also included were Tyson and Peter Loader, making their England debuts. Cowdrey was twelfth man. Doubts about Hutton's appointment were revived as England contrived to lose by 24 runs. In their first innings Pakistan scored 133, Evans conceding no byes. England made 130. The match was lost during the Pakistan reply of 164, which, in Evans's view, 'should have been less than fifty'. On the turning wicket then characteristic of The Oval, McConnon continually dropped the ball short, at one stage admitting to Evans, 'I've lost it'. One is tempted to speculate on what Lock and Laker might

'I feel that you know all there is to know about him' – In action against Pakistan, 1954. (Press Association).

have achieved in similar conditions. McConnon's inclusion at their expense was, says Evans, 'madness', and owed much to the influence of Wilfred Wooller on the Committee. Even so, England began their second innings needing only 168 with four sessions to play. Evans was party to the decision to attempt to win that evening, and admits that the prospect of a 'free day' may have obscured the team's objectivity. As at Headingley in 1948, England embarked on the last stage of a Test convinced of success, and as on that occasion failed. At 115–4 Evans joined Compton at the wicket, promoted by Hutton with the instruction to 'get them quickly tonight'. The first ball he received from Fazal lifted and burnt past his nose; Compton and he exchanged significant glances. England were dismissed for 143 and Pakistan squared the series. During it Evans conceded a total of 26 byes and took seven dismissals. The last, Kardar, was his 131st Test victim, a world record. It compensated for an otherwise abject England performance.

A week later Pakistan defeated Kent, whose season showed marked improvement under Wright's equable captaincy. Still more than 100 points separated them from Surrey, then in the midst of a record seven-year winning sequence, and Cowdrey, for one, appreciated the effort with which the wicketkeeper adapted to the vagaries of County Cricket. In early September, Evans declared himself 'exhausted' after three successive seasons' play. A week later he was on board the SS *Orsova*, bound for Australia.

A huge, swaying figure, bedecked in luminous sailcloth, listing under the weight of a stone of exotic headgear; that, for some, was the first sight of the England wicketkeeper. Evans's representation of Carmen Miranda was inevitably the *pièce de résistance* of the outward voyage; that and his ingratiating habit of appearing in the guise of 'Onest Evans', the people's bookmaker, at moments of otherwise stultifying boredom. If early September had seen him exhausted, then within days of embarking on his third Australian tour he was again the life and soul of the party. In Tyson's words, 'everything he touched seemed to be charged with dynamism'. It would remain so throughout the tour.

Evans's own outstanding memory of the voyage was passing through Suez; the British troops lining the Canal Zone cheered as the team appeared on deck. Below it Bedser was suffering from a listlessness later diagnosed as shingles. It was the one discordant note as the party arrived at Perth, where Cowdrey was informed that his father had died. When he went into dinner that night, he recalls, 'Hutton said nothing. It was only after the meal that he came round the back of my chair, put his hand on my shoulder and said, "I'm sorry." There were tears in his eyes.' A month later Cowdrey scored 110 and 103 against New South Wales and Hutton would ask him to open the batting for England.

More ominous was the condition of Bedser, who, after attending the Melbourne Cup with Evans, played his first match of the tour against an Australia XI in late October. It was clear that the bowler's form was critical, and the committee of Howard, Hutton, May, Edrich and Evans spent the evening of 25 November deliberating the side for the first Test at Brisbane. Earlier Hutton had spent the day staring fixedly at the wicket in the State match against Queensland. The outcome was a decision to invite Australia to bat; the outcome of the selection to omit Wardle and

Appleyard in favour of an all-pace attack. 'Good God,' said Bailey, when informed. 'The last time we did this, we lost by a mile in Melbourne.'

England lost by an innings at Brisbane. On the morning of the Test Evans contracted 'flu and spent the first day of the match in bed with a temperature of 102°. The news from the ground did nothing to cheer him. England went into the field on Friday morning and were still there the following Monday lunchtime. Harvey scored 162, Morris 153 and Australia eventually declared at 601–8. In all England dropped fourteen catches. Andrew, deputizing behind the stumps, missed Morris off Bedser. 'It was hardly a chance,' says Tyson, 'but substitutes for Godfrey Evans should expect comparisons.' One such was Andrew's inability to sustain the morale of a losing side in the field. 'I wasn't like Godfrey,' he concedes, 'and never could be. I only developed as a player when I learnt that.'

The Test brought a rare note of dissent between Evans and Bailey. The latter's repeated reference to the Melbourne Test of 1932–33 influenced, Evans believes, 'other members of the side who were inclined to agree with him, and, in consequence, team spirit was not all it should have been'. 'Team spirit', to Evans, was paramount. After the match, Cowdrey found Hutton 'unapproachable' and 'the team's spirits at zero'. While the party flew 200 miles north to Rockhampton in a plane of dubious vintage, Evans recuperated at Rose Bay Golf Club in Sydney. The four days he spent there returned him to match fitness. He rejoined the side against the Prime Minister's XI at Canberra, where MCC won by 31 runs. In the nets behind the ground Alf Gover, travelling as a journalist, could be seen demonstrating to Tyson the virtues of a shortened run-up. The results were dramatic. Against Victoria at Melbourne, Tyson took 6–68, hitting the stumps five times. The bowler had experimented with a diminished run at Brisbane, but now, directed by Gover and Hutton, determined to 'adapt my technique to meet the conditions'. Dalton, the team's masseur, was instructed to devise a training regime accordingly and on match days Tyson's diet consisted of exotic concoctions of raw eggs. A week later, on the eve of the second Test, lightning struck and thunder rubbed the windows of the team's hotel. Inside Tyson rubbed his hands, 'imagining the condensation that would be forming under the covers'.

On the morning of 17 December light rain was falling on Sydney and the ground was damp and dripping; ideal conditions for Bedser, one of the twelve players selected. Hutton, Edrich, May, Evans and Bedser himself inspected the wicket. There was a shortage of time before the start and the upshot was that, at the last moment, Bedser was informed he had been omitted. With Wardle and Appleyard both included, the final place had been between himself and Tyson. In private, Evans had lobbied for the latter by asking his fellow committeemen whom they, as batsmen, would rather face; the unanimous, if unwilling, verdict was 'Bedser'. The first Bedser knew of it was when the manager pinned the team sheet to the dressing-room door. It was the end of an illustrious career overseas.

Earlier in the series Bedser had been taken aside by Hutton and asked not to fraternize with the opposition. His reply was to ask how fraternal an aggregate of 69 wickets in two series could be. Throughout the tour Hutton exuded a kind of nervous intensity at odds with those for whom hostilities ceased at the close of play. The second Test was a case in point. Hutton took the field on the first morning as though in a different dimension. He and Bailey opened the England innings. Bailey was bowled and replaced by May, whom the captain seemed surprised to see at the wicket. Hutton was then caught by Davidson and returned muttering about the new tendency towards leg-slips. England were 60–4 and 99–8; Evans contributed three. There then followed, in Tyson's words, 'one of the most amazing cricket interludes yet witnessed'. It featured Statham and Wardle, who, in their contrasting styles, withstood the Australian attack for a stand of 43. The total reached 154 before Wardle skied the inevitable catch to mid on. Immediately the heavens opened.

On the second day Australia encountered Tyson for the first time. Employing his abbreviated run, he and Bailey contained the home lead to 74. As Lindwall walked to the wicket, Tyson reasoned that 'a man who has scored 60 in the previous Test can expect a bouncer early in his innings'. This one saw Lindwall dynamically caught by Evans. In the England reply Tyson quickly learnt the folly of bowling bouncers at opposing fast bowlers. The height of Lindwall's hand 'seemed to suggest a different ball'; Tyson had just time to turn before being struck on the back of the skull. On his return from hospital, he found Australia facing a target of 223. Tyson's target was revenge.

At this stage the consensus was in favour of Australia. They started the final day needing 151, with eight wickets in hand. As the England team took the field on the morning of 22 December, Evans delivered his immortal remark: 'We shall be there at the finish.' With the third ball of his second over, Tyson yorked Burke. This, in the bowler's view, was 'the psychological moment'; in Evans's, 'the beginning of the end'. With the total at 127–6 Davidson snicked the ball hard towards first slip; Tyson, at third man, had the impression of a 'bird veering in flight, the extension of an enormous glove, a heaven-shaking shout, and the departure of the crestfallen batsman'. It was Evans, who in his own recollection, 'dived in front of first slip and caught the ball with my left hand. As I hit the ground it was dislodged. . .I caught it with my right.' Davidson departed disconsolately. A few overs later Johnston snicked Tyson down the leg side and Evans took the running catch. England had won by 38 runs.

It was not a great team performance. May scored a hundred and Tyson took ten wickets. In the end the result owed much to the tail-end heroics of Wardle, Appleyard and Statham. That and the sustained brilliance of Evans, who, in addition to two critical catches, conceded no byes in the Australian second innings. Later in the tour he obtained a translation of his maxim and a special tie, imprinted *Perduravimus*, was struck. He wears it to this day.

Christmas was spent in Sydney. Evans orchestrated the festivities at the Oceanic Hotel, which he remembers Hutton 'enduring rather than enjoying'. An unlikely participant was the American industrialist Henry Sayen, to whom Cowdrey recalls the captain 'explaining the tricks of the trade with rare patience'. Sayen's enthusiasm soon extended to distributing substantial financial bonuses to the players for special performances. Tyson, May and Evans duly prospered.

The team arrived in Melbourne on 30 December convinced that the tide had turned. The bookmakers had reduced the odds on the series to evens. In Tyson England possessed a bowler of a sort not encountered since Larwood (whom Tyson had met during the Sydney Test). Unfortunately none of this communicated itself to Hutton, who, on the morning of New Year's Eve, announced that he was unfit to play. For some time it had been clear that he was feeling the strain of captaincy; now, two hours before the Test, he was locked in his room, morbid with fibrositis and shivering. Evans took charge. Pausing only to collect Edrich, he arrived in Hutton's room. The captain seemed to be on the verge of collapse. In a hoarse, quivering voice he announced that May should captain the side. 'Exactly what the Aussies want,' said Evans. Reluctantly Hutton agreed to dress and appear at the ground.

In the event the only notable absentee was Bedser. As at Sydney, he was included in the twelve; as at Sydney, he inspected the wicket. Again he was omitted. Compton replaced Graveney, and before a crowd of 70,000 Cowdrey proceeded to score 102 of the England total of 191. At lunch Miller had figures of 3–5 in nine overs; his doctor had recently told him not to exert himself. Evans scored twenty on a wicket 'you could pick lumps out of'. In the pavilion Appleyard and Wardle waited.

On Monday 3 January the shade temperature reached 105°. The England team arrived expecting the same arid pitch they had encountered the previous Saturday. To their amazement, the cracks on the playing area had narrowed; while, from the pavilion, black patches, not previously apparent, were visible on the square. A posse of players sought out the groundstaff. Hutton brooded.

Was the wicket watered? The journalist Percy Beames in *The Age* categorically said so. This was promptly denied by the authorities, who issued a statement indicating the ground had 'sweated'. Though an official enquiry revealed nothing, no legal action was taken against Beames; the most likely explanation remains human error. In the altered conditions Australia were left requiring 240 to win on the final day. The critical moment came at 77–2 when Harvey shaped to leg glance Tyson. Evans ran forward, propelled himself to cover the remaining distance and clutched the deflection at full-stretch. At the end of his follow-through Tyson froze in disbelief. 'If ever there was a turning point,' he said, 'that was it.'

England won the Test by 128 runs. Tyson's analysis of 7–27 had never been bettered by a fast bowler between the two countries. The victory, wrote Swanton, was due entirely to England's attack 'and, incidentally, to Evans, whose performance backed it up so brilliantly'. Cowdrey felt that Hutton 'had caused a crisis by not wanting to play, yet his captaincy was magnificent'. The other stalwarts were Bailey, Statham and May. Inspired by Evans's example, the fielding, he recalls, was 'outstanding. . .The spirit was wonderful and every one of us was convinced from the first ball that "we should be there at the finish". We were.' Over five days the match was watched by 300,000 spectators who paid £47,933; this despite the rival attraction of the nearby Davis Cup. At the end of the match Robert Menzies congratulated Hutton while, in the dressing-room, a hastily clad Carmen Miranda distributed champagne. It was a new year.

It appears that at this point the Australians knew the despair more familiar to their opponents. Between the third and fourth Tests the selectors dropped Morris and then reinstated him when Lindwall was unable to play. When the day dawned Morris was included and Favell, of the original twelve, omitted. The selectors further failed to endear themselves to the Adelaide public by dropping Langley. Evans remembers him being cheered when he entered the ground as a spectator.

The fourth Test began, in a week of century temperatures, on 20 January. It was Hutton's intention to limit the Australian scoring to a maximum of 180 a day, duly achieved in their eventual total of 323. For England Evans struck an even-time 37, engaging in a stand of 51 with

The shot that clinched the Ashes, Adelaide 1955.

Bailey. When Australia batted again they collapsed to 111. At this stage, facing a target of 94, Evans was convinced that England would 'walk it'. Miller, critically, demurred. Only three runs were on the cathedral-shadowed scoreboard when Edrich was bowled; Hutton and Cowdrey followed. Evans, more subdued, lay in the shadows of the dressing-room. An emetic roar heralded the return of May, caught dubiously at cover. At 49–4 Hutton delivered his epic remark, 'The buggers have done us', and retreated to the dressing-room. Compton and Bailey held firm until the latter was out to Johnston. At four o'clock on 2 February 1955, Evans – in Tyson's words, 'cocksure, aggressive and confident' – came to the wicket. The first ball he faced brought a bye. To the second, off Miller, he ran two. The third he struck with an almighty smash for four. England had won by five wickets.

The most disconsolate man in the ground was Compton. 'Do you know what you've done?' he asked. 'Won the Ashes' must have suggested itself, but Evans forbore. It transpired that Compton had been offered £100 (a month's salary) if he achieved the winning run, but only on condition that he informed no one. On reflection, his enthusiasm for his partner's second run off the penultimate ball *had* been subdued, which Evans attributed to 'Denis's normal eccentricity between the wickets'. Not so. Compton for once had actively sought the strike – although in radically different circumstances than in his stand with the same player eight years before. It took several bottles of champagne at the Pier Hotel that night to convince him of the merits of team success.

At the height of the revelries, Evans himself was wagered £100 against his ascending a pillar in the hotel lobby. He did so. No sooner had he slid groggily to earth than the stakes were raised to 'double or quits' on the toss of a coin. He lost. Events might have proceeded indefinitely but for the return of Hutton, May and Howard from an official dinner. The last visibly blanched when informed of the number of champagne bottles attributed to his account. The total, Evans believes, was 96.

The fifth Test at Sydney was anti-climactic. Monsoon conditions not witnessed for half-a-century delayed play until the fourth day. England scored 371–7, of which Graveney contributed 111. Australia replied with 221, and, following-on, were 118–6 when proceedings ended. The match was memorable as the only occasion on which Bailey deliberately sacrificed his wicket in international cricket. When, on the fifth day, Evans was dismissed for 11, it represented Lindwall's 99th Test wicket against England. Believing the bowler's retirement to be imminent, Bailey promptly provided the 100th; 'a magnificent action', wrote Miller, 'to honour a great fast bowler'. So great, in fact, that in Melbourne, four years later, Lindwall was to take his *final* wicket against England. The victim? Bailey.

The fifth Test ended on the evening of 3 March 1955. That night the party flew to New Zealand, where play was scheduled to start 36 hours later. The jet age had arrived; as had Jean Evans and Dorothy Hutton. They saw England win the first Test at Dunedin by eight wickets and the second, at Auckland, in extraordinary circumstances. In their second innings, New Zealand were dismissed for 26, the lowest total in the history of Test cricket. It was to be Hutton's last Test (he scored 53), and immediately afterwards the two families embarked on a fishing expedition to Mayor Island. Overnight facilities were spartan and the upshot was that the four found themselves sharing a single wooden hut of military decor. As the light was extinguished they lay, in adjoining bunks, as the stripes of sailing masts fluttered through the window.

Finally Hutton spoke: 'You know, Dorothy,' he said, 'it's the first time ah've been to bed with two women.'

The tour was over.

For Hutton it was the last. Australia had exhausted him, mentally and physically. Cowdrey, himself no stranger to the vicissitudes of captaincy, believed that 'this kind of stress was more likely to occur in someone with less experience of leadership'. Hutton, after all, had come to the England captaincy at the age of 36, never having led a cricket team before. He relinquished it without having lost a series. In Australia his own form had deteriorated to an average of 24, yet even in this the journalist Alan Ross took solace in that 'for the first time since the War, England had not relied exclusively on Hutton, Compton, Bedser and Bailey'. The five key players he nominated were May, Cowdrey, Tyson, Statham and Evans, the last of whom 'held thrilling catches'. In fact he took thirteen in his four Tests, and a total of 34, excluding seven stumpings, on the tour. Evans's dismissal of Harvey at Melbourne was described by Keith Andrew as 'arguably the greatest wicketkeeping catch ever'. Tyson, the bowler, was more explicit: 'It decided the Test. . . . After that, and the heart it put into the whole side, I never doubted that we would win.'

The England party arrived home on 5 April. After having twice defeated Australia (and despite the success of the West Indies in 1950) Evans felt that 'we were now indisputably the leading cricket country in the world', and looked forward to meeting the touring South Africans. England's intention was to persevere where possible with the established side and team spirit was maintained by a celebratory dinner at The Dorchester Hotel. To emphasize the sense of continuity, Hutton was confirmed as captain on 23 May during the MCC fixture against South Africa. The next day he was stricken with lumbago and wrote to Allen, the Chairman of Selectors, that 'for some time now when playing in England I have suffered from rheumatic pains. . . . During the past three weeks I have been far worse than before.' The result was that May was invited to lead England in his place.

'Both players,' wrote Swanton, 'were serious, reserved, difficult to penetrate – and both in turn had the added burden of carrying the England batting on their shoulders.' The parallel can be extended in that May, like Hutton, suffered a physical breakdown and retired when still full of cricket. May without doubt owed more to his predecessor's influence than that of Stuart Surridge, then still captain of Surrey. 'He was,' says Graveney, 'a man who came alive the moment he strode onto a pitch, yet strangely shy and uncommunicative away from it. . . That was his weakness as a captain.' Evans confirms that May lacked the ability to mould a winning team, being 'found out' later in his career, most notably in Australia on the tour of 1958–59. On the other hand, Benaud himself places May 'at the top of the captaincy tree during my time, ahead even of the victorious Hutton'. On the latter's retirement, he must indeed have seemed the natural successor: 25 years old and a veteran of 24 Tests; three summers down from Cambridge, yet ingrained in the England team. In Allen, May had a sympathetic Chairman whose time in office exactly coincided with his own. 'There grew up between them a particularly close understanding,' wrote Swanton, and for five series England's unbeaten sequence continued. Thereafter nothing was to be quite the same again.

Evans primed himself for the first Test by scoring 40 of a Kent total of 119 against Derbyshire in late May. On 9 June he reported to Trent Bridge where Kenyon, the Worcester opener, had been selected to replace Hutton. In middle order was the 24-year-old Ken Barrington, who would represent England twice that summer and not again until 1959. 'It was during this period,' wrote Bailey, 'that he began the systematic tightening-up of his game' that was to accumulate 6,806 Test runs; at Trent Bridge Barrington began with nought.

In arctic Nottingham conditions England achieved a score of 334. The South Africans' high reputation in the field was mitigated, Evans believes, by the need to wear two, or even three, sweaters; the captain, Cheetham, resembled the Michelin Man in profile. Over the week-end South Africa were 46 for no wicket. On the Monday, Tyson (still in what he classified as his 'Australian period') and Statham reduced the opposition to 153. The Nottingham crowd, always appreciative of hostile bowling other than Australian, signified approval. In the second innings Tyson took 6–28 in 21 overs, in his own words, 'not only hitting the stumps, but sending them cartwheeling into the ever-open arms of Godfrey Evans'. Evans himself recalled that the tourists 'though beaten by sheer pace, showed no lack of courage. They got behind the ball every time.'

During the Test, his 64th, Evans took his 150th dismissal. Tyson, meanwhile, in the nine months since first playing for England, had taken 52 wickets. The tourists' response came in the form of Neil Adcock and Peter Heine, the former of whom Evans recalls as 'an enormous man who brought the ball down out of the sky'. Hutton's absence was keenly felt, and in the five Tests England reverted to three separate opening partnerships. The Nottingham Test also saw the breakdown and virtual disappearance of Appleyard, whose bowling vagaries, says Tyson, 'left Evans behind the stumps black and blue'. Little did they know that Appleyard's ramrod action had affected his shoulder muscles to the extent that he was to spend much of the next year in hospital.

By now the weather was improving and the tourists were beginning to blend into a team. At Lord's England were without Appleyard and Tyson and it was South Africa's turn to attack. In the England innings of 133 (Evans second-top-scoring with 20) Heine took 5–60; the fielding was electric. In reply South Africa scored 304, after being 7–2; both openers caught behind – the second, Goddard, playing a legitimate leg glance to which Evans dived and caught an inch off the ground. Eventually Heine was stumped off Wardle and England batted again, leaving South Africa a target of 182. They might have achieved it had Cheetham not been struck by a ball from Trueman and forced to retire. The incident engendered considerable controversy and contributed to the 'Fiery Fred' persona, although to Evans it was a clear case of the batsman 'allowing the ball to him him'. The upshot was that Cheetham withdrew, and from there Statham proceeded to reduce the opposition, Evans holding three catches. The bowler's analysis was 29–12–39–7, and, according to Swanton, included 'scarcely a ball off the mark'. The light was dull but not dangerous. At 78–6 an incident occurred that illustrates the spirit in which even Tests were then played. Graveney appeared to make a dramatic catch at slip, falling as he did so. The batsman, Keith, enquired if the ball had carried and, informed that it had, left, in Swanton's words, 'with a smile of congratulation to the bowler'. South Africa were dismissed for 111 and the match was won by 71 runs. For England Evans took six catches and a stumping; from the Long Room, two bowed old men watched approvingly. Sydney Barnes and Wilfred Rhodes, 82 and 77 respectively, admired the ancient virtues.

Changes were rung before the third Test at Old Trafford. Bedser returned for the unfit Statham, while Cowdrey was included for his first home Test. More dramatically, Lock replaced Wardle after being surreptitiously vetted by two of the England selectors. Immediately prior to the Test Kent played Surrey at Blackheath, and there Allen and Ames viewed the bowler from every angle. According to Swanton, 'they thought that at times his action looked 'a bit funny', but neither could see that his elbow was bent prior to delivery'. These being the days before photography was introduced as evidence, Lock passed the inspection; and, incidentally, took 5–43 in eighteen overs.

At Manchester England scored 284; Compton, ambulatory or not, made 158, which was to be his last century for England. Cowdrey, whose success in Australia had derived from playing forward, soon learnt that, against Heine and Adcock, defence was the best form of attack. In doing so he emerged so bruised that it was winter before he was fully fit again.

For the tourists McGlew, Waite and Winslow made centuries. Bedser was not the partner that Tyson might have chosen. One blow to the outfield found him 'circling cumbrously and failing by yards to reach it'. It was to be his last Test. During the first session on Saturday 9 July Tyson produced an in-swinger to the left-handed Goddard. In diving to prevent byes Evans twisted his hand and the ball struck the back of his little finger. 'Something's wrong,' he remarked to Graveney. The match continued.

When, at the fall of the next wicket, Evans took the opportunity to inspect his finger, he found it 'bent, swollen and jet black'. May approached him and suggested he left the field. 'No fear,' said Evans. He learnt later that the finger was broken in two places and that, continuing to play all day, the marrow had been literally squeezed from the joints. His hand was encased in plaster that night.

On 11 July Evans reported to the ground and was bowled at in the nets. Having improvised a batting glove able to accommodate his cast, he was surprised at the apparent ease with which he could play. At 274–6 Evans returned to the dressing-room. Three wickets later May turned to him and asked if he felt able to bat. 'Of course,' he replied. 'And make some runs, too.'

He made 36. His last-wicket stand with Bailey contributed 48, and, according to *Wisden*, 'Evans hit powerfully despite injury.' The runs were critical in setting South Africa an eventual target of 145. That they reached it, with three minutes and an equal number of wickets to spare, was due in part to Graveney's performance behind the stumps. With no disrespect, allowing the batsmen a bye when retrieving the ball off Tyson was hardly restrictive. Ironically Graveney, too, damaged a finger, as did Cowdrey, May and Compton. In the last over Waite drove Tyson through the covers and South Africa had won. Tyson himself injured his ankle at the close and was not selected again until the final Test against Australia the following year. It was the end of an era.

It was the end, too, of Evans's season. He withdrew from the Gentlemen v Players match the following day and watched the remaining Tests (a South African and England win respectively) from the dressing-room. In his abbreviated three-match series he achieved ten dismissals and a batting average of 16.40. His final innings at Manchester accounted for nearly half his total runs.

During the season Kent fell two places in the table to thirteenth. They were hindered more than most by injuries and absences, and, according to *Wisden*, 'Any team deprived for most of the season of its best batsman, its only bowler of genuine pace and a wicketkeeper of supreme quality may be excused some shortcomings.' The bowler was Fred Ridgway; the batsman Cowdrey, who finished second in the first-class averages with 49.42. Evans himself appeared in only eight matches; of the remainder, Ufton played thirteen and Catt seven. Surrey, for the fourth time, were Champions.

In the winter of 1955–56 an MCC 'B' team under Donald Carr toured Pakistan. The wicketkeeper was Swetman. At home in Aylesford, Evans exercised his injured finger and played squash and hockey. He also purchased a motor cruiser named *Angela* at the Shipwright's Arms at Faversham Creek, a desolate place concealed by a dyke at the far end of a deserted marshland. Evans moored the boat there, its bows angled out towards the Medway and the Isle of Sheppey. On weekends he, Jean and Howard motored to Herne Bay pier (scene of his earlier incarnation as 'Geoff' Evans) and picnicked before returning at dusk. It was an agreeable diversion from the most pressing thought then on his mind: the arrival of the Australians that spring. Despite having won the two previous encounters, Evans asserts that England were 'anything but confident' about the coming series. In addition to Miller, Lindwall and Harvey, the opposition included a player of recognizable genius, Benaud, and a wicketkeeper, Langley, who retains the highest average number of victims per Test. In the West Indies, Australia had recently defeated the opposition by three Tests to nil. 'We knew that all of us, especially the bowlers, would have to perform,' says Evans. Little did he know.

England began their defence of the Ashes at Trent Bridge on 7 June 1956. It was raining. Two declarations by May failed to bring a result; for England Cowdrey and Richardson shared opening stands of 53 and 171, and to some extent

Kent C.C.C. under Wright.

compensated for the void left by Hutton. Richardson became the first batsman to score 50 in each innings of his Test debut against Australia without making 100 in either. A foretaste of the series was provided by Laker's 4–58 in the Australian first innings; previously he had taken 10–88 against the tourists for Surrey. 'Uncanny length and flight,' recalls Evans, 'with spin you could *hear* as it left his hand. On the right wicket, Jim was unplayable.' Such a wicket failed to materialize at Nottingham, where play was restricted to seventeen hours. At the close Evans felt moved to offer Miller odds of 2–1 against an Australian victory in the following Test at Lord's. 'Agreed,' said Miller, whereupon he took 5–72 and 5–80, capturing ten wickets in a Test for the only time in his career, and abetting an Australian victory by 185 runs. The other factor was a score of 97 by Benaud in the Australian second innings. The two all-rounders were mutual admirers, and Benaud had arrived in England in April with the intention of 'following Miller into the media world'.

The wish was in time granted, although at Lord's Benaud's innings was tempered by a roaring appeal by Evans off his first ball. It was refused. Afterwards both Benaud and Miller confirmed that the ball had touched the batsman's glove on its way to the wicketkeeper; the umpire, Emrys Davies, admitted that he saw only a deflection off Benaud's shirt. 'It was the right decision under the circumstances,' says Evans. 'What an umpire can't see, he can't give.' Given were nine dismissals to Evans's counterpart Langley, who thus established a world Test record. Evans's own wicketkeeping was, he feels, 'back on song', and he himself took seven dismissals. In the Australian first innings of 285 there were no byes. 'A good match for the stumpers,' he recalls; and, undoubtedly, for Miller, who prospered by £50 as a result of his wager. The final Australian plaudits belonged to Mackay, who contributed a painstaking 32 to counterbalance the more mercurial Benaud. The previous week at Canterbury, Mackay had made 113 in the drawn match against Kent. 'An Australian Bailey,' says Evans. 'Every side should have one.'

In the fortnight before the third Test it was agreed that, for England, one down in the series, radical measures were required. The appropriate minute of the Selection Committee reads:

> When it was agreed to omit Graveney and Watson and to include five batsmen instead of six, it was decided that one of the three in middle-order must be a player with Test match experience. When it was appreciated that the choice lay between Washbrook and Simpson, Washbrook [a member of the Committee] was asked to leave the room.

The upshot was that at the age of 41, having last played for England on the tour of 1950–51, Washbrook was recalled. The batsman's comment, 'One will do one's best, but it won't be easy,' typified the moment; other reactions ranged from May's lukewarm acceptance to Evans's delight at the return of a player whom he describes as possessed of the 'usual attributes you expect of a Lancastrian'.

The third Test began on 12 July 1956. Within an hour Washbrook was walking to the wicket with the score at 17–3. By close of play he and May had put on 187 for the fourth wicket. 'Thank God I listened to you,' May told the Chairman. The captain scored 101; Washbrook 98; and Evans 40, 'through the courtesy of Ian Johnson, who foolishly kept the spinners on while I enjoyed myself'. Johnson himself believed that 'the 1948 team would have won the Lord's Test, as we did, saved Nottingham, Manchester and The Oval, but may have been beaten at Leeds'. The key qualification was whether Bradman, Hassett, Morris, *et al* would have allowed Laker to bowl as well as he now did. The off-spinner finished the match with figures of 11–113 off 70 overs, and in the two Australian innings only Harvey (69), Burke (41) and Miller (41) batted with confidence. In mitigation, Swanton asserts that the pitch 'certainly had not the lasting properties that all concerned had a right to expect'. The former Australian spinner Arthur Mailey agreed that 'the state of the wicket did, of course, favour Laker', while conceding that 'no bowler in the world could have made better use of the advantage'. Rain had appeared, as if on cue, at the conclusion of the England innings, allowing Lock and Laker to perform in optimum conditions. And perform, in Johnson's words, they did, 'their contrasting methods dovetailing perfectly'. With unconscious irony, *Wisden* labelled the match, won by England by an innings and 42, as the turning-point of the series.

Benaud confirms that the Australian momentum now halted. 'The team was unable to play good off-spin bowling on turning pitches. . . . for much of the series batsmen needed time as much as runs, and it was Laker, landing on or just outside the off stump, that caused by far the most trouble.' Laker, in short, made the batsmen *play*; Lock, in contrast, although endeavouring to do the same, frequently spun past the edge either to Evans or direct to first slip. With the pitches that summer remaining uniformly slow, Evans remembers that even the ball finding the edge off Lock would frequently fall harmlessly short of slip. Standing up to the left-armer was as arduous in its way as to Bedser. Lock, Evans recalls, had the endearing habit of pushing the ball through with velocity proportionate to his partner's success at the other end; the better Laker's analysis, the faster Lock's action. It was a formula that kept the wicketkeeper, quite literally, on his toes.

Between the third and fourth Tests Evans appeared in the 150th Gentlemen v Players match at Lord's. It was drawn. As he prepared for the climactic Manchester Test, he seems to have shared the general belief that the initiative had been wrested by England. There comes a point in every series when, for a variety of reasons – luck, ability umpiring, injuries – one side appears to yield to the momentum established by the other. Evans believes that the Australians now did so. With Lindwall and Miller appearing in harness for the last time, much of the solidity of the team was expected to have been supplied by the batsmen. It was not. In the event, Burke topped the averages with 30.11; Benaud was second on 25. Critically, Harvey had a bad year. Despite a double century against MCC at Lord's, he lapsed into relative obscurity in the Tests, emerging with an average of 19.70. 'Gradually,' according to his captain, 'failure ate away the confidence around which Harvey's style [was] built.' The same evaluation might be applied to the team as a whole. 'By Manchester there was a sense that the tide had turned,' says Evans. 'Though none of us knew how far.'

It was his 70th Test. The wicket at Manchester on 26 July looked brown and dry; England proceeded to make 459 in 491 minutes. Evans, sent in at 339–6, was dispatched with the almost superfluous instruction to 'have a go'. He struck 47 in 28 minutes and, according to *Wisden*, 'hit lustily, revelling in the situation'. Evans's enjoyment was tempered only by his surprise that, yet again, Johnson persevered with his spinners at a critical moment. Three runs would have equalled the fastest Test half-century then recorded, and Evans was duly stumped reaching for the sky. After that, he recalls, he began to wonder if Johnson were much of a captain; some had expected Miller, or even Benaud, to assume the leadership. Earlier in the innings Richardson and Sheppard – recalled after adopting Holy Orders – had made centuries.

On the second day Laker dismissed Australia for 84. It was a spinner's wicket, dry and crumbling, yet earlier in the day England had scored 152 in two hours against Johnson and Benaud. Nonetheless, speculation arose about the undoubted suitability of conditions for Lock and Laker. According to *Wisden*, 'mutterings about the pitch could be heard'; Miller himself made a reference to wearing dark glasses 'to keep the sand out of my eyes'. On the other hand, Laker swore that on the first morning Bradman, travelling with Australia as a team official, had asserted 'this is just the sort of wicket we've been waiting for'. Incredibly, conditions at that stage were thought to predominantly favour Lock, who, in Evans's words, 'bowled throughout a fraction too short . . . and although turning enough to beat the bat, did so on the outside, the ball passing harmlessly outside off stump'. He finished the innings with 1–37; Laker took the remaining nine for the same number of runs.

Australia followed on and were 53–1 that evening. The following day clouds scudded across Manchester and seams of flinty sunlight illuminated the sizzling sky. Then and on the following Monday there was a mere hour's play; during it Laker took the wicket of Harvey for nought. The next day was, in his own account, 'among the most memorable' of Evans's career. If Laker's first-innings performance was, in the *Telegraph*'s phrase, 'clouded by the deficiencies of the Australian batting' (considered by Mailey to have been the equal of any village team in England), then there was no refuting his performance in the second. On a damp, disjointed pitch, McDonald and Craig withstood the session until lunch. At that stage, Swanton noted 'Evans and Lock, those tireless propagandists when the latter was bowling, trying their hardest by expression and gesture to suggest that the dormant pitch was stirring'. The truth was different. Evans was inwardly amazed at May's decision to employ Laker from the Stretford End, and considered that 'so long as McDonald remained . . . the odds were evenly balanced'. After lunch Craig was twice beaten by lifting balls from Lock, and then, after an innings of four hours twenty minutes, fell lbw to Laker. It was the turning point. Resentful at seeing his rival capture a wicket he might reasonably have considered his own, Lock visibly accelerated his action. At the other end Laker proceeded to take the remaining seven wickets. Granted the ball was turning perceptibly in answer to shafts of drying sun; it

Catching McDonald off the outside edge – Trueman gives full vent to his emotions. Headingley, 1956.

still spoke volumes for Laker that he kept his head while about him the Australians, and Lock, were losing theirs. The latter seems to have been driven by his compulsion to compete not only with the opposition, but Laker. 'Slow down,' said Evans. 'Let the wicket do the work.' 'I can't,' came the reply. At 130–6 Benaud came to the wicket, and, in Swanton's words, 'took guard sometimes once or twice an over, as though suspicious that Evans might have surreptitiously moved the position of the stumps'. Still McDonald endured; May belatedly exchanged his spinners and introduced Bailey and Oakman. In the event it was Laker who trapped McDonald and followed by bowling Benaud. At this point Johnson demonstrated the tactical acumen not always apparent in his captaincy by appealing against the sawdust. The umpires, straightfaced, refused. Minutes later Maddocks was lbw; the match was won by an innings and 170 runs. Bailey left the field 'repeating to myself that it was all a dream'; Evans applauding 'the finest piece of bowling that I, or any of us, had seen'. Laker took his sweater and turned.

For the fifth Test Compton returned. He top scored with 94 in England's first innings before becoming one of Archer's five victims – six, including Langley, who retired after being struck attempting to take a rising ball. Harvey deputised behind the stumps. Heavy rain curtailed play and on the rest day Evans invited Miller to Faversham Creek to inspect the *Angela*. There were no hard feelings about the match at Manchester; although Miller, like others, expressed curiosity as to how Laker would perform on a good wicket in Australia. On a damp wicket in Kennington Laker took 4–80, and on the last day May declared the England innings at 182–3. Sheppard made 62 re-appearing in the Test side with Evans, who, in his own words, 'behaved impeccably'. A draw looked a formality until Australia collapsed to 27–5 at the close, engendering criticism that May had mistimed his declaration. A target of 228 in two hours was not, Evans concedes, 'the most generous ever made, but under the circumstances Peter had nothing to gain'. The Ashes were retained, and Evans and Sheppard were seen in animated discussion at the celebration.

In the series Evans took nine dismissals – of which, incredibly, seven were at Lord's – and scored 115 runs at 19.16. More notably, Laker took 46 wickets, second only to Barnes's 49 as the highest recorded in a rubber. At least part of this was attributable to the opposition, and it is hard to refute *Wisden*'s assertion that 'the gradual decline in Australia's cricketing strength since the retirement of Bradman . . . was not halted by the team led by Johnson.' Notwithstanding which, Laker was magnificent. He was an artist. Like many such, he demanded perfection in the field and greeted the occasional dropped catch or missed stumping by gently tapping his foot and glancing Heavenward as if imploring justice. In 1956 he had little cause to do so.

Hitting out against Middlesex, 1956. Murray is wicketkeeper, Compton at slip. (Sport & General).

The distinction of England's performance was matched by the inadequacy of Kent's. They fell to sixteenth in a Championship again won by Surrey. For his County Evans scored 685 runs at an average of 24, and, according to *Wisden*, 'at times showed glimpses of his most punishing form.' One such was a fixture against Glamorgan in early May when Evans scored 50 of a Kent total of 308–8, again applying his philosophy of maximum velocity. On the whole, however, it was difficult to deny *Wisden*'s review of the year ('another bad season'), and it was to prove Wright's last as captain. In the close-season the Committee turned to Cowdrey, 24 and established as an England regular, who in time presided over a gradual recovery in fortunes. The appointment was made when Cowdrey was on tour with MCC in South Africa, and his first action was to ask Evans 'how men of his calibre would react'. The reply was unequivocal: 'We're all behind you, master.' If Evans himself harboured ambitions of captaincy, he artfully concealed them from Cowdrey, to whom he gave 'nothing less than the promised hundred per cent.' At the same time, it is safe to conclude that the Kent Committee 'played safe' by reverting (as had England) to a man of amateur background, denying one whom Wright himself thought 'might have made an outstanding captain.' In recognition of his service to the County, the Committee subsequently raised Evans's basic annual salary to £600; that and the income from his second book, *Action In Cricket*, at least keeping him in the style to which he had become accustomed.

The 1956 season ended on a sunless afternoon in Scarborough, when, 'in conditions scarcely fit for cricket' (*Wisden*), Evans hit 26 runs in an over off his favourite captain, Ian Johnson. Had Miller, leaning back over the boundary fence, not caught his attempt at six off the last ball, it would have been 32 and a world record. The Australians applauded him all the way back.

Chapter Six

Swansong

SIX WEEKS LATER the MCC party left Southampton on the SS *Edinburgh Castle*, bound for South Africa. The series was, to Swanton, tempered not only 'by each side's aiming to grind the other down', but by 'the helpless feeling of being in a lovely country divided and rent in spirit by the various racial frictions'. Allowing that social conditions had materially altered since his previous visit, Evans maintains that excellent cricket was played by both sides with he himself enjoying his most prolific series. His performance in at least one Test was, under the conditions, miraculous.

A strong side, captained by May, was managed by Freddie Brown, who duly styled himself 'Boss'. Compton, despite his medical history, was included; Graveney and Tyson not. Evans's deputy was the 24-year-old Essex player Brian Taylor, whose selection he considered, 'with respect, a mistake'. *Wisden* agreed, allowing that Taylor 'tried hard, but came nowhere near challenging Evans, who maintained his astonishingly high standard behind the stumps.' Taylor's inclusion, which owed much to the influence of Bailey and Insole, proved the truth of Evans's contention that 'great wicketkeepers are great to *all* bowlers, not just those they're familiar with'. His own Test career was a case in point: from 1951 onwards, he kept exclusively to bowlers from counties other than his own. Few ever had cause to complain.

Evans's style suited South Africa. Against Rhodesia in late November he scored 50 in 45 minutes of an MCC total of 501 (May made 206). In the first Test at the new Wanderers' Stadium in Johannesburg, Evans baptised the ground by hitting the first six. It provided relief from a match in which the scoring rate averaged 28 runs per hour, and which England won by 131 runs. In the first innings Richardson scored 117 in a numbing eight hours, atoning, Evans believes, 'for his more swashbuckling approach the previous summer'. Bailey, not to be outdone, produced an

Centre stage – on the Edinburgh Castle *to South Africa.*

epic performance in the South African reply – 5 for 20 in fifteen overs. As in Jamaica in 1954, he again excelled in unfavourable conditions, although the rarefied atmosphere (6,000 feet above sea level) may have helped; the wicket-keeper took two catches off deliveries that 'seamed a mile'. Throughout Evans noted 'a certain difficulty' about the South African captaincy, which he assumed arose from personal animosity towards McGlew. Never one to curry favour, the captain promptly ordered his team into the field for net practice over the New Year's holiday; by the time they appeared for the second Test at Cape Town there was a mutinous atmosphere which England could hardly fail to exploit.

Their own New Year was spent at the Kelvin Grove Club, where Brown tried 'as much in hope as expectation' to curb the antics of Evans, Bailey and Compton. Having terminated proceedings at four o'clock that morning, Evans was appreciative of May's decision to bat when the captains tossed seven hours later. Of the England total of 369, Evans made 62 in 50 minutes, according to *Wisden*, 'being one of the few batsmen who attempted attacking strokes'. In the South African reply of 205 there was a single bye.

On the final day the home team was bowled out for 72 by Bailey and Wardle and lost by 312. The 84 journalists variously reporting the tour could find little to criticize except perceived technical flaws in individual players; Insole, the vice-captain, could be seen every morning poring over the comments of one critic who implored him to tighten up his technique. The result was that Insole became nervous, and his nervousness in turn affected the team. The situation was such that May and Brown held a meeting to discuss the matter. As a result several players (Evans not among them) refused to talk to the critic in question, despite whose attentions Insole recovered to score a century in the drawn third Test.

Two coincidences illuminated the match at Cape Town. It saw the first dismissal at that level for 'handling the ball', when Russell Endean deflected it with his hand after padding off a delivery from Laker. Endean had been the man waiting to make the catch when Hutton was given out 'obstructing the field' at The Oval in 1951. Secondly, the South African second innings reached the same abject total as at Johannesburg: 72. On this occasion Wardle took 7–36. Bailey broke a bone in his right hand but remained on the field, appearing in all three subsequent Tests.

At this stage, with the temporary exception of Insole, the party registered two pressing concerns. The first involved May. Despite the enviable position of leading two-nil after two Tests, Evans detected 'reticence' on the captain's part to fully establish English supremacy; his tactics, though sound, lacked flair or imagination and tended towards the dilatory in the field. As a batsman, despite his double century against Rhodesia, May proved alarmingly fallible in the Tests and eventually ended the series with an average of 15.30.

England's other consideration was the bowling of Hugh Tayfield. The off-spinner was to collect May's wicket on no fewer than four occasions, and finished the rubber with 37 victims at 17.18. He subsequently appeared in the Lancashire League to little effect. Compton, on his last overseas tour, empathized with May's relative decline, recalling his own in the 1950–51 series in Australia. His suspicion that 'the round of official functions and parties was not Peter's scene', is echoed by Evans, who adds that, 'if Peter had a weakness, it was against top-class off-spin. Tayfield on that tour mesmerized him.'

The third Test at Durban began on 25 January. Its features were a score of 110 by Insole in the England second innings; that and the inability of South Africa to reach a final total of 190 to win. An incident occurred when Wardle was bowling to Ken Funston that not one of the assembled press reported, or apparently observed; after dropping a simple return catch, Wardle, instead of the normal histrionics, 'turned round, picked up the ball, juggled with it for a moment and quickly sent down another delivery'. It was as good a piece of deception as Evans had seen. Wardle got away with it that day – as, in the past, had Evans.

The tide turned in the fourth Test at Johannesburg. Despite the relative ease of the tour thus far, Evans remained concerned that England had failed to dominate, reiterating that 'most series are won by breaking the opposition's will'. This England had conspicuously failed to do. Now South Africa counter-attacked with a first innings total of 340. McLean made 93, after, in Evans's words, 'being almost certainly' lbw to Statham before scoring. There were no byes. The England reply was 251; Insole was run out for 47 after edging the ball to slip; May made 61; Evans 7. On a ruined pitch South Africa scored 142; the eventual winning target was 230. That England failed to reach it was due to 'fantastic fielding' encouraged by a fiercely partisan crowd. On the critical fifth day, Evans remembers 'an incredible atmosphere. . .the crowd leaning forward in their seats to applaud the home team, who bowled and fielded like tigers'. The England score rose by increments; May departed for nought, Evans for eight. Finally South Africa prevailed by seventeen runs.

The fifth and climactic Test was played on the worst wicket in the country. The square at Port Elizabeth had recently been relaid, and, according to Evans, 'in the course of the match deteriorated from bad to atrocious'. Under the circumstances, McGlew must have hesitated all of a second before electing to bat: South Africa scored 164, of which, incredibly, there were no byes. Incredibly because, according to Bailey, 'the pitch made the "beach" at Old Trafford where the Australians were "Lakered" appear reasonable by comparison. At least two balls per over shot straight along the ground, and from the point of view of the wicketkeeper it would be difficult to imagine worse conditions.' England replied with 110. On a wicket now comfortably the worst he had witnessed in ten years as a Test cricketer, Evans allowed a single bye in the South African second innings; 'not merely good, but superb,' says Bailey. He then 'hit powerfully' (*Wisden*) for 21 in the losing England reply before being caught off the one ball that lifted in an over of ankle-high shooters. *Wisden* offered the following summary:

> At the close the crowd swarmed on to examine the unusual pitch and several people took away pieces of the ground as souvenirs. Special praise was earned by Evans for his magnificent wicketkeeping under extremely difficult conditions. He allowed only one bye, an extraordinary performance by an extraordinary man.

Thus England contrived to draw what, up until the fourth Test, had appeared a winning series. Again the momentum of the side had been arrested at a critical moment, and at Johannesburg and Port Elizabeth Evans felt a certain defeatism had been allowed to develop. Typically, he failed to share it. In the course of the tour he took 40 dismissals, of which exactly half were in the Tests. More remarkably, in the course of ten completed South African innings, Evans conceded a total of fourteen byes – an astonishing achievement in view of conditions on at least two occasions. At 36, and whatever the vagaries of his performances for Kent, he remained comfortably the supreme Test wicketkeeper in the world.

Kent was a subject much on Evans's mind when approached by Cowdrey at the time of the latter's appointment to the County captaincy. Guessing correctly that much of the team took their lead from Godfrey, Cowdrey sought out his wicketkeeper's endorsement and was duly encouraged by the response. His own view confirms the belief that Evans at times struggled to motivate himself at County level, despite which his very presence 'galvanized the fielding' beyond recognition. Cowdrey himself had been electrified by Evans's performances in Wartime cricket and remembers especially the attribute, noted by Arlott, of his gathering throws from the field one-handed. Cowdrey's theory was that this was in conscious effort to develop comparable muscles in both arms, 'much in the manner of a footballer learning to kick with either boot'. The truth was more dramatic. Evans had learnt early on the artifice of catching the ball in one hand while signalling frantically for its return with the other. The running batsman was thus liable to be hoodwinked into believing the ball to be still in flight while it in fact nestled in Evans's glove. More than one learnt otherwise to his cost. Despite which, Cowdrey asserts, 'Evans was never a show-off. . .everything he did was for effect, not affected. If he dived for a ball, it was because he genuinely thought he could catch it.' And frequently did.

Evans himself supported the appointment not least because he felt Wright to have accepted the captaincy under duress. The circumstances surrounding Murray Wood's dismissal in 1953 had left an impression that only a man of Cowdrey's equanimity could correct. And equable he was, despite a tendency to inexplicably lose confidence. Evans found it extraordinary that at times Cowdrey would appear to undermine his own authority, a condition that periodically communicated itself to the team. As Bailey noted of the same player: 'A team should have faith in itself, even when it is not entirely justified. This is hard to achieve when the skipper has certain reservations which, because he is an open, honest individual, he cannot conceal.' In 1957 Cowdrey, by his own admission, found it daunting to retain authority in the presence of established players like Evans, Wright and Fagg. It was a feeling he never entirely lost.

The reverse applied to Evans himself. In South Africa he exhibited the usual ebullience, not least in his eternal conviction that 'we'll be through them tonight', even when the match situation scarcely warranted it. It was, for him, a supremely successful tour. It ended on a note of unexpected nostalgia, when, after dinner at a private party in Cape Town, he was invited upstairs by his hosts to say goodnight to their young children. On the bedside table was an air letter, the return address of which immediately caught Evans's eye. It was from friends who ran 'a flourishing antique business. . .in an old house in Kent called Lords.'

'I know the place,' said Evans.

The party returned with a profit of £26,500; Evans with a reputation triumphantly sustained. In 1957 England faced the first home series against the West Indies since the fateful debut of Ramadhin and Valentine. Both were included in a team again captained by Goddard, which, according to Sobers, entered the first Test 'with the feeling that we might well repeat the success of 1950'.

They did not. The critical difference was the performance of May, who on the eve of the Birmingham Test – the first on the ground in 28 years – issued the directive: 'Don't get out to Ramadhin'. The spinner promptly took 7–49 in 31 overs, dismissing England for 186. At this point, and when West Indies replied with 474, it appeared that yet again an England captain had woefully misjudged the opposition. When Cowdrey joined May at noon on the fourth day, the score stood at 113–3. When they parted on the final afternoon it read 524–4. Critically, Ramadhin was allowed to bowl a record 98 overs in the innings, in the latter stages of which, according to Swanton, 'he went through the motions of bowling, floating about like a sleepwalker'. In the event, May scored 285, Cowdrey 154; when the latter was out, Evans was promoted with the by now traditional directive to 'have a go'. He did so by nearly running out May off his first ball. At the end of the over the captain modified his statement to include 'within reason'. Thereafter, in Swanton's words, Evans 'cut and carved and ran for everything', achieving a rapid 29 before the declaration. Ramadhin left the field a broken man.

May's (and, to a lesser extent, Cowdrey's) tactic had been to use the pad as an adjunct to the bat. Sobers called it 'one of the most depressing sights' ever witnessed in a Test; to Swanton, 'as a captain's effort, it stood alone'. Evans's own view was that the policy 'may have drawn the game, but it won the series'. Thereafter the West Indies were terminally demoralized, and in their second innings (72–7,

One that got away, Lord's 1957. (Sport & General).

defeat looming) batted as if in a trance. To Swanton it was a 'fabulous' Test, unprecedented as one 'wherein the fortunes changed with such utter completeness from one side to the other'. As at The Oval in 1956, May delayed his declaration to the point where the opposition's subsequent collapse could not fully be exploited. To Evans, the captain's strategy was itself counter-productive: 'My experience was that you sometimes didn't get a batsman out if you pressurized him, whereas if you gave him enough rope he'd likely hang himself. Peter gave no rope.'

England nonetheless entered the second Test at a moral advantage. At Lord's the West Indies were dismissed for 127, thanks largely to figures of 7–44 by Bailey, comparable to his feat against the same opposition at Sabina Park three years earlier. England's reply was 424, of which Evans made 82. His seventh wicket stand with Cowdrey was worth 174 and owed much to the West Indies' frailty in the field. In *Wisden*'s words, 'Evans made the most of his luck'; in Sobers's, 'we must have missed him at least eight times. I did so myself.' The aggrieved bowler was Roy Gilchrist, who, according to Evans, began to vent his frustration on Cowdrey. So much so that questions were raised about the legality of Gilchrist's action, which, in the batsman's view, 'remained something of a mystery'. To Evans, the bowler was 'fast, not over-intelligent, hostile – and dangerous'. The scampered single or edged four left him 'pawing the ground' in frustration.

More temperate was Bailey, who took a further four wickets in the West Indies' second innings. It was his 50th Test. England thus won in four days a match attended by 99,000 spectators who paid £43,976. 'From then on, the series was over,' says Sobers.

To celebrate, Evans returned to Kent and scored 61 of a total of 198 against Yorkshire at Tunbridge Wells; his 50 came in 28 minutes. That spring the County had taken the initiative of appointing Ames as Cricket Manager. Retired to hotel management in Hastings, the wicketkeeper-batsman was persuaded to return to a position then unknown in County cricket. It was a resounding success. Among the measures undertaken by Ames was the development of the Association of Kent Cricket Clubs, established by

Valentine in 1950, with the purpose of identifying young players of promise throughout the county. Both manager and captain agreed that it would be a decade or more before success could be expected in the Championship, but in the meantime players like Evans detected a new sense of purpose in the dressing-room. Its first tangible result would ensue the following season, although, in the event, the Championship proved elusive for longer than the predicted decade.

The third Test began at Trent Bridge on 4 July 1957. Its chief feature was the selection of Dick Richardson, of Worcester, to appear alongside his brother – the first such instance since the Hearnes in 1891. In the England innings of 619–6, Graveney scored 258, described by *Wisden* as both 'brilliant' and 'determined'. To Evans it was 'as elegant a piece of batting as you could see. . .Graveney had a high backlift which on occasion proved his undoing against fast bowling, but which provided the full, flowing drive that was his trademark.' To Sobers the innings was evidence that 'here was the best front-foot player I ever saw'. The West Indies replied with 372, of which Worrell scored 191 not out. There were no byes. 'Another magnificent performance behind the stumps,' says Graveney, 'which magnified the West Indies' deficiencies in the same area.' In 1957 Kanhai and Alexander alternated as wicketkeeper, highlighting Sobers's lament that 'in this particular area, we missed more than we caught'. With Ramadhin and Valentine becalmed and pace provided exclusively by Gilchrist (Sobers himself restricted to left-arm spin), the West Indies' sole advantage lay in batting. In the second innings they scored 367. England had time to reach 64–1 before the close, the near-defeat exacerbating, in Sobers's words, 'the growing factions and loss of form throughout the team'.

The fourth Test at Headingley will always be associated with the exploits of Peter Loader. He it was who, in Swanton's view, 'achieved one of the more remarkable feats of bowling when he dismissed a strong West Indian batting side for 142'. In grey light and leaden atmosphere, Loader took 6–36, including a hat-trick comprising Goddard, Ramadhin and Gilchrist. After a moderate tour of South

Running out Sobers at Headingley, 1957. Trueman looks on. (Hulton-Deutsch).

Africa in which he took nine wickets in four Tests, the Surrey bowler yorked Goddard, bringing to the wicket Ramadhin, 'whose batting capacity,' opined Arlott, 'may be searched'. It was; Trueman taking the catch at square leg. A minute later Loader produced the perfect delivery to bowl Gilchrist and record the first Test hat-trick since Goddard's for England against South Africa on Boxing Day 1938.

It was Evans's 80th Test. In catching Collie Smith in the West Indies' second innings he recorded his 200th dismissal (70 ahead of Oldfield's career total), adding to his achievement of conceding no byes throughout the match. Significantly, it was at this point that he admits to 'occasionally wondering' if he would achieve a century of international appearances. The odds seemed to favour it. A month short of his 37th birthday, he was sighting the ball as well as ever, and, alongside May and Cowdrey, represented an automatic England selection. His enthusiasm for the game, at least at the highest level, remained undiminished, and he himself saw no immediate prospect of retirement. Graveney, who achieved an average in the series of 118, felt that Evans was 'absolutely at his peak, whether chivvying the bowlers or advising the captain. . .the first man you looked to for motivation'.

The West Indies had no such character. They arrived at The Oval in late August drawn and depressed. England scored 412 on a pitch described by Weekes as a 'beach'. Graveney made 164; the combined totals mustered in both West Indies innings was 175. Ramadhin, Smith and Sobers between them bowled 127 overs at a rate in excess of twenty an hour. According to Sobers, the team knew what to expect when his second delivery to Sheppard 'turned a foot, took the edge and flew between wicketkeeper and slip. If I could turn it that much, what would Laker and Lock do?'

The answer, in the latter's case, was to return figures of 11–48, while Laker 'gave an exhibition' at the other end. England won by an innings, extending their crushing superiority. In Evans's view the mood of the series had been established as early as Edgbaston, resulting in an 'increasingly morbid' West Indian approach to the subsequent Tests. His own series produced the notable average of 50.25 (higher than that of Sheppard, Bailey and Close) and a total of fifteen dismissals. Bets began to accumulate on his reaching a hundred appearances.

For the West Indies Sobers established a reputation to be fulfilled by his record Test score the following year. To Evans he was established already as a batsman of 'power and charm', attributes which also characterized Sobers personally. His 66 in the Test at Lord's, on a pitch of uneven bounce and temperament, was 'clearly the work of genius'. In time Sobers was to incorporate wrist spin and fast-medium bowling to his other attributes; in 1957 he remained 'the star of an otherwise indifferent team. . .shy, reserved and uncertain of himself, though with a sense of humour' who shared with Evans an appreciation of the turf.

Similarly inclined was Compton, for whom the close-season brought retirement. He remains 'the supreme sportsman' of Evans's era: the most brilliant cricketer; a Cup Final winner; twice elected Sportsman of the Year. When first encountered in Wartime cricket, Compton (already 'impressed greatly' by his Aldershot colleague) was a slow left-arm bowler who subsequently developed a Chinaman in the fashion of the Australians Fleetwood-Smith, Tribe and Walsh. His batting was inimitable. According to Evans, 'at the wicket you never quite knew what he was going to do. He never knew himself.' Compton also possessed a 'bloody-minded' streak, typified by his altercation with Bradman at Adelaide in 1947; 'his smile,' says Evans, 'belied his determination.' Of the decade in which they shared the reputation as the 'golden boys' of English cricket, Evans nominates 1947 as the apogee of a relationship that continues today. It began with the epic at Adelaide and ended in the drawn Test at The Oval in which Compton scored 113 and Evans himself made 84 in two innings. At Adelaide, while watching Compton score 147, Miller was heard to observe that 'this bugger isn't the worst player in the world.' It was, all agreed, the understatement of the century.

Wright, too, retired at season's end. To the last he remained capable of sporadic genius, tempered by almost perverse inconsistency; characteristics also apparent in his captaincy. Under Cowdrey the County rose to fourteenth in the Championship. Evans scored 624 runs at an average of 24, without, as he puts it, 'imposing myself with the bat'. In his absence Ufton and Catt were considered by *Wisden* to have proved adequate deputies.

Evans's own wicketkeeping was confined only by the occasional listlessness he now admits to suffering. His assertion that 'no player can keep at his maximum indefinitely' found expression in certain fixtures in which he was patently not firing on all cylinders. The converse was that, at Test level, he was at the peak of his career. At 37 Evans seems to have resolved to keep his most

Kent C.C.C. under Cowdrey.

notable performances for international cricket, although, as Cowdrey said, his very presence remained an inspiration. In 1957 there is evidence that, for the first time, Evans himself realized it.

The winter provided an opportunity to consolidate business dealings with Yates. Evans attended trade fairs both at home and in Europe and continued to devote the same enthusiasm to the commercial aspects of life as to the sporting; Brian Johnston recalls him 'bringing a small case of jewellery in which he was financially interested' into the England dressing-room. No sale was recorded. At home in Aylesford Evans cultivated his garden, exercised and played squash; in April he presented himself at Canterbury, convinced that the next year would be critical. It would culminate in his eighth overseas tour; for Evans, and many others besides, it was to be the last.

When in 1949 New Zealand had last appeared in England, there had been insufficient time to complete a single Test. Now, nine years later, the reverse applied; four of the five matches were finished within three days. The pattern was established at Edgbaston, where the home side won by 205 runs. New Zealand were dismissed for 94 and 137, at least one batsman suffering the wrath of the now finally established Trueman. 'England,' in *Wisden*'s words, 'were never extended'; nor, for that matter, was Evans, who found the match lacking in prestige or passion. Interest was sustained by the inclusion of a 24-year-old batsman, two years down from Oxford, where he had scored three successive centuries and played fly-half for the University XV. M.J.K. Smith, strong, affable, determined, had, says Evans, a tendency to hit across the line; to all but the fastest bowling his technique was sufficient to compensate. Smith went on to captain England 25 times and was recognized, like Brearley after him, for his inspired leadership. Now, the junior member of the England side, he was in turn inspired by Evans, who remained, in his 38th year, 'unafraid of anything'. Himself an outstanding close catcher, Smith recognized the virtue of making the batsman aware of the field. His assessment of Evans in this respect is illuminating: 'He never let a batsman relax, either by word or deed. The dialogue wasn't malicious. It just let you know he was there.' Evans himself had the ability to unwind completely between deliveries while remaining attentive at the critical moment. 'I *did* like to talk,' he admits. 'It relaxed me.'

At Lord's, New Zealand totalled 47 and 74 against the combined talents of Laker and Lock. England won by an innings on the third morning, when, with 25,000 spectators present, both sides indulged in an exhibition match to finish the day. Evans bowled – 'and very respectably too' – while Richardson kept wicket. A fortnight later the farce resumed at Headingley, where Arthur Milton made his Test debut. Not only was he on the field throughout the match, but in opening the innings with Smith, he ensured that the England order was led by, respectively, a soccer and a rugby international. After heavy rain, New

Zealand were dismissed for 67 and 129, the damage again inflicted by Laker and Lock. England won by an innings. 'It was getting monotonous,' says Evans. 'There was a feeling that the selectors should experiment.'

They did. At Manchester Smith was dropped. His replacement was a 23-year-old recently down from Cambridge. Throughout the first three days of his first Test, Ted Dexter sat, in his own words, 'peering through the teeming rain'. On the fourth, 27 July, the names of the MCC party to Australia were announced, his not among them. Not untypical was the reaction of the *Daily Telegraph* correspondent who wrote: 'The omission of Dexter from the team is the biggest clanger I have known selectors anywhere to commit.' Similarly inclined was Evans, who heard the news at Mere Country Club in the presence of, among others, Dexter. 'We'll get you there if it kills us,' he announced, before adding his own views on the vagaries of selection. Allen himself expressed regret that no place had been found for the player, who promptly scored 52 the following morning on a sodden pitch.

Included on the tour was a young opening batsman also making his debut at Old Trafford. Raman Subba Row, who finished the season with 1,810 first-class runs, duly celebrated by borrowing Evans's prize 1936 Bentley to reconnoitre the nightlife of Manchester. Both batsman and Bentley returned substantially impaired, adorned, in the latter's case, by a crumpled front wing. Evans's reaction ('That's life') was, says Subba Row, 'the quote of the season. No one else could have made it.' That morning, he recalls, he took to the field under the influence of numerous aspirin and a hastily remodelled hairstyle to conceal a bruised forehead. 'What's wrong with Raman?' asked May. Evans shrugged.

The Manchester Test was won by an innings. Shortly thereafter the composition of the touring party was unsettled when Wardle was sacked by Yorkshire. Having put his name to a vitriolic column in the *Daily Mail*, the player was informed that his invitation to Australia had been withdrawn. No replacement was announced, and in consequence the party included only two spinners. To

'It just let you know he was there' – against New Zealand, 1958. (Sport & General).

many, including Evans, it seemed an ominous note on which to depart.

'On paper, it looked a strong team. It also contained a number of individuals not slow to speak their minds,' says Evans. In addition to Wardle, Laker – excluded from two previous tours to Australia – had expressed reservations about playing under May, his County captain. The bowler eventually relented. In conjunction with Dexter's exclusion, the party announced on 27 July, and its immediate amendment, was the most controversial selected since the War. The eventual sixteen names were: May (captain), Bailey, Cowdrey, Evans, Graveney, Laker, Loader, Lock, Milton, Peter Richardson, Statham, Subba Row, Swetman, Trueman, Tyson and Watson. Swetman was rewarded for his consistent season with Surrey and for his familiarity with at least three of the England bowlers. A final omission was

Illingworth, who, like Subba Row and Dexter, had made his debut at Old Trafford, returning figures of 45–18–59–3. 'A mixed blessing,' he says; 'had I toured, my wedding plans would have had to be postponed.' Illingworth's turn would come in 1959 and beyond.

The fifth Test at The Oval was decided, as was much else that season, by rain. New Zealand, who scored 161 and 91–3, at least achieved a draw. So ended a series as monotonous as any that decade. From it Evans emerged with 28 runs at an average of 5.60 and seven dismissals. For New Zealand the captain John Reid scored 1,429 first-class runs at 39.69; MacGibbon took twenty Test wickets. To be fair to the tourists, it was unfortunate that a relative decline in New Zealand batting coincided with an upturn in English bowling, spearheaded by Trueman, Laker and Lock. Moreover, Sutcliffe, who injured himself in the field early on the tour, never fully regained match fitness. Finally, the rain that fell incessantly all summer meant that the rhythm of the side was never established, and public interest in the series declined proportionately. The tourists returned with a profit of £4,000.

From The Oval, New Zealand travelled to Canterbury for the traditional fixture with Kent. Of the home side's 140, Cowdrey scored 57 before rain intervened. This was the year when, according to *Wisden*, 'the long awaited Kent revival took place'. The County rose to eighth in the Championship and boasted a batsman (Cowdrey) and two bowlers (Ridgway and David Sayer) in the top first-class averages. Evans scored 545 runs at 20.96, and, by his own admission, had an indifferent season behind the stumps. The decline was observed by *Wisden*, which remarked, 'Evans did not always live up to his own high standards of excellence.' The criticism reflected the trend established the previous year of Evans's 'listlessness' at County level. The distinction between this and his performances for England bears repetition; in the 1958 series Evans conceded no byes in three completed (if modest) New Zealand innings, and his keeping to Lock on a turning wicket was, according to the bowler, 'superlative'. Evans himself declared the series disappointing for players and spectators alike, yet contributed significantly both on and off the field. Swanton's account of the 'marvellous cheerfulness and optimism [he possessed] even when things looked at their darkest' applied in 1958 just as it had in 1954 and 1946; the difference being that Evans's field of concentration now lacked the depth of previous years. By his own admission, returning to Kent after performing heroics for England became increasingly a lesson in self-motivation; and to perform at his peak Evans required the stimulus of external factors. In his own words, 'In my twenties, enthusiasm alone meant I could play all day, every day, throughout the year. Later I found the strain greater. . . it affected my performance at certain times during the season.' 1958 was the first such when official note had been made of the consequences.

The season ended for Evans when he appeared for T.N. Pearce's XI against New Zealand at Scarborough. In somewhat more positive vein than before, the tourists scored 303–8 declared, leaving a target of 259 to win. On no more strategic basis than having a train to catch, Evans was promoted and scored 69, engaging in a stand of 77 in 32 minutes. Whatever the relative decline of his performances for Kent, he was still capable of outstanding brilliance when the situation required. Evans caught his train and was in London before he learnt the result of the match he had so decisively transformed. It was a tie.

The twelfth MCC party to Australia set sail, according to Swanton, 'in a dangerous mood of over-confidence'. Benaud, too, recalls that 'at a time when some of his players, ability-wise, were on the way down rather than on the way up, May was ill served by the pre-tour publicity which listed his team as the greatest ever to leave English shores. They had an enormous amount to live up to and sometimes that kind of adulation can be worse than criticism.' In fact the mood of the party, in the wake of the Wardle débâcle, was dangerously volatile, and, in Tyson's words, 'to the practised observer it was clear, even at the outset, that all was far from well in the English camp.' The obvious ill-will that existed between Laker and May, following the latter's remark that the off-spinner 'hadn't tried' during a

Surrey v Kent fixture that summer, ensured the party had little chance of establishing an *esprit de corps*. To Tyson, 'it was obvious that commonsense should have told May that he was not going to get the best out of his senior bowler'.

The pattern of the tour was established when the S.S. *Iberia* was a day out of Tilbury. During dinner Tyson happened to refer to the captain as 'Peter', prompting the manager, Freddie Brown, to deliver a lecture concerning the virtues of formality; henceforth May was to be referred to exclusively as 'Skipper'; Brown himself reverted to 'Boss'; while, almost surreally, Desmond Eagar, in charge of financial arrangements for the tour, became 'Cash'. To Tyson, an intelligent man who had known and played cricket with May long before he became captain, the imposition merely 'opened up a gap between the leader and his followers'.

Evans worked hard to establish a link between the two. As the senior professional he was aware of his responsibilities regarding team spirit and motivation; yet this did nothing to deter his ability to inject a note of genuine anarchy. The saloon of the *Iberia* saw the resumption of Evans's rendition of the 'German Band', a community song acquired from a Canadian Sergeant during the War. It began with the assertion, '*Ich can de musica*' and went on to enumerate various musical instruments which Evans would vigorously mime, with considerable audience participation. On the *Iberia*, too, he, Bailey, Tyson and Subba Row initiated the Bowers Club, subsequently electing Brian Johnston an honorary member. It was a male-only association, which, in Johnston's recollection, 'would meet once a week and carry out various rituals invented and conducted by Evans, accompanied by the odd glass of wine'. Throughout the three-week journey, in fact, he seems to have consciously attempted to improve the spirits of the party and was the first tourist ashore when the ship docked in Bombay with the cry, 'We'll murder them.' From there the party flew to Ceylon, where rain restricted the traditional one-day fixture and Evans distinguished himself by appearing on an elephant. When the *Iberia* was reboarded for the final journey to Freemantle he, at least, felt that the tour was off to 'a flier'.

The feeling altered in the course of a State match against Victoria at Melbourne. With Swetman selected behind the stumps, Evans took the opportunity of a round of golf, returning to the ground to catch his first sight of a young Victorian fast bowler. Ian Meckiff, fresh from a tour of South Africa in which he and Mackay established a record ninth-wicket partnership while achieving little with the ball, now provided 'the most extraordinary sight' of Evans's career. Meckiff threw. More graphically, 'he took a short run, left-arm over the wicket, checked, stretched and released, exactly like a fielder picking up a ball and throwing it in'. Tyson, watching from the pavilion, was similarly convinced: 'Meckiff's run-up was a mere apology. . .he ambled to the wicket before pitching the ball at the batsman as fast as he could. We were all of the opinion that he threw.' After the shock had subsided, Evans immediately approached Brown with the assertion that 'something has to be done'. Brown agreed to speak to May. A day went by. Then another. Evans again expressed his views to the manager, who replied, 'We've decided to let the matter rest. Peter says he doesn't want to create an incident. Besides which, he isn't that good a bowler'. Evans reeled. In his four Tests that series, Meckiff took seventeen wickets at an average of 17.17, including 6–38 at Melbourne. 'It was,' says Evans, 'the crime of the century.'

Cowdrey (promoted to vice-captain over Bailey) led the team at Melbourne. At a critical moment in the Victorian second innings he did an extraordinary thing; despite the presence of Statham and Lock, Cowdrey invited Graveney to bowl. He promptly dismissed McDonald and Victoria collapsed. According to Evans, it was the most imaginative piece of captaincy of the tour; that in contrast to May, who soon indicated that the pressures of leadership were affecting him. In Evans's words, 'Peter didn't seem to like us to relax on the field, perhaps because he himself didn't do so.' In fairness to May, who finished the tour with a Test average of 40.50, the additional burden of captaincy was hardly alleviated by the speculation concerning the presence of his fiancée, Victoria Gilligan. 'Wives on tour' suddenly became an issue and a photograph of the two sunbathing beside a swimming-pool was produced as evidence that May was aloof from his team. It led to a suspicion of certain elements of the press that remains today. Although Cowdrey asserts that no captain took more care to look after his team, the mere fact of the allegation was damaging.

Against New South Wales MCC encountered the twenty-year-old Gordon Rorke, who added a new dimension to an already suspect action by his use of 'drag'. According to Swanton: 'When a man of Rorke's speed drags so far you think he's never going to let the ball go, and on his delivering it at last from some eighteen yards you then get a delayed sight of it, the scales are heightened against the batsman, to say the least.' To Evans it was 'another example of blatant cheating, which, to our cost, we chose to ignore', a view shared by observers both in and outside the party. At Brisbane, Lindwall re-introduced himself to the team as 'the last of the straight-armers'.

Against a Combined XI at Perth the party had witnessed a more orthodox talent: Norman O'Neill, a 21-year-old New South Welshman 'built like a young Compton' and with the same range of orthodoxy and improvisation. After Evans had watched him at Perth, he came to the conclusion that O'Neill 'was the most polished young player I'd ever seen', a status confirmed by his 104 against an attack including Statham, Loader, Bailey and Laker. O'Neill was never to fully realize his youthful potential, despite an eventual Test aggregate of 2,779; that series he averaged 56, and, according to Evans, 'had the world at his feet. He was the most exciting prospect on either side.'

Evans himself scored 55 at Perth, incredibly accounting for nearly half his total runs on tour. His timing was propitious. As he approached the first Test at Brisbane, notwithstanding the presence of Meckiff (though not Rorke), Evans asserts the mood of the team to have been confident. 'After all, we held the Ashes. Our record in recent years was outstanding. We still had every reason to be optimistic.'

England lost the Test by eight wickets. Having trailed Australia by 53 in the first innings, the critical phase came on the fourth day, when the tourists were dismissed for 198. So dire were both sides' performances that the *Telegraph* felt moved to ask whether victory 'was worth the cost in terms of the sterile play that makes one sick at heart to watch'. Its centrepiece was Bailey, who batted for seven-and-a-half hours for 68: 'A classic,' says Evans. 'The public were gravely disappointed,' reported Swanton.

The result was not entirely representative of the sides' abilities. *Wisden* duly noted that 'England, contrary to expectations, were beaten'; Evans that various elements of the team's play were disturbing, rather than the performance itself. Among the liabilities, he believed, was the insistence that May and Cowdrey bat at numbers four and five respectively, with very little (Evans himself appeared at seven) to follow. The inference was that the responsibility of being the last accredited batsmen in the side inhibited the captain's and vice-captain's play. The journalist Ray Robinson agreed, noting that 'Australia gained an enormous advantage by having an opening pair, McDonald and Burke, who usually saw the new-ball bowlers off. . .In contrast, England enjoyed neither a steady start nor the subsequent depth to sustain it.' According to Evans, his suggestion to May that he and Cowdrey consider their positions was met with a polite 'thank you', and, incredibly, the decision to bat one place lower in the second Test.

One down in the series, a further crisis presented itself when no fewer than four players – Watson, Subba Row, Milton and Bailey – reported unfit, while a fifth, Laker, nursed an injured spinning finger. The upshot was that, on Graveney's advice, the Gloucester bowler John Mortimore was sent for and joined the team against South Australia at Adelaide. Also included was Dexter, who, after an epic journey encompassing Paris, London, Frankfurt and Bahrain, arrived in Australia 'exhausted, dazed, light-headed and mute into the bargain'. Despite having fulfilled his promise to 'get you there if it kills us', Evans had reservations about Dexter's introduction in mid-tour; even Allen thought it 'no way to blood a young cricketer of high potential'. Dexter himself asserts: 'I had no confidence whatsoever.'

Evans, meanwhile, noted a disconcerting change from the routine established on previous tours. Gone were a number of the enjoyable up-country matches, replaced by repeat fixtures against the States, which left the players physically and mentally exhausted in the run-up to Tests. What Evans was witnessing was the genesis of an itinerary that, by the 1970s, would dispense with up-country matches entirely. Now, already, 'some of the charm of touring had vanished'; and that from the world's most gregarious tourist.

Christmas was spent at the Glenelg Hotel in Adelaide. It was memorable for a light-hearted football match involving MCC against the press. At some stage the distinctive figure of Bill Edrich, accompanying the party, appeared on the pitch. Lacking definite affiliation to either side, Edrich contented himself, in Evans's words, to 'meandering amiably about the pitch, occasionally aiming a kick, missing and falling flat on his back. . . .He was quite different when he used to play for Spurs.'

The second Test began at Melbourne on 31 December 1958. After being 7–3, England were redeemed by May, who scored 113; according to *Wisden*, the captain 'fell to a ball which moved in quickly'; in Dexter's more explicit view, 'Meckiff ran, or rather ambled up, and May, halfway through his backlift, lost his middle stump. He looked astonished, as did those of us watching.' For the record, it was the first century by an England captain in Australia since MacLaren's at Sydney in 1902. For Australia Harvey made 167 of a total of 308; there were no byes, despite which Evans admits he found it hard to motivate himself in a side 'lacking direction' by the captain. Again the critical phase came when England batted in the second innings and were dismissed for 87; critical, too, for Evans, in that attempting a short single, he checked, turned and dived for home only to see the ball brilliantly fielded and returned to the wicket. In his own words:

> I dived to get back into my ground; as I did so I stabbed the little finger of my left hand in which I was holding the bat into the ground with a great deal of force, and felt a pain shoot up my arm. When I took my glove off afterwards the finger was swollen, but not bad enough to prevent my continuing in the game, which I did, stumping Wally Grout. But the finger continued to bother me, and X-ray showed that the bone was chipped.

The upshot was that, before 50,000 spectators, Australia won by eight wickets; Meckiff took 6–38. According to Swanton, 'MCC made a tactical error by not registering their doubts about the bowler the first time they met him. . . .When, a couple of months later, he was taking nine wickets in a Test, bowling out England for 87 on a plumb wicket, and more or less clinching the rubber in an afternoon, England could only grin and bear it – or at least bear it. They weren't exactly beaming.'

The recriminations began after Melbourne. Evans continued to rue the lost opportunity of May's policy of passive resistance; Dexter, too, felt that 'surely some comment would have been reasonable'. To complicate matters, counter - allegations were now raised about Lock, who later in the tour was presented with documentary evidence about the dubious nature of his own action. In the four days prior to the third Test the mood in the England camp turned irrevocably sour; the conviction that Meckiff had 'stolen' the Test, bolstered by growing doubts about the Australian officials, in particular Mel McInnes – in Dexter's view, 'a great umpire when the tour began, who finished up a moderate one'. Dexter himself had been gently upbraided when entering the dining-room of the team hotel in Melbourne dressed in shorts, only to read the next day of his being evicted from the premises. To compound matters the press now published their photograph of May sunbathing with his fiancée, and the general impression was that the 'enemy' now encompassed more than the thirteen opponents on the field. In such cases resentment becomes rife and the mood of the party in the first week of 1959 bordered on the paranoid. When, at that very moment, the management issued a directive limiting the activities of the ubiquitous Saturday Night Club, it must have seemed like a Fifth Column attack on an already beleaguered army.

Swetman made his debut in the third Test at Sydney. He scored 41 and dropped two catches – 'standing too close to Trueman'. After emerging with a draw, England were upbraided by Swanton for technical deficiencies: 'The general axiom is that once a man has become a Test cricketer he 'knows it all', and that it is henceforward up to him. I believe this is a foolish theory.' More ominously, the same correspondent noted that 'the [public relations] arrangements on the tour have turned out badly because the manager, who has relieved the captain of all press liaison, is not well cast for this particular aspect of his job', a view echoed by Laker, who wrote that 'Brown, to be frank, was not exactly the most diplomatic man to be in contact with the press, and, leaving aside his personal manner, was not competent to tell them a lot that they wanted to know' – that in contrast to Benaud, whose avowed policy was 'to invite any journalist who wished to do so to come to the dressing-room at the close of play for a drink'. The results were self-evident.

On the morning of 30 January the Committee met to determine the team and tactics for the fourth Test at Adelaide. Both were immediately jeopardized when, minutes before the start, Laker declared himself unfit. In the fortnight since Sydney, Evans had received treatment for the chip in his finger; unfortunately Laker had no such remedy for the same affliction on his shoulder. While the bowler himself asserted that 'had I played I would have been letting down England', Evans and others believed it to be a case of Laker losing heart at the critical moment. Mindful of the injustice of his omission from the two previous tours of Australia – and of his still simmering resentment against May – Laker, Evans believes, 'decided to make his point in the most dramatic way possible'. As the team took the field on the first day, they attempted to put the bowler's 'shattering blow' behind them.

The first ball from Statham pitched, seamed and lifted over the top of McDonald's middle stump. The batsman went on to score 170. Had the ball been a fraction lower, and McInnes concurred with Evans's raucous appeal against Burke off Tyson, the Australian total would never have reached 476. As it was, by the end of the first day the series was effectively over; as was Evans, when, on the second afternoon, he dived to take a ball off Tyson, was struck on the finger and uttered his memorable understatement, 'something's wrong.' After taking his 76th and final dismissal against Australia, Evans handed the gloves to Graveney and sought confirmation that his finger was again broken. He batted – virtually one-handed – in the two England innings, scoring four and nought; on 5 February Australia won by ten wickets and recovered the Ashes. May, recalls Dexter, 'paid a gracious tribute to the better side' and the party returned to Melbourne. By now Evans realized that, for him, proceedings were over. They seemed to have been almost from the outset. As early as Brisbane, his suggestions regarding field and bowling changes – eagerly solicited by captains from Hammond to Hutton – had been met by May with 'immense courtesy . . . and complete inaction'. Bailey, too, felt his position to have been undermined once superseded as vice-captain by Cowdrey, a decision even the latter considered a mistake. The upshot was that England's two senior players found themselves virtually redundant off the field and confined by injuries on it; Bailey appeared throughout with a strained back and returned to England believing 'my image no longer fitted'. The same was evidently true of Evans, who recognized early on that 'Peter's style and mine would never be one'. While the team remained successful there was room to accommodate both; after surrendering the Ashes, in Cowdrey's words, 'everything became disseminated. In the inquest which followed there seemed to emerge a line of thought which was to have a profound effect on English cricket for the next decade. It was held to be high time that certain players were brought down to size.' Evans, Bailey and Laker would never tour for England again.

Australia won the fifth Test by nine wickets, thus inflicting a four-nil defeat on a side which had itself recorded a similar result six months previously. In his three Tests Evans scored 27 runs at an average of 4.50 and took six dismissals. The figures were taken by *Wisden* as proof that 'Evans was another stalwart who gave evidence of a decline in power'; and the unpalatable fact is that, at 38, his reflexes had slowed appreciably. His mental approach, too, had altered. Throughout his career Evans found it easier to motivate himself in sides which, if not successful, at least pulled together. In 1958–59 the side pulled apart. May, and to a lesser extent Cowdrey, 'didn't listen' to their senior professionals, some of whom in consequence adopted a less than wholehearted attitude. The results were self-apparent. In his own analysis of the tour, Ray Robinson concluded that '. . . in the key wicketkeeping post, Grout's twenty wickets equalled Tallon's Australian record for five Tests against England. . . Only one chance escaped Grout's gloves, whereas English wicketkeeping errors almost equalled the wickets taken behind the stumps.'

In retrospect it appears that the tour was blighted from the start. The Wardle saga established a mood exacerbated by *Wisden*'s claim that 'England stand at the top of the world'; in consequence there was only one direction to go. The subsequent descent was a traumatic one. Evans, like Bailey, Graveney, Watson, Tyson, Loader, Laker and Lock, proved himself capable of sporadic brilliance during the tour, without ever showing the consistent excellence characterizing his three previous visits. Under the circumstances minor irritations developed into serious grievances, and by the fourth Test relations with May had deteriorated to a level of frosty civility. As the tour ended there was a definite sense that an era had ended.

Evans began the 1959 season having played 89 Tests, whereas, with a full complement in Australia and New Zealand, he might have expected to reach 93. Nonetheless he remained confident of being the first player to 100 appearances. A further twelve months would have seen him achieve it, and in April 1959, his finger healed, Evans felt confident 'of another year, if not two' at the top.

The immediate concern was whether he could motivate himself sufficiently for another year at Kent. Catt was entering his sixth season as Evans's sometime deputy and there was concern by Cowdrey that, without the opportunity of regular cricket, the reserve player would be lost. Evans readily agreed to stand down on certain occasions, a decision misunderstood by some who believed the England wicketkeeper to have thus been 'dropped' by his County. 'Not so,' says Evans. 'The arrangement was that Tony would be gradually phased into the side, just as I'd been before the War. The officials and players all understood.' To reinforce the cyclical nature of the agreement, the team continued to be managed by Ames, who had himself stood down in 1939 to accommodate Evans and Levett. 'It made perfect sense,' he asserts. 'Godfrey was still the finest Test wicketkeeper in the world. At the same time we were naturally planning for the future.'

Evans himself declared his total commitment to co-operating with Ames and Cowdrey; 'I was looking forward to building on the progress Kent had made in 1958.' At the same time the strain of daily cricket, both on and off the field, was now undeniable. In 1959, for the first time, Evans expressed disenchantment at 'life out of a suitcase', a condition aggravated by a decision taken that spring to which he reacted angrily. From April all Kent players, when appearing outside the County, were to stay in the same hotel, which was in turn nominated by the Committee. To Evans, 'while the intention was clearly to safeguard the interests of the younger and less well-paid players, the rule came rather hard on the more senior professionals who had been on the circuit for years and who liked to make their own arrangements, especially in places where they had friends'. More profoundly, perhaps, he felt that, as senior professional, he might have been consulted. 'It seemed my views were no longer required,' he says. 'That hurt.'

The transitional state of English cricket was reinforced by the MCC team selected to play the touring Indians in May. Murray was wicketkeeper. A fortnight later Evans was included in the first Test at Nottingham. Also selected were Tommy Greenhough (Lancashire), Ken Taylor (Yorkshire) and Martin Horton (Worcestershire). In the England first innings of 422, Evans scored 73; his fifty came in 42 minutes, and, at one stage, he witnessed Compton (commentating on television) signalling from the pavilion that the fastest century of the season was in sight. It proved elusive, but Evans's score was acknowledged by *Wisden* ('Desai suffered severely') as a return to his highest form. 'I felt absolutely marvellous', he says. Evans enjoyed playing India.

Somehow the story got around that Evans, far from feeling 'marvellous', had emerged from the Test exhausted. His own view is different. 'I *was* exhausted,' he admits, 'for about ten

The penultimate Test – against India at Trent Bridge, 1959.

minutes. I got into a bath, stayed there, got out and dried myself and dressed. Then I was back to normal again.' The first person to greet him was May.

The captain's own performance in Australia had, meanwhile, been minuted by the Selection Committee with unusual clarity:

> Before formally inviting Mr P.B.H. May to be captain, the chairman informed him of the Committee's determination to instil into the team, through the captain, a more aggressive approach to the game. Particular reference was made to the number of overs bowled per hour, fielding and the tempo generally. In the light of Mr May's undertaking to do his best to achieve improvement in these departments of the game, he was invited to captain England for the whole series.

The vexed question of 'brighter cricket' had been extensively aired in Australia, where Robinson noted that 'England mostly fell below twelve eight-ball overs an hour and averaged only 474 balls a day in the Tests. . . . Every aspect of this problem of diminishing play calls for attention.' Not the least of Evans's frustrations had been attempting to synchronize the field to his own energetic tempo at a time when, he felt, 'there was a tendency to dawdle when things were going against us'.

No such tendency was apparent against India, with whom the second Test began at Lord's on 18 June. In the tourists' first innings of 168 there were no byes. Nonetheless, the first afternoon contained the – as it transpired – critical last phase of Evans's career. In the space of four overs he missed an equal number of stumpings off Greenhough, the Lancashire leg-spinner. Two of the chances were googlies, and lifted sharply; the other two, outside the leg stump, kept low. All came through unexpectedly between bat and pad. In Evans's view, 'that type of chance is undoubtedly the most difficult to take, since the bat invariably covers the pitch of the ball'. Nonetheless the lapses marred an otherwise meticulous performance, and *Wisden* felt moved to record that 'Evans, who otherwise kept well, had a bad quarter of an hour.' The player himself felt he 'would have learned to pick Greenhough, given another match.' Only, for Evans, there were no other matches.

On 19 June England replied with 226. Evans was bowled by Surendranath for nought. In the Indian second innings there were again no byes; Evans's assertion that he would 'learn to pick' Greenhough was fulfilled when he stumped Gupte off the same bowler. England duly won by eight wickets and on Saturday 20 June 1959 Evans completed his ninety-first Test, coincidentally against the same opponents as his first. Shortly thereafter May, for whom Evans continued to find it 'difficult' to motivate himself, suggested he 'rest' during the remainder of the series while retaining fitness for the winter tour of the West Indies. Allen, Evans's captain on his first such excursion in 1947–48, felt moved to state: 'Evans has been omitted from the team so that another wicketkeeper may be tried in the interests of team-building.'

The chosen player was Swetman, who appeared in the

three remaining Tests, achieving an average of 57 and taking eleven catches. When the MCC party was announced in late July he and Andrew were included as wicketkeepers. Evans, who had taken May's remark concerning fitness as a 'broad hint' of his selection, was mortified. It is hard, at a distance of 30 years, to reflect the exact nuances of what was said, but Evans remains adamant that 'an inference' was definitely made; May that the subsequent announcement was 'a unanimous decision of the Committee' and, more cryptically, that 'every player has an end'. This was Evans's. Convinced that his England career was over, he returned to Kent only to face renewed pressure to 'consider the position' of his deputy. The evidence of the Australian tour was that Evans's reflexes were not what they had been, and, denied the stimulus of Test cricket, he found it hard to reconcile himself to life on the circuit. Throughout August, Cowdrey was to remind him that Catt, now 25, was impatient for first-class cricket; although there was 'no direct suggestion' that Evans retire (indeed he was to captain Kent in Cowdrey's absence), he spent much of the rest of the season pondering his options.

On 29 August India appeared at Canterbury and Evans held three catches in the tourists' first innings. He took his 1000th first-class dismissal and shortly thereafter wrote to Ames, the man who as much as any had inspired him to play cricket, announcing his retirement. As Cowdrey says, 'For Godfrey it was the top or nothing.' In early September he appeared for the last time for the Players against the Gentlemen at Scarborough, scoring 65 and being 'raucously received' by the crowd, elements of whom may have guessed what was happening. On 12 September Evans appeared at The Oval for the Rest of England against the Champion County – which, to general surprise, was Yorkshire. After Wardle's acrimonious departure, it said much for the spirit of a team which the previous season had finished eleventh. Evans scored 10 and 27, took no dismissals, and on 15 September left the ground realising it to be 'the last time I would look at that unlovely gasometer and be paid for it'. The next day he formally announced his retirement. Kent organised a subscription and presented him with a

'Good for another year or two' – Evans in 1959. (Sport & General).

cheque for £1,100. In his last season Evans had scored 528 runs at an average of 15.08 and saw the County decline to thirteenth in the Championship; the revival heralded in 1958 had proved illusory. In his two Tests he scored 73 runs and took four dismissals, the last his 219th in international cricket. Appropriately enough, it was a stumping.

In late 1959 Compton was invited by the Transvaal cricket authorities to organise a Commonwealth tour of the province. Evans was appointed vice-captain. Among the players was Roy Marshall, the West Indian batsman appearing for Hampshire; Bert Sutcliffe of New Zealand; and Ian Craig, captain of Australia in South Africa two years earlier. The Commonwealth side won three of its five fixtures and drew the remainder. Evans appeared in all five, and, in Compton's view, 'never kept better'. The captain himself showed touches of his old form and to the thousands who packed the Wanderers Ground in Johannesburg it must have seemed like a return to another era. The party left in early December, convinced, in Evans's words, that the visit had been beneficial 'for players and spectators of every persuasion'.

On 8 December Evans and Compton drove to the Great Western Hotel, Paddington. The lobby was teeming with the chairmen and managers of professional football clubs, who, it transpired, were holding their annual meeting. Immediately apparent was Tommy Trinder (representing Fulham), who raucously greeted his old acquaintance. Evans's reaction was more subdued. Also assembled in the hotel was the MCC party setting out for the West Indies. Evans spoke to May and to Walter Robins, the team manager, who took personal possession of the Godfrey Evans Cricket Shirts supplied to the tour. He wished well to Swetman and Andrew. Trueman was there, and the two recalled the previous tour of the Caribbean in which the 'Fiery Fred' persona had been forged. There were the usual high spirits, now tinged with regrets, as when Trueman, observing the assembled team, remarked: ''Twere never a dull moment when you were around, Godders.' It was, in its way, as fitting an epitaph as Cardus's in the following edition of *Wisden*:

> Godfrey did not just wait for chances which any competent keeper could take. He was creative. . . . Cricket is the poorer for his retirement at the early age of thirty-nine. Most of us had thought that time would toil and pant after him in vain.

After a time the party walked to the waiting train. Among the wives and children Evans stood beaming through the smoke and steam. Swetman, a diminutive figure who might almost have been someone's child himself, appeared at a window. He seemed to mouth something through the filmy glass; Evans cupped a hand to his ear. Just then the train gave a jolt and started.

Chapter Seven

The Gloves Are Off

EVANS'S INVOLVEMENT WITH cricket continued. From the Transvaal tour emerged the idea of the International Cavaliers, so named after the personality of the captain. Another of that ilk was Colin Ingleby-Mackenzie, captain of Hampshire, who inherited the County after a long period of decline and led them to the Championship in 1961. Ingleby-Mackenzie's oft-quoted decree 'that all my players be in bed before breakfast' typified the spirit of the Cavaliers. 'It was good Club-level standard,' says Evans, 'which we took, within reason, seriously'; his kind of cricket.

Recognition of his former career came on 16 February 1960, when Evans was invested with the CBE by the Duke of Edinburgh. The two talked cricket for some time, the Duke commenting on the then current MCC tour of the West Indies (the tourists won one-nil). The MCC itself elected Evans an Honorary Life Member, as did Kent. His affection for his old County remained undiminished and with the passage of time he grew nostalgic even for the Canterbury pavilion described by Cowdrey as possessing 'a splintered floor roughed up by the studs of Frank Woolley'. Evans professed still to miss the variety of playing on nine different grounds, admitting that 'even for Blackheath I finally formed an affection'.

The Cavaliers toured Jamaica under Compton in 1963–64, and the other Caribbean islands under Bailey the following winter. The latter, recalling a fixture against Barbados, wrote:

> We were so badly hit by injuries that we couldn't raise a fully fit side. In order that the game should not peter out into a draw I declared, leaving our opponents a total to make against the clock, although my attack had by that time been reduced to only two recognized bowlers. Godfrey, despite a painful septic knee, insisted

Godfrey, Howard and Jean Evans at the Palace, February 1960. (Press Association).

In action for the Cavaliers

> on keeping wicket and proceeded to pull out all the stops. For some two-and-a-half hours the crowd saw the one and only 'Godders' in action. Increasing age and girth could not disguise the fact that here was a great personality and a superb craftsman, the like of which we are unlikely to see again.

At home Evans himself adopted the captaincy of the Cavaliers, sponsored by Rothman's in a series of 40-over Sunday matches. Among regular players were Compton, Trueman, Graveney and a young South African named D'Oliveira who appeared when not representing Middleton in the Lancashire League from 1961–64. Evans remembers commending the all-rounder to Ken Graveney of Gloucester, only for his brother Tom, recently transferred to Worcester, to recruit the player for his adopted County. Evans had been impressed by D'Oliveira's assertion that 'the first hour

Loosening up before the comeback, August 1967. (Hulton-Deutsch).

belongs to the bowler. After that I'm in charge', allied to his own marked proficiency with the ball. Socially, too, the pair were far from dissimilar. Stories abound.

From 1964 the Cavaliers' home fixtures were to be broadcast, wholly or in part, on television, thus returning Evans to the spotlight. As captain and sometime manager of the team, his role was to strike the balance between providing entertainment and cricket, a parity to which his own career was testament. In time the Cavaliers were succeeded by the (then) John Player League, to which the side duly applied for membership. At an advanced stage negotiations broke down, and in 1969 the Cavaliers disbanded. In addition to providing a curtain-call for Evans and others, the team supplied a valuable source of income for County beneficiaries, most notably Tom Cartwright for whom 20,000 witnessed a Cavaliers fixture at Edgbaston.

On 7 August 1967 Evans received a message from Ames. Alan Knott had been selected to play his first Test, and in the absence of reliable deputies (Catt having retired) Evans was invited to represent the County against Yorkshire. His first reaction was shock, followed by the realization that 'attempting to reach match fitness would be futile'; he contented himself with a sauna. Thus it was that on 9 August, the week before his 47th birthday, Evans returned to Canterbury. In the Kent first innings of 223 he scored 10, being greeted with a flourish by Trueman. The next day he took two catches, and, in Ames's words, 'performed magnificently'. In the Kent second innings Evans scored 6, caught by Padgett off the son of his former captain, Hutton. In the final innings there were no byes.

> One of the most successful Canterbury Weeks of all time [wrote *Wisden*], some 40,000 people attending over the six days, ended with Kent gaining only two points from the first game. Evans reappeared after retiring for eight years in place of Knott, who was playing for England. Moreover, Evans kept wicket superbly.

For the occasion Evans was paid £40 by the Kent Committee, comparing favourably, he noted, with his fee as a professional. In the interim the distinction between Gentlemen and Players had been abolished, an initiative long advocated by Evans himself. In 1956 he had written of his belief that 'all first-class cricketers should be classed as players, not as amateurs or professionals, according to their status in the game. . . . Each should be paid a specified amount for a match, whether he wants it or not. The man who wishes to remain an "amateur" could always donate it to charity.' On overseas tours Evans had noted the imbalance of maintaining separate arrangements for two sets of players, the chief distinction being that the amateur received more in expenses than the professional in salary. The change, in short, was overdue.

In 1969 Evans played his final first-class fixture, for the Cavaliers against Barbados at Scarborough. The following year he was approached to play for the Whitbread Wanderers, a precursor of the Courage Old England XI. The latter, established in 1981 under the captaincy of Trueman, raised

After catching Taylor (Yorks.) off Alan Brown, August 1967. (Hulton-Deutsch).

£16,000 for charity in their first season, and included stalwarts such as Graveney, Titmus and Swetman at various times throughout the '80s. Swetman himself had played his last Test in March 1960, raising questions about the principle of team-building held responsible for Evans's retirement. The two, along with Parks and Murray, continued to alternate for Old England, which in September 1982 played a fixture against an Old World XI at The Oval. Press reports refer to Evans's 'outstanding' work behind the stumps.

On 26 August 1973, the XI played an England Ladies XI at The Oval. The Ladies had recently won the first World Cup competition, defeating Australia in the final at Edgbaston. Among those appearing were Hutton, Compton, Simpson and Shackleton. Evans, in Compton's view, 'kept brilliantly' throughout the opposition score of 171–6, said

Old England XI v England Ladies, The Oval 1973: Hutton's last match.

to be punctuated by lively dialogue on both sides. It was Hutton's last representative fixture.

In March 1977 Evans, and, among others, Hutton, Compton, Dexter, Statham, Trueman, Lock and Laker were guests of the Australian Cricket Board at the Centenary Test in Melbourne. In the course of a fortnight at the Melbourne Hilton, he encountered Bradman and Harvey; entertained Miller and Lindwall; and found time even to watch the Test, which, remarkably, was won by the same margin as 100 years before. For England Derek Randall scored 174; 'a remarkable innings,' says Evans, 'by someone who seems to be always either "up" or "down". On this occasion he was up.' More poignantly, on the outward excursion Evans was approached by a bowed, emaciated man who introduced himself with the phrase, 'You won't remember me.' He was right. After some time Evans was forced to ask the identity of the only wicketkeeper to appear for England both before and after the War. It was Paul Gibb. The two reminisced about their joint tour of Australia 30 years previously, before Gibb excused himself with the words, 'I'm feeling rather tired.' By year's end he was dead.

In August 1980 the return fixture was staged at Lord's. It was preceded by a veteran's match at The Oval, in which Old Australia (average age 43) defeated Old England (50) by seven wickets. A crowd of 5,000 saw a match in which Cowdrey, Barrington, Simpson and Harvey all excelled. According to Brian Scovell in the *Daily Mail*, 'Godfrey Evans, at 60 the oldest player on the field, gave England the edge in one department – wicketkeeping. His stumpings of Simpson and Ian Redpath were so quick that Alan Knott would have been hard pressed to surpass them.' Simpson himself recalls that 'Evans was the same as ever – talkative, determined and brilliant'. Towards the end of the Australian innings he was replaced by Parks, and left the ground to sustained applause. 'Marvellous,' he says. 'Trueman was actually *moving* the ball, the so-and-so.'

Next day the official teams embarked on a match distinguished only by controversy. In its report of the fixture, *Wisden* remarked:

> It had been hoped that England's Centenary Test might be played in late summer sunshine with many a nostalgic reunion, some splendid fighting cricket and a finish to savour.
>
> Over 200 former England and Australian players assembled from all over the world; it was impossible to move anywhere at Lord's without meeting the heroes of yesteryear. The welcoming parties, the dinners and the take-over by Cornhill Insurance of a London theatre for a night were all hugely successful. Sadly, however, the party in the middle was markedly less so.

The chief complaint was that, on the critical Saturday, with 20,000 present and a television audience of millions, play was delayed until 3.45 pm; and then only after a scuffle following the umpires' fifth pitch inspection of the day. Two MCC members were questioned by the Secretary and a statement issued:

> Enquiries instituted today into the behaviour of certain MCC members towards the umpires and captains on Saturday leave no doubt that their conduct was inexcusable in any circumstances. Investigations are continuing and will be vigorously pursued with a view to identifying and disciplining the culprits. Meanwhile the Club is sending to the umpires and to the captains of both sides their profound apologies that such an unhappy incident should have occurred at the headquarters of the game and on an occasion of such importance.

Evans's observations are threefold: firstly, that an attack on the umpires, however provoked, was unconscionable; second, the decision to suspend play for several hours after the groundsman himself had indicated that conditions were fit was, under the circumstances, 'disgraceful'. Finally, after a match designed to represent the best in cricket, and watched by some 85,000 spectators, England's decision to ignore the last innings challenge and instead grind out a draw was sadly indicative of the current state of the game. In a phrase: 'The fun seemed to have gone out of it.'

The reverse was true of Evans's antics during the Test. Among those present were, of former captains, Allen, Mann, Yardley, Brown, Hutton and May; they in addition to Compton, Edrich, Bedser, Tyson and Wright ensured that the celebrity enclosure in 'Q' Stand was rarely untenanted. There was a reunion with Miller; and with Loxton, Morris and Hassett. Tallon, and, more notably, Bradman declined to attend. The latter had been in ill-health for some time, but had given Evans a warm reception in Melbourne. Indeed their friendship remains one of cricket's more enigmatic relationships: 'I don't know why Don was considered cold,' says Evans. 'He never was to me.'

The new decade saw Evans gradually restrict his appearances to the Old England XI, the Lord's Taverners and the occasional charity match. Of these Brian Johnston has written: 'Evans still crouches close up to the stumps and brings off miraculous stumpings, often down the leg side, which were his speciality. He keeps for about an hour and then goes off, having shown to an admiring younger generation what *real* wicketkeeping looks like.'

Evans's ties with the past have physical manifestation. He has neckwear designed by Ames and Levett, ties commemorating all eight of his MCC tours, including his maxim *Perduravimus* struck in scarlet; ties for the Cavaliers, for Kent and England. The Wombwell Cricket Lovers Society, which exists in celebration of any cricketer breaking a record, provided a tie; Evans has spoken at the Society's dinner, an experience he at first compared unfavourably to going in to bat in a Test. A cricketer is invited to such functions all over the country. A tie comprising Father Time and a pair of thistles indicates the national character of the game. The insignia of the Wig and Pen Club in Fleet Street denotes Evans's career as a broadcaster and journalist.

On New Year's Eve 1948 Evans was invited to a party in Johannesburg hosted by the cast of the touring musical *Oklahoma*. He left with a prize collection of the show's music, after having rendered his own version of the 'German Band' to rapturous applause. Among his souvenirs have been bats and balls, stumps and bails, and even a stuffed alligator purchased in British Guiana. Most, if not all, have evaporated over the years, as have the photographs and memorabilia of his career. Evans's life has never been a monument to itself.

The journalism began on his retirement in 1959. The *Sunday People* contracted him for a series of articles and for some years Evans wrote weekly about cricket in London and the South, while Trueman aired his views concerning the North. He broadcast for independent television and for Channel Nine in Australia. In 1986, following a call 'from a new publication, for whom Bobby Moore was writing about football', Evans resumed his weekly column, perceptively analysing the modern game while eschewing nostalgia. For a while all went well; until, in fact, Evans happened to purchase the publication to which for nearly two years he had lent his name. It was *Sunday Sport*.

His own publications concluded with *The Gloves Are Off* in 1961. In it Evans combined criticism of May ('Peter seemed to have no humour in him') with appreciation of his undoubted ability as a player. Cowdrey was 'a very sound individual [who] sometimes, in quite an extraordinary way, didn't look like a very good batsman at all'. Hutton, at least on occasion, 'didn't handle people very well'. Written as it was shortly after his retirement, Evans made uncharacteristic censure of certain colleagues while not abandoning his distinguishing attitude to the game: 'I had a wonderful run, over a period of fifteen years, and there was no point in being depressed.' The book was a substantial success.

In the winter of 1963–64 Evans was on tour with the Cavaliers in Jamaica. One evening he and Ingleby-Mackenzie were invited to dinner by William Hill at the latter's residence in Montego Bay. It was there that the notion of becoming formally involved in cricket bookmaking was first raised, although in the event it was another concern – Ladbroke's – that subsequently contracted him. After meeting Cyril Stein, the Chairman, Evans was introduced to Ron Pollard, director designate of Ladbroke's cricket betting, and from 1971 was to advise the firm on odds at all major domestic fixtures. Evans's views on bookmaking are illustrative:

> There are ways of trying to beat the punters – not just who will win the match, but the number of wickets to fall or runs scored in a particular session, who will be the highest-scoring batsman in the match, and so on. The idea is to *involve* the public at every turn. Cricket betting, for me, should be fun.

The fun reached its apogee on 20 July 1981, when, in the third Test at Leeds, Evans was responsible for establishing odds of 500–1 against England. The match situation at that stage read: Australia 401–9 declared; England 174 and 135–7. In *Wisden*'s words, 'the distant objective of avoiding an innings defeat seemed [England's] only available prize'; in Evans's, 'someone had to win – and it didn't look like us'. Hence the odds, which preceded an 'astonishing' unbeaten 149 by Botham and Willis's last-day heroics of 8–43 to win the match. According to Allan Border, the mood in the visitors' dressing-room 'deteriorated visibly' with the return of the Australian coach driver, who, in tandem with Lillee and

Marsh, had availed himself of Ladbroke's generosity the previous day. The three profited to the tune of £7,500. 'We lost a bundle,' admits Evans. 'But the publicity for cricket betting was marvellous' – particularly when Lillee himself admitted the story in print.

Evans today can be seen, in Johnston's words, 'bustling into the commentary box with the latest odds for the day's cricket. . . .Still the eternal optimist.' His involvement with cricket was extended by his appointment as consultant to the Asda Trophy in Scarborough, and, in 1982, as adviser to the Gordon's Gin Wicketkeeper of the Month Award. The idea originated with an approach by Roy Mantle of Counsel Ltd, the agency acting for Gordon's, and involved Evans's chairing a panel to nominate both monthly and seasonal awards. The other members were Murray, Andrew, Dexter, Trueman, Laker and Reg Hayter. At the inaugural lunch it was agreed that 'a wicketkeeper's ability with the bat should be considered only if every facet of his game behind the stumps is equal to another player's'; so-called 'wicketkeeper-batsmen' need not apply. The first winner was Derek Taylor of Somerset, at 39 hardly a representative of the younger school, but the following three months saw recognition for Bob Taylor, Bruce French and Jack Richards. Taylor was the seasonal winner. A prizegiving dinner was held at The Ritz, at which John Holbeach, managing director of Gordon's, presented a cheque for £2,000. 'Class told,' says Evans.

May 1983 brought recognition for Alan Knott. 'Like myself,' says Evans, 'he rose to the challenge and often played better for England than for Kent.' Knott was especially useful in a crisis. As a batsman he combined 'rock-like defence with improvised attack. He had an instinct for survival together with genuine flair.' As a wicketkeeper, Knott possessed 'a wonderful pair of hands and a great gift for anticipation. Some of his work was outstanding, especially when standing back.' For Knott, like many in the modern game, was essentially a 'percentage player', eschewing the quickfire stumping in favour of a policy of safety-first. 'I often spoke to him about it,' says Evans. 'His reply was always: "I'm not as strong as you were. I couldn't stand up without eventually injuring myself. Besides which, I catch more by standing back." It's hard to argue with a man who took 1,344 dismissals.'

The remaining monthly awards went to David East, Chris Maynard and Bobby Parks; the seasonal trophy to East. Throughout that season and the next, Evans travelled the country in an Autostrada, a type of mobile home, which allowed him to see more cricket than at any time since his retirement. His conclusion was that the standard of wicketkeeping had 'risen dramatically' over the past decade, notwithstanding the tendency to stand back. 'Players are fitter than in my day; they play a tighter game, although the spontaneity seems to have gone out of it. It's harder to be a character.'

When subsequently reporting on the general standard of first-class wicketkeeping, Evans concluded:

> The main difference is that, in my day, the keeper stood up to the stumps whenever possible. To my mind, standing up gave the bowler something to aim at, encouraging him to pitch the ball up and committing the batsman to a stroke. As a result the batsman tended to be cautious when playing forward for fear of lifting his back foot.
>
> Modern-day players will claim that standing back means they drop fewer catches and concede fewer extras. Today the ball is a different texture from my day – the shine lasts longer and it tends not to get soggy and soft in wet conditions. Consequently, it stays newer and swings for a longer period – another reason for standing back.
>
> I always maintain that if a player has the ability and confidence he should stand up whenever possible. Some catches might go down, but he compensates by making the occasional stumping. His very presence is an additional distraction to the batsman. Standing up also eliminates the run to the stumps to gather each return from the field. In some cases, the fact that the keeper is already at the stumps will lead to a run-out.
>
> As I say, there are pros and cons on both sides. But, if a keeper is standing up and the going gets tough, he shouldn't allow his pride to rule his head. He should drop back to where it is comfortable.

Evans continues to chart the course of first-class cricket, chiefly through his work with Ladbroke's and his appointment as adjudicator of certain limited-overs matches. His view on the latter is direct: 'One-day cricket is here to stay. People should make the most of it and not offer excuses about the difficulties of playing three- or five-day cricket one week and a limited-overs match the next. Cricketers play cricket. It's as simple as that.'

Evans's commercial dealings have been the most trying of a life not unused to challenge. Having been refused by Whitbread, he was appointed in 1966 to the tenancy of a pub in New Milton, Hampshire. For three years (encompassing the comeback to Kent) he was the landlord of the Milton Hotel, happily entertaining visiting cricketers and having recourse to a small armada of motor-boats and cruisers. In 1969 he took possession of the Jolly Drover, a pub immediately north of Petersfield, at which, in Brian Johnston's words, 'one was wary of calling in to see him, as Evans would greet you warmly and announce to the assembled crowd that the drinks were on you'. During his years as landlord the premises were renovated and extended to include a dining-room over which Evans presided genially. To stimulate trade he frequently appeared at a nearby sauna, issuing at the psychological moment an invitation to 'have one at a little place' he knew in the vicinity. It was rarely refused.

For some years Jean Evans, after a marriage of intermittent separations and long absences abroad, had experienced difficulty in adapting to the life of a publican's wife. Evans himself concedes that, particularly during his overseas tours, he hadn't been a saint, while Howard Evans recalls the distance that increasingly separated his parents. During their time at the Jolly Drover the couple divorced, Jean perhaps ironically re-marrying another publican, Tony Smith. In 1977, to Evans's immense sadness, she suffered a stroke and died. In the meantime he himself had met Angela Peart, daughter of a family of Hungerford trout farmers, and in November 1973 they married. A daughter, Abigail, was born on 21 July

The Jolly Drover.

1975. That marriage, too, ended in separation and mother and daughter returned to Hungerford, where the latter shows an aptitude for equestrianism arguably attributable to her great Uncle Jimmy. Evans's one remaining ambition is to attend an event opposing Abigail with Peter May's own horse-loving daughters; as yet it remains unfulfilled.

Howard Evans married and settled successfully to a life of antique furniture restoration. In his youth, according to Evans, he showed 'distinct promise' as a batsman and fast bowler, while lacking the competitive spirit to excel at either. 'Perhaps because I was challenged so much as a boy,' says Evans, 'I never did so as a father.'

Evans's own steel as a sportsman had been forged largely at the family home at Sheldwich. The 'friends who ran a flourishing antique business' revealed in South Africa were called Cropley; under their tenure Lords one night burnt to the ground. Evans passes the village still on his visits to Canterbury and travels the same roads as on his excursions as a boy. His brother and sister have moved from the area and his son resides not in Kent but neighbouring Hampshire. Still the county has him in its hold and Evans remains, as a player whose art existed in a game rather than in the expression of words or music or commerce, a man of Kent. Few have deserved the description more.

Shortly after his retirement from first-class cricket, Evans appeared on *Double Your Money*, successfully answering questions on jewellery and winning £1,000 – half of which was donated to David Sheppard on behalf of Islington Boys' Club. The title of the programme was ironic. So far from doubling his money, the majority of Evans's commercial exploits have left him appreciably poorer, perhaps fulfilling Cowdrey's affectionate description of him as 'naïve', and Bailey's that 'Evans's instinctive generosity, combined with his inborn impetuosity, is why some of his ventures have failed to turn out as successfully as hoped'.

Prominent among them was the relationship with Yates. After a successful transition from Reeve Carter to Yates & Evans, the company dissolved in some acrimony when, in

Doubling his money, with Rev. David Sheppard.

Evans's words, he discovered his partner 'to be almost as big a scoundrel as myself'. An investment in a battery farm near Banbury dissipated when the chickens were found to have the croup; that in a dice game when the venture failed to secure sufficient backing. John Murray recalls an attempt to patent an Evans pitch-drier, which on trial promptly scorched the practice area at Canterbury beyond recognition. Most spectacular of Evans's debacles was the abortive purchase of Walton-on-the-Naze in Essex. This coastal property was, in his own words, 'crying out' for development into a resort and leisure complex, and a substantial deposit was duly placed. The plan was, after reinforcement of the exposed coastline, to establish a community of 500 holiday chalets; unfortunately the scheme presumed planning permission by the local authority, which, after a long debate, was unforthcoming. The area remained undeveloped and Evans lost his deposit. If it is difficult not to sympathize, then Bailey's words again come to mind: 'There are times when it is essential to wait in business, but waiting is foreign to Godfrey's temperament. He always wanted to make the first million within six months, and was not prepared to wait a year.' Or Johnston's: 'In spite of – or perhaps because of – all Evans's varied activities, I doubt if he will ever become a millionaire, but he will continue to bring fun and laughter to all his countless friends and to every stranger he meets.'

In 1966 Evans was elected a founder member of The Sportsman's Club in Tottenham Court Road. He, Compton and Jimmy Hill were appointed non-executive directors of the establishment which, at that stage, existed to serve the clientele implicit in its name. A 'Sportsman of the Month' award was established in recognition of outstanding achievements, and over the years Tony Jacklin and James Hunt were among those honoured. Brian Johnston recalls Evans as 'the genial host. . .greeting all and sundry as if he had known them all his life', a congeniality soon extended to the gaming-room inside the club. Here Evans established his 'system' for certain success at roulette, applying the same combination of precision and inspired guesswork characterizing his work for Ladbroke's. At the time of writing, the 'system' has failed to secure Evans's first million, while undoubtedly financing a number of otherwise rewarding evenings.

At the time his formal arrangement with The Sportsman ended, Evans joined the staff of the Skew Bridge Country Club in Rushden, Northants. So-called for the ungainly railway bridge under which access to the Club was originally gained, it lies in 300 acres of reclaimed land surrounding a series of lakes designed for water-skiing of all levels. From 1978–81 Evans was gainfully employed as Public Relations Officer, greeting friend and stranger alike and staging an Old England v Lord's Taverners fixture which, in his own estimation, helped put the place on the map. The establishment has particular significance because, on the termination of his contract, Evans elected to settle in the area and remains there still; 'the centre of England', as he puts it, and convenient for his then regular excursions in the Autostrada. Residents of Skew Bridge recall him with undiminished affection.

Evans was not a commercial success. Not so in the sense of failing to achieve his ambition of financial independence, in which respect the remarks of Bailey and Johnston may be taken as read. On the other hand few, if any, sportsmen have been more generous with their time and enthusiasm; Evans has sorted his way through life experiencing frustration upon fortune. In retirement he has devoted himself to colleagues, to charities and causes – few requests for a personal appearance have been denied. His cry 'Happy Days' has been applied to friend and foe alike; the passing stranger greeted as affably as a Miller or Compton. Any village cricketer or schoolboy could ask him for advice and be answered with genuine interest. He believes in an honest profit, but no percentage was ever added because he was Godfrey Evans. Bad debts were forgiven, if not forgotten.

Evans's life chronicles a half-century of professional cricket. The greatest batsmen he saw were Bradman, Hammond and Compton; the greatest bowler Lindwall. As a wicketkeeper Tallon, 'a player who could make the most improbable dismissals look outrageously simple', stood alone. The

Australian played much of his cricket at Brisbane, where chances were at a premium; in consequence Tallon acquired a reputation for gamesmanship. But nobody denied his brilliance.

Decades later, Evans remains mystified by the decision to omit Tallon from the touring team to England in 1938. The following winter he broke two world records. Tallon would assuredly have played in 1942 but for the intervention of War. When Bradman led his triumphant side in 1948 he was an automatic choice.

Although relatively tall for a wicketkeeper, Tallon was exceptionally fleet of foot. He moved to take the ball late, not committing himself before any movement off the pitch, and, in Evans's words, 'remaining largely unnoticed – a sure sign of a class player' (himself excepted). At Sydney in 1946, Evans watched Tallon catch Compton from a rebound off slip's chest; 'No one else would have considered it a chance.' When, at the end of the tour, critics like O'Reilly and Armstrong compared the two players, Evans regarded it as the greatest compliment. Tallon, simply, was 'the most complete wicketkeeper' of his time.

Then there was Ames. 'Les,' says Evans, 'would have excelled in almost any team for his batting.' Against Gloucestershire at Dover in 1937 Kent, in the form of Ashdown, Woolley and Ames, scored a matter of 218 in 70 minutes; manning the scoreboard was a seventeen-year-old Colt, who, in his own recollection, never worked so hard in his life. As a wicketkeeper Ames was of a more sedate nature than Levett or Evans, notwithstanding his athleticism to the bowling of Larwood and Voce. Socially he was anything but; Evans recalls an occasion when the pair were called before the Kent secretary to explain why the team was no longer welcome at a certain Bristol hotel. 'After a hard day,' says Evans, 'we'd apparently disturbed a few residents' evenings. The next day Les scored a century to compensate.' On another occasion Ames, anxious to cross a road, found his way blocked by a succession of cars. Rather than walking round, he leapt over them. Under his and Levett's influence it becomes apparent where Evans adopted his own approach to cricket.

With Jim Laker and Tom Graveney – minutes before the German band struck up, 1985.

Of more recent vintage, Evans admires John Murray – 'a man who found it impossible to be inelegant'. Murray was a proponent of the old school and, like Evans, elected to stand up whenever possible. He and Tallon played the same derisory number of Tests – in the former's case largely due to the emergence of Knott. Taylor was another to suffer the same fate: 'a genius in footwork, handling and concentration,' says Evans. 'One of my favourite players.' One of Taylor's attributes was consistency, in which he compares favourably to Evans – even relinquishing the captaincy of Derbyshire because he felt it to be affecting his performance.

Of bowlers to whom Evans kept, Wright remains 'the best, on occasion, in the world'. Less eminent if not exuberant was the Kent seamer Fred Ridgway. According to Evans, he was 'small of stature, but well-proportioned, with a cramped, unattractive run which nonetheless left him side-on at the moment of delivery. Fred, on his day, could make it wobble, float, dip, and because of his size, keep low. The lot'. For England, Evans nominates Bailey's performance at Kingston in 1954 as 'the match of a lifetime'; Trueman 'possessed a marvellous run-up and sideways action, allowing him to bowl the perfect outswinger. You never knew what Fred would produce next – a swinging full-toss, yorker, bouncer. He wasn't always sure himself'. Statham was a stalwart who swung little in the air but possessed genuine speed and unerring accuracy; 'the perfect foil' to Tyson, 'comfortably the fastest' to whom Evans ever kept.

Bedser, despite a flawless action, rarely produced an outswinger – but in mitigation developed a devastating leg-cutter. Like Maurice Tate before him, he seemed to gain pace off the pitch, and Bedser's request that his wicketkeepers stand up was fulfilled by some of the most spectacular catches of Evans's career. Laker, himself possessed of a copybook action – right arm brushing his ear, pivoting at the moment of delivery – was among the most awkward for friend and foe alike. He made the ball bounce. Even on the fated Australian tour of 1958–59, says Evans, 'he evoked memories of 1956' and took fifteen wickets in four Tests. One wonders what he might have achieved in a fifth.

Overseas, four bowlers are normally associated in pairs: Keith Miller was, and remains, the master of the unexpected; 'you had the impression he never knew what he was going to do', a supposition confirmed by the bowler himself. Miller varied his run-up and the ensuing delivery at will; he remains the only fast bowler in memory to 'drop the ball in mid-run, retrieve it and carry on as if nothing had happened'. Moreover, Miller was a fighter of causes – witness the second innings at Adelaide in 1955. Lindwall, his partner, 'had everything': hostility, control and speed, the last never more evident than on the MCC tour of 1946–47. Unlike Miller, Lindwall's routine never varied: a short, fluent approach culminating in a sideways action and follow-through. *Like* Miller, the end result was rarely predictable. Lindwall possessed genuine variations of pace, which allied to his tendency to 'drag' made him 'the most devastating new-ball bowler of his – or any – generation'.

Sonny Ramadhin began life as a caddy in Duncan Village, Trinidad, and developed his singular action by practising with a golf ball. Singular in that he bowled genuine leg-and off-breaks – Ramadhin's palm was pointing downward at the moment of delivery, and his action made it impossible to determine the direction of the ball in the air. In 1950 he took 33 wickets in four Tests. Only three Englishmen scored centuries in the series: Hutton, Washbrook and Evans, the last on a wicket on which, in Bailey's words, 'no one should have scored fifty, let alone a hundred'. At the other end Valentine, more orthodox in method, delivered spin audible to the batsman. Between them they accounted for 59 wickets and decisively changed the West Indies' status in world cricket.

Behind the stumps Evans admired Bradman ('dispatched the ball mercilessly'); Hutton ('a complete stylist'); and Hammond ('about the best all-round cricketer this country has seen'). Compton was 'an artist' whose batting was in some ways comparable to Miller's bowling: incomparable. Neil Harvey, first encountered as an eighteen-year-old on the tour of 1946–47, was a genius possessed of an 'unflabbable temperament'. His footwork, both at the crease and patrolling the covers, was inimitable. The first time Evans saw Harvey bat he announced, 'I'll see you next year' – meaning the 1948 tour of England; on the last the players were 60 and 51 respectively. Harvey scored 29 for Old Australia and, in Brian Scovell's words, 'would not have disgraced the Test side the next day'.

Finally, Sobers. Despite his assertion that 'some of my friends tell me that Godfrey was the best, although I didn't see enough of him to make a judgement', Evans himself has no such reservations. Sobers was the greatest. In addition to batting characterized by perfect timing and acute power, he possessed three separate bowling actions and fielded with animal grace. Sobers had two consuming passions outside cricket: horse racing and golf. Evans shared both. 'After all, most cricketers are gamblers. Who else has as much time on their hands?'

How, technically, has the game changed since Evans's debut? Firstly, notwithstanding the tendency of wicket-keepers to play the 'percentage game', the general standard of fielding has risen dramatically. The level achieved by, say, the 1955 South Africans is now prevalent throughout. The players are fitter. One of the contributory factors has been the advent of one-day cricket, which, Evans asserts, 'I would have loved'. The record certainly suggests it. Even though, perversely, he retains the record for inactivity in a Test, Evans's philosophy was that 'a bat is for scoring with.' Nor does he sympathize with the debate concerning the apparent strain of adapting from five- to three- to one-day cricket and back, typically turning the argument on itself: 'What could be better than getting runs, wickets *and* a result all on one day?'

Other developments have proved less agreeable. The impregnated leather used in the manufacture of cricket balls has led to a product 'encouraging the swing bowler and, disappointingly, a type of medium-pacer whose sole aim is to restrict runs. The spinner has become all but extinct.' While registering Evans's claim that the latter 'preferred the old-fashioned ball', it is hard not to draw the connection between the spin bowler's demise and the 'loveable' one-day format just extolled. By his own account the spinner (and particularly leg-spinner) is at a disadvantage with the newer ball; hence a decline in accuracy; hence decline. Some might argue that the last derives equally from the unnatural restrictions imposed on the bowler by the nature of one-day cricket. In either case the result has been uniform. England awaits its Wright.

The seamer's ascendancy has been due additionally to the quality, or reverse, of first-class pitches. Evans is not alone in observing the 'obvious doctoring' undertaken to bestow the illusion of greatness on certain technically inferior bowlers. *Genuine* pace, as he says, is all too often provided by those 'born under a bluer sky than ever seen at Canterbury'.

On the vexed question of overseas players, Evans observed:

> Not that I would stop good cricketers coming in from abroad, but the registration rule needs to be applied. If

> overseas players were allowed into County cricket in unlimited numbers, chances for home lads would be even more limited than they are now.

The interesting thing about the above is that it was written in 1956. 'Chances for the lads' was evidently an issue more than a decade before the decision to permit immediate registration, and it was in deference to it that Evans ended his career with Kent. Not long afterwards the structure of the Championship altered in a way to encourage negative cricket. It was the origin of a trend that found expression in the leaden tempo and ponderous tactics of which Evans wrote:

> A major change is that teams tend now to set out not to lose, rather than to win. I would have thought – and I'm sure the spectators paying for entertainment would feel the same – that it should be a case of try your damnedest to win and, if that becomes impossible, settle for a draw. Perhaps the pressures of money, television, sponsorship and the mass media have been responsible.

Hence the lament that 'the fun seems to have gone out of it' during the Centenary Test and thereafter. For Evans the joy of cricket was paramount. Regardless of the derisory wages, the seven-month tours undertaken in anything but luxurious conditions, Evans possessed that priceless attribute of any profession: enjoyment. Few of today's cricketers appear to share it. Botham is one Evans admires. Of an earlier generation, Milburn ('a loss to the stage') and D'Oliveira derived more pleasure than most. Recent examples are conspicuous by their absence.

Two modern masters illustrate the point. Barry Richards joined Hampshire in 1968 and scored 2,395 runs in his inaugural season. He was, says Evans, 'about the most proficient opener ever', with a temperament to match. Unfortunately over the years he became sardonic. Richards admitted he was 'bored' by County cricket and was known to adopt the attitude of a father playing against the boys in a parents' match. Dennis Lillee, meanwhile, possessed of an action 'equal to Lindwall's' (though lacking the latter's variations in pace) seemed to motivate himself by antagonism. The Saga of the Tin Bat was, says Evans, 'funny for the first thirty seconds'. Both players seemed to possess instincts 'other than an inherent love of cricket'.

Others whom Evans admired from a technical standpoint included the Chappells, Pollock, Lloyd, Gavaskar, Zaheer and Boycott, and, of contemporary players, Greenidge, Border, Viv Richards and Miandad. Bowlers, in his own phrase, he 'would have loved to have kept to' embrace McKenzie, Thomson, Holding, Roberts, Garner, Marshall, Kapil Dev, Imran, Hadlee, Procter, Snow, Willis, Underwood, the Indian quartet of Bedi, Venkataraghavan, Prasanna and Chandrasekhar, Gibbs and Abdul Qadir – the last in the conviction that 'I would have picked him'. More in sorrow than anger, Evans adds: 'It would have been laughable, thirty years ago, for a batsman to have appeared for England without having faced a genuine "leggie". Every team had one.'

Evans himself knew the vagaries of selection. He was dropped by England in 1949 and '51 and omitted from the MCC tour of 1959–60; the last, ironically, under May, who became Chairman of Selectors in 1982. The ensuing six years proved, says Evans, 'the futility of rule by committee'. His own proposal for a 'supremo' reinforced by a network of regional advisers was to some extent achieved in 1989. His strong preference for the job was Illingworth; as a player, 'aware of his limitations' for which he compensated with tactical acumen; as administrator, 'tough, direct and no-nonsense'. The eventual appointment of Dexter was something of a shock, particularly accompanied by the terms apparently denied Illingworth. 'I rang Ted to congratulate him,' says Evans. 'I've not heard from him since.'

The Selectors' judgement had been questionable for some years before; never more than when, under May, the Committee selected only one specialist wicketkeeper to tour New Zealand and Pakistan in 1983–84. That particular economy was, says Evans, 'madness'.

> After all, Taylor was 42. Fowler, the Lancashire opening bat, was to step in in an emergency and Downton was in South Africa, ready to appear if anything happened. But joining a tour midway through is never satisfactory. Personally, I was disgusted with the decision. A second

> player should have been included – and money no object. The wicketkeeper is one of the most important men on the field, and the two best available should always tour.

Similar reservations were expressed in September 1989 when, on successive tours to India and the West Indies, the Selectors nominated Alec Stewart, 'a competent bat, with no great pretensions as a wicketkeeper', in preference to the 'infinitely superior' Steven Rhodes. The incumbent, meanwhile, remains 'Jack' Russell, a player nominated by Evans more than two years before his eventual debut. Russell, in the modern idiom, is 'probably the best percentage player in the world'; notwithstanding a tendency to 'allow batsmen liberties' unthinkable by Evans. His appointment in 1988 heralded the end of a long era of mediocrity since the retirement of Taylor; when the latter reappeared briefly in 1986 it represented the highlight of an otherwise monotonous series.

Of remaining players Evans admires Robin Smith, in whom there are traces of the 'authoritative cutting' of Weekes, and Fraser, a 'more accurate' (though duller) version of John Warr. For the future he has hopes for Malcolm, Medlycott, Hussain, Atherton and Afford. Pringle, perhaps surprisingly, he describes as 'capable of great things – if sufficiently motivated', a condition unlikely to occur under the captaincy of David Gower. The latter was and remains 'a superlative bat, reminiscent of Graveney' who, as captain, 'seemed to let the game run'. Others to whom the accusation applies have included Hammond and Compton. In 1989, faced with an Australian team 'led from the front' and against the backdrop of inducements from South Africa, Gower lacked the willpower to impose himself. The results were self-evident.

On South Africa Evans is unequivocal: a cricketer has but a short time to play and it is full of sorrow. Given the vagaries of selection and modern tendency to injury, players are advised to 'take what chances they can'. In 1989 three front-line bowlers, Thomas, Dilley and Foster, duly did so. A fourth, Jarvis, pleaded impecuniosity. The answer, says Evans, is to offer such players annual contracts; those on the fringes of the team in particular. Failing which, he adds, 'you can hardly blame them for looking elsewhere. I would have done so myself.'

Evans admired the captaincy of Mike Brearley. As early as 1964, recently down from Cambridge, he was scoring 2,000 runs for his County and remained, says Evans, a 'much underestimated' opener. As a captain he was peerless. Brearley's approach was based on the psychology of the individual: 'he studied each player separately and decided how to handle him'. In the 1950s Stuart Surridge adopted the same strategy at Surrey. 'It worked for him,' says Evans; and for Brearley – a record of six successful series is almost miraculous by modern comparison. 'That kind of attitude is what England need – and lack – now. I can only think of a single better skipper.'

Hutton. The Yorkshireman reigns supreme of those under whom Evans played. 'Len was a genius, to whom cricket was essentially a business. As a captain he had limitations, as a batsman almost none. Everyone in the team respected his ability and played out of their skins for him.' Never more than on the West Indies tour of 1953–54. England emerged from the Barbados Test in something approaching a crisis. Against a backdrop of political hostility, the team had impeded its own chances by adopting an approach typified by Hutton's dictate, 'Don't get out.' In consequence strokeplayers like Graveney felt unnaturally restrained. After representations by Evans and Compton the captain relented and England won two of the remaining three Tests to level the series. Hutton himself scored 169 and 205. The mood of the party perceptibly altered, having played, according to the *News Chronicle*, 'the best cricket of any English side since the Jardine and Chapman era'; in short, a classic example of being led from the front. Evans remains convinced that Hutton's play would 'inspire today's team, just as it did ours'. A Hutton, unfortunately, occurs once in a lifetime.

Of those currently available Evans nominates a perennial leader of England 'A' teams and successful County captain – Mark Nicholas. In ascending order, Nicholas is 'a respectable bat', who finished 1989 with an average approaching

40; 'someone who, like Ingleby-Mackenzie, knows how to enjoy himself'; and critically, 'a leader of men', a quality not always apparent in Graham Gooch. As to whether Nicholas represents that peculiar English phenomenon, the Captain Not Worth His Place In The Team, Evans cites Hampshire's recent performance in Championship and one-day cricket. 'A good captain is one who wins matches. Nicholas's record speaks for itself.'

Another so qualified was Keith Miller, described by Benaud as 'a magnificent cricketer and a great captain .... No one under whom I played sized up a situation more quickly and no one was better at summing up a batsman's weaknesses. He had to do it for himself when he was bowling and it was second nature for him to do so as captain' – a view upheld by Bailey, who wrote: 'Miller would have responded to the responsibility and might well have become an outstanding Test captain. I certainly would have liked to play under him.' All the more credence, therefore, to Miller's remark at the end of the 1989 Ashes débâcle: 'What this (England) team needs is a skipper like Godfrey Evans.' He added:

> 'The man never gave up. He was made for a crisis – always bustling, chivvying the field, talking the batsmen out. As a wicketkeeper, Bradman and I agree – a first in itself – Tallon just had the edge. As a competitor, Evans stood alone.'

As to whether he himself harboured ambitions of captaincy, Evans is ambiguous. In 1957 the Kent Committee turned to Cowdrey, a man twelve years younger, who promptly sought his senior professional's endorsement. Evans's reply – 'We're all behind you, master' – concealed a number of mixed emotions. When in 1959 he deputised in Cowdrey's absence, Evans's captaincy displayed the same forthrightness exhibited as a player. By then it was too late. But in seeking former examples of the spirit now lacking in English cricket, it is hard to escape Evans's name. As Miller says, he stood alone.

In 1990 Evans was asked to play the perennial game of My Greatest XI; the terms of reference being Test cricketers from 1946 to the present. In batting order, his selection read:

Honour party to Boulogne, 1989. Levett and Ames are seated centre.

Hutton, Gavaskar, Bradman, Compton, Hammond, Sobers, Tallon, Laker, Lindwall, Lillee, Holding; reserves included Barry and Viv Richards, Wright and Trueman; 'near-misses', Harvey, Walcott, Miller, May, Cowdrey and Botham. He has no illusions about the superiority of one era over another and concedes that 'the bulk of those just outside the team' would be of modern vintage: Pollock, Lloyd, Zaheer, Boycott, Border, the Chappells, Knott, Marsh, Roberts, Marshall, Procter, Hadlee and Imran. Notwithstanding the technical changes over the years, only one immutable fact of modern cricket depresses him: 'The fun seems to have gone out of it. That's sad.'

Evans divides his time now between charity matches and major first-class cricket, where, as Johnston says, he cuts 'a bustling figure with enormous grey mutton-chop whiskers'.

The whiskers go back to the time when Evans and the late Graham Hill appeared on an early edition of *A Question Of Sport*. The hirsute racing-driver challenged Evans to 'let your hair down'; the response being the luxuriant foliage that now serves as his trademark. Hill's response was not recorded.

No one has been more generous with his time or interest. Evans sustains charities and causes the length of the country, invariably ebullient and (unlike another of his era) punctual to the minute. In the summer of 1989 it was reported that Statham – 'the straightest of bowlers' – was suffering from osteoporosis. At 58 he had little chance of working again. A testimonial dinner was organized at which the nine survivors of the triumphant 1953 Test team and 500 lesser mortals gathered to pay homage. No one received a warmer reception than Evans; no one, not Hutton, nor May, nor Dexter, remains as true to the memory of what they once were. Tom Graveney expressed the sentiment to perfection: 'Whatever you do,' he implored, 'don't change.'

Later that summer news was received of another former comrade. Gerry Chalk, Evans's County captain who first recognized the boy's ability, had enlisted in the RAF in 1939. For nearly half-a-century it was assumed that he was lost to enemy fire over the Channel in 1943. Then an extraordinary rumour began to circulate. It seemed a farmer outside Boulogne had discovered metallic deposit in one of his holdings. The authorities were alerted and the field duly excavated; therein were the mortal remains of Chalk, still encased in his skeletal Spitfire. Word reached the ground at Canterbury and an honour party including Evans, Ames and Levett assembled to pay its final respects. On the crossing the three reminisced about an era now archaically distant; it was Chalk who in July 1939 conceived a side in which Evans would co-exist alongside his two peers. The War disrupted that, and much else besides, but the outcome was no less dramatic. After the simple funeral ceremony the three convened to a local pub where a toast was drunk to their captain's memory. Despite the solemnity of the occasion the mood was essentially light-hearted. 'After all,' said Evans, 'that's the way we played it.'

Statistical Index

by Chris Taylor, Kent C.C.C., and Nicole Broderick

GODFREY EVANS – TEST CAREER

		M	I	No	R	Hs	Ave	Ct	St
1946	India	1							
1946/7	Australia	4	8	2	90	29	15.00	9	
	N.Zealand	1	1	1	21	21*		2	
1947	S.Africa	5	7	2	209	74	41.80	10	4
1947/8	W.Indies	4	7	0	128	37	18.28	6	1
1948	Australia	5	9	2	188	50	26.85	8	4
1948/9	S.Africa	3	4	0	49	27	12.25	5	5
1949	N.Zealand	4	4	0	61	27	15.25	8	4
1950	W.Indies	3	6	0	224	104	37.33	3	6
1950/51	Australia	5	9	1	144	49	18.00	11	
	N.Zealand	2	2	0	32	19	16.00	2	1
1951	S.Africa	3	4	0	7	5	1.75	4	1
1952	India	4	4	0	242	104	60.50	4	4
1953	Australia	5	7	2	117	44*	23.40	11	5
1953/4	W.Indies	4	6	0	72	28	12.00	5	1
1954	Pakistan	4	5	0	63	31	12.60	6	1
1954/5	Australia	4	7	1	102	37	17.00	13	
	N.Zealand	2	2	0				3	1
1955	S.Africa	3	5	0	82	36	16.40	9	1
1956	Australia	5	7	1	115	47	19.16	7	2
1956/7	S.Africa	5	10	0	164	62	16.40	18	2
1957	W.Indies	5	6	2	201	82	50.25	14	1
1958	N.Zealand	5	5	0	28	12	5.60	7	
1958/9	Australia	3	6	0	27	11	4.50	5	1
1959	India	2	2	0	73	73	36.50	3	1
	TOTALS	91	133	14	2439	104	20.49	173	46

* *signifies not out*

SUMMARY

Opponent	*M*	*I*	*No*	*R*	*Hs*	*Ave*	*Ct*	*St*
Australia	31	53	9	783	50	17.79	64	12
S.Africa	19	30	2	511	74	18.25	46	13
W.Indies	16	25	2	625	104	27.17	28	9
N.Zealand	14	14	1	142	27	10.92	22	6
India	7	6	–	315	104	52.50	7	5
Pakistan	4	5	–	63	31	12.60	6	1
Home	54	71	9	1610	104	25.96	94	34
Overseas	37	62	5	829	62	14.54	79	12
TOTAL	91	133	14	2439	104	20.49	173	46

GODFREY EVANS – FIRST-CLASS CAREER

	M	I	No	R	Hs	Ave	Ct	St
1939	5	7	0	50	22	7.14	4	
1946	27	40	2	737	72	19.39	58	12
1946/7 Aust./N.Z.	16	22	6	438	101	27.37	29	5
1947	28	45	5	1110	74	27.75	68	25
1947/8 W.Indies	9	15	1	300	53	21.42	14	3
1948	27	42	3	754	75	19.33	40	17
1948/9 S.Africa	11	14	4	288	77	28.80	13	11
1949	31	54	2	1090	76	20.96	59	22
1950	21	37	2	1021	104	29.17	42	17
1950/1 Aust./N.Z.	14	20	3	357	49	21.00	24	9
1951	30	53	2	871	101	17.07	47	12
1952	31	56	0	1613	144	28.80	49	19
1953	28	48	3	984	93	21.86	38	20
1953/4 W.Indies	6	8	0	72	28	9.00	9	1
1954	26	41	1	625	109	15.62	42	10
1954/5 Aust./N.Z.	13	20	2	244	40	13.55	34	7
1955	11	19	0	209	40	11.00	17	4
1956	25	42	2	929	93	23.22	34	9
1956/7 S.Africa	12	19	1	354	80	19.66	31	9
1957	25	42	5	953	84*	25.75	47	8
1958	26	39	2	731	69	19.75	45	7
1958/9 Aust.	7	10	0	124	55	12.40	8	3
1959	25	44	2	766	73	18.23	39	8
1959/60S.Africa	3	4	0	32	18	8.00	9	2
1960	1	1		37	37	37.00	4	
1961	1	2	1	105	98*	105.00		5
1963	1	0	0				1	2
1963/4 W.Indies	2	4	1	54	36	18.00	8	3
1964/5 W.Indies	1	1	0	14	14	14.00		
1967	1	2	0	16	10	8.00	2	
1969	1	2	2	4	4*		1	
TOTALS	465	753	52	14882	144	21.22	816	250

* *signifies not out*

MATCHES FOR KENT 1939–1967

	M	*I*	*No*	*R*	*Hs*	*Ave*	*Ct*	*St*
1939	5	7	0	50	22	7.14	4	
1946	24	37	1	707	72	19.39	52	10
1947	17	29	2	691	61	25.59	46	14
1948	17	28	1	526	75	19.48	28	10
1949	23	42	1	870	76	21.21	41	13
1950	16	28	2	768	98*	29.53	36	7
1951	23	43	2	817	101	19.92	38	8
1952	22	43	0	1241	144	28.86	38	8
1953	16	28	0	650	93	23.21	20	8
1954	18	30	1	480	109	16.55	24	7
1955	8	14	0	127	40	9.07	8	3
1956	16	29	1	685	93	24.46	21	3
1957	15	27	1	624	84*	24.00	26	3
1958	17	27	1	545	55	20.96	35	4
1959	20	37	2	528	58	15.08	32	5
1967	1	2	0	16	10	8.00	2	
TOTALS	258	451	15	9325	144	21.38	451	103

* *signifies not out*

Index